THE SILVER WREATH

Being the 24th Regiment at Isandhlwana and Rorke's Drift, 1879

Being the 24th Regiment at Isandhlwana and Rorke's Drift, 1879

THE SILVER WREATH

Being the 24th Regiment at Isandhlwana and
Rorke's Drift, 1879

NORMAN HOLME

Samson Books

By the same author

MEDAL ROLLS (1793–1889) of the 24th FOOT, SOUTH WALES BORDERERS

MEDAL ROLLS 23rd FOOT – ROYAL WELCH FUSILIERS, NAPOLEONIC PERIOD

(with Major E. L. Kirby)

———————

ISBN : 0 906304 04 0

First Published in Great Britain by Samson Books Ltd.
13–19 Jamaica Road, London, SE1 2BY

Printed in Great Britain by Gee & Son (Denbigh) Ltd.

Contents

ISANDHLWANA

1st BATTALION

2nd BATTALION

1st BATTALION

RORKE'S DRIFT

1st BATTALION

2nd BATTALION

PHOTOGRAPHS IN CENTRE SECTION

ISANDHLWANA (Killed in Action)

1st Battalion
Lt. Col. H. B. Pulleine
Capt. W. Degacher
Capt. W. E. Mostyn
Capt. R. Younghusband
Capt. G. V. Wardell
Lt. E. O. Anstey
Lt. C. J. Atkinson
Lt. C. W. Cavaye
Lt. N. J. A. Coghill, V.C.
Lt. J. P. Daly
Lt. G. F. J. Hodson
Lt. T. Melvill, V.C.
Lt. E. P. Porteous
2 Lt. E. H. Dyson
Py. Mr. F. F. White
Q.M. J. Pullen

2nd Battalion
Lt. H. J. Dyer
Lt. E. Godwin Austen
Lt. C. D'A. Pope
Sub-Lt. T. L. G. Griffith
Q.M. E. Bloomfield

RORKE'S DRIFT

The Memorial
Lt. G. Bromhead, V.C.
C/Sgt. F. Bourne, D.C.M. (in 1905 when a Major)
Cpl. W. Allen, V.C.
Pte. F. Hitch, V.C.
Pte. A. H. Hook, V.C.
Pte. R. Jones, V.C.
Pte. W. Jones, V.C.
Pte. J. Williams, V.C.

FOREWORD

by

Major G. J. B. Egerton, DL.

This book is the result of fourteen years of painstaking research into the lives and military service of those officers and men of the 24th Regiment who fought at the battles of Rorke's Drift and Isandhlwana in the Zulu War and I am more than pleased to write the Foreword to it. Not only do I know the author well, but from my experience over the last twenty-three years, first as Regimental Secretary and then as Curator of the South Wales Borderers Museum, know that there is a crying need for just such a book as this. What more appropriate time could there be for its publication than in the centenary year of the Zulu War.

The intimate details which Norman Holme has collected from the documents of those who fought in the two battles will be of inestimable value and interest to their descendants and to historians, medal collectors and the general public, giving, as they do, an insight into the lives of soldiers in the late Nineteenth Century.

Until now there has been doubt concerning the names of those who actually fought at Rorke's Drift because the roll of the defenders compiled by Major Bourne, DCM, who was the Colour Sergeant of 'B' Company 2/24th Regiment, differed in a number of instances from that produced by Lieutenant Chard, V.C., R.E., who commanded in the battle. As the latter was apparently signed by Chard only two weeks later it has always been accepted as correct, but the author's penetrating research has now proved that it was neither compiled nor signed by Chard and not entirely accurate. However, the use of the Christian names of almost all members of 'B' Company could be said to prove that it was compiled by a member of that Company and therefore must be at least near correct.

Norman Holme has left no stone unturned. By discovering an amended and as yet unpublished roll made by Bourne, and by checking the service details of all soldiers of 'B' Company whether they appeared on either of the rolls or not, he has now produced a final analysis the accuracy of which I am sure cannot be questioned.

G. J. B. EGERTON,
Major (Retd.).

Brecon.
31st January 1979.

BIBLIOGRAPHY AND SOURCES OF REFERENCE

PUBLISHED SOURCES

ABBOTT, PETER : 'N Battery 5th Brigade R.A., at Isandhlwana'. *Journal of the Society for Army Historical Research*, Autumn 1978.

ADAMS, JACK : *The South Wales Borderers* (London, 1968).

ATKINSON, C. T. : *The South Wales Borderers, 24th Foot, 1689–1937* (Cambridge, 1937).

COUPLAND, SIR REGINALD : *Zulu Battle Piece – Isandhlwana* (London, 1948).

EMERY, FRANK : *The Red Soldier* (London, 1977).

JACKSON, F. W. DAVID : 'Isandhlwana, 1879 : The Sources Re-examined' (*Journal of the Society for Army Historical Research*, 1965, Nos. 173, 175 and 176).

MACKINNON, J. P. and SHADBOLT, S. : *The South African Campaign, 1879* (London, 1880).

PATON, GLENNIE and PENN SYMONS : *Records of the 24th Regiment* (London, 1892).

UNPUBLISHED SOURCES

Rorke's Drift Orders Book (Regimental Museum, South Wales Borderers, 24th Foot).

The contents of this work are based primarily on Crown documents contained in the following classes : WO.12, WO.16, WO.25, WO.32, WO.100, etc.

The transcripts/translations of the above Crown-copyright records in the Public Record Office appear by permission of the Controller of H.M. Stationery Office.

Lieutenant Chard's hitherto unpublished letter to H.M. Queen Victoria, and its accompanying sketches, appear by gracious permission of Her Majesty Queen Elizabeth II.

PREFACE

One hundred years ago today, on Wednesday, 22nd January 1879, a force consisting chiefly of five companies of the 1st Battalion and one company and a composite company of the 2nd Battalion 24th Regiment of Foot, whilst guarding the camp of number three column at Isandhlwana Mountain, came under attack by a large and powerful Zulu army. The Zulus, in overwhelming numbers, launched a highly disciplined assault, and in spite of a gallant resistance the defenders were virtually annihilated and the camp occupied by the enemy.

During the afternoon of the same day a small garrison, mainly consisting of B Company of the 2nd Battalion 24th Regiment of Foot, defended the Mission Station at Rorke's Drift against vastly superior numbers of Zulus. The battle, which lasted continuously until the early hours of the next morning, finally resulted in the repulse and subsequent withdrawal of the enemy. The great courage displayed by the defenders of Rorke's Drift was reflected by the large number of decorations for gallantry conferred upon the garrison. Of the eleven Victoria Crosses awarded for the action, no less than seven of these were won by men of B Company.

The battle of Isandhlwana and the defence of Rorke's Drift have been frequently and on occasions somewhat controversially described in various works relating to the Zulu War of 1879. It is not appropriate that this work should contain a description of the battles other than in the form of personal narratives, as provided by men who actually participated in the actions.

Many officers and men belonging to various regiments and corps, both Imperial and Colonial, served with gallantry and distinction at Isandhlwana and Rorke's Drift. Whilst this fact is duly acknowledged, it is not within the defined purpose of this work to include, with the exception of two noteworthy instances, references in respect of these men.

Battles are often remembered when those who fought in them are long forgotten. This book, which in addition to providing a means of recording the available biographical details of the individual officers and men who embodied the 24th Regiment, is also intended as a tribute to their memory in the form of a Roll of Honour.

.   .   .

The 24th Regiment of Foot, afterwards the South Wales Borderers, has for a considerable number of years represented the focal point of my interest in British military history. This personal interest in the regiment has manifested itself in a variety of ways, the principal one taking the form of research in connection with the service careers of individual officers and men; a subject which is closely allied to medal collecting.

The results of my original findings appeared in published form in 1971 as 'Medal Rolls (1793–1889) of the 24th Regiment of Foot, South Wales Borderers'. As the title implies, the contents relate to a period of some ninety-six years of regimental history, as expressed in the award of various decorations and campaign medals. That part of the book devoted to the battle of Isandhlwana and the defence of Rorke's Drift would appear to have engendered by far the greatest amount of interest. It is largely because of this and the fact that the several lists of defenders of Rorke's Drift contain many anomalies, as outlined in my previous work, that further research has continued up to the present time.

Soon after embarking on the original project, it became apparent that the regimental medal rolls, which formed the basis of the subject, contained numerous irregularities and omissions. As a result of this, it became necessary to consult other documentary sources which included pay and muster rolls, credits and effects lists, casualty lists, records of service, and, where applicable, the depot description book. Additional information was obtained from official correspondence including dispatches, medical reports, etc., and various narratives in the form of statements and letters were also utilised. This information, together with details extracted from soldiers' papers and an additional series of muster rolls, constitutes the basis of the present work.

It would have been impossible for me to have undertaken this research without the considerable amount of assistance which I received from many other sources. Captain W. A. Morgan, Lieutenant-Commander M. Godfrey and Mr. P. R. Meldrum were instrumental in providing the initial copies of documents from the Public Record Office, London, and I am most grateful for their help.

I owe a special debt of gratitude to the descendants of men who fought in the defence of Rorke's Drift. Mrs. L. Bunting, daughter of Private Henry Hook, V.C., kindly supplied valuable information concerning her father; as did Mrs. D. Partridge in respect of her great-uncle, Private William Jones, V.C. The late Mr. James Keefe, who served for many years in the South Wales Borderers, was extremely helpful in matters relating to his father, Drummer James Keefe; whilst Elizabeth Ann Jones ('Miss Wales' and 'Miss United Kingdom') generously provided me with information on her great-grandfather, Private Evan Jones. I owe a tremendous debt of gratitude to Mrs. Mary F. Whitby, daughter of Lieutenant-Colonel Frank Bourne, O.B.E., D.C.M., formerly Colour-Sergeant of B Company, 2nd Battalion, 24th Regiment. In addition to generously supplying me with photographs and unlimited information from her late father's effects, Mrs. Whitby has patiently and uncomplainingly responded to a multitude of questions, and her contribution to this work cannot be overstated. My thanks are also due to Lieutenant-Colonel W. W. M. Chard for his kind assistance in respect of his forebear, Lieutenant J. R. M. Chard, V.C.

Lieutenant-Colonel Jack Adams, M.B.E., B.A., author of *The South Wales Borderers* and a serving member of the regiment for thirty-seven years, was instrumental in providing guidance, for which I am most grateful. The late Colonel A. South, R.E., was most helpful in obtaining valuable information on my behalf and my thanks are due to him. A particular debt of gratitude is owed to Major Peter Abbott, R.A., author of 'N Battery 5th Brigade R.A., at Isandhlwana' (*Journal of the Society for Army Historical Research*, Autumn 1978), for his understanding and kind co-operation.

I am greatly indebted to Mr. Derek Davis, M.Sc.G. M.Inst., M.S.M., for his generous assistance in undertaking a comparison of various documents in connection with the several lists of Rorke's Drift defenders. His professional expertise in the science of forensic handwriting has proved indispensable to the outcome of my investigations.

The defence of Rorke's Drift was briefly described by Lieutenant Chard in his concise dispatch to Colonel Glyn. A more detailed and informative account of the battle is contained in a letter submitted by Chard to Queen Victoria. This hitherto unpublished narrative appears by gracious permission of Her Majesty the Queen.

It was my original intention to include within this work a selection of letters by soldiers of the 24th Regiment, which are in the possession of the Regimental Museum. The publication in 1977 of *The Red Soldier* by Frank Emery provided a far greater source of reference material, and I am totally indebted to Frank for his overwhelming kindness in allowing me to quote the relevant letters from his book.

It would be impossible to name and thank individually the many people who have generously contributed photographs, documents and additional information; suffice it to say that I am indeed most grateful for their kind assistance.

My special thanks, as always, are due to Major G. J. B. Egerton, D.L., Curator of the Regimental Museum of the 24th Regiment, the South Wales Borderers. In addition to placing the contents of the Regimental archives at my disposal, George Egerton has also provided me with every conceivable facility for research. The Museum Staff, in particular Mr. John Marsh, have patiently dealt with my countless letters and telephone calls, and on the frequent occasions that my wife and I have visited the Regimental Museum we have been received with warmth and courtesy.

I owe the greatest debt of all to Mr. Gordon R. Everson, who, when the conventional means of my obtaining information from the Public Record Office ceased to be available, generously offered to undertake the work on my behalf. In addition to devoting countless hours, totally without recompense, to the mammoth task of obtaining this information, Gordon also provided a considerable amount of vital documentation. It would have been impossible for this work to have been completed in the form in which it now appears had it not been for the contribution made by Gordon Everson, and it is impossible to thank him sufficiently for his valuable assistance. The quality of the photographs is solely due to the expertise of Mr. John Ormond-King.

The contents of this work are based on the results of research which has continued throughout a period of fourteen years, during which time every effort has been made to ensure the accuracy of the information. It has, however, become apparent that certain previously published material contains information which is at variance with that resulting from this research. Amendments appropriate to these instances have been included in the work, and those details which cannot be substantiated by means of the relevant documents have been omitted.

NORMAN HOLME.

Over Hulton,
Bolton.
22nd January 1979.

The biographical details in respect of the officers and other ranks are sectionalised by battalions in order of precedence, the names of the individuals appearing in alphabetical order under strict sequence of rank as at 22nd/23rd January 1879.

In comparison with certain other regiments, the 24th Foot cannot be regarded as being particularly well documented. A depot description book/regimental register does not appear to have been instituted until 1881, and consequently it is virtually impossible to obtain detailed information relating to non-commissioned officers and men during the period circa 1855–1880. This deficiency, together with a total lack of service papers in respect of men killed in action, has resulted in only minimal biographical notes in the majority of instances. In order to obtain the maximum amount of available information, it has been necessary to utilise alternative documentary sources. These sources contain a number of errors and omissions which only become apparent during the process of comparison, however material relating to pay, allowances, credits, pay deductions and forfeitures represent a series of documents which were carefully audited since each item was accountable, and therefore this source of information may be considered as being accurate. The pay rolls clearly indicate the precise dates of service for which a soldier received payment, and in this respect they are invaluable in not only establishing the names of casualties but also in identifying the men joining, leaving, or becoming temporarily absent from the active strength of the regiment.

It is obviously essential to correctly identify each individual soldier, both by name and service number, prior to attempting to establish his record of service, biographical details, entitlement to medals, etc. In the case of the 24th Regiment the basic means of identification are rendered more complex by two factors, both of which are considered to be deserving of a comprehensive explanation. One of these relates to a common error which is to be found throughout all the documentary sources, including soldiers' papers, and concerns variations in the spelling the same name. Examples of this error are contained in the roll of Rorke's Drift defenders, where a number of men are found to have served for many years under names which only approximated to their own. Several other instances, again involving the defenders of Rorke's Drift, reveal a confusion of entries in the records of service relating to men with identical or similar names. As a result of this it has not been possible to determine the correct spelling of names in every case and appropriate notes have been included in these instances.

The second factor which tends further to complicate the process of identification concerns the allocation of service numbers to individual soldiers. Prior to April 1873, the 1st and 2nd Battalions each maintained an entirely separate series of numbers. On joining the regiment, men received a service number from the sequence allocated to the particular battalion to which they were posted. In all instances these numbers were prefixed by the indicator '1/24' or '2/24' respectively. On the comparatively rare occasions when men transferred from one battalion to the other, providing their existing service numbers did not duplicate one already in use in that battalion, they were apparently allowed to retain the original with a changed prefix; however, if a duplication did occur a new number was then issued. On 1st April 1873, as part of the Army Reform Act, the 24th Regiment was designated as the 25th Brigade and allotted to a permanent depot at Brecon. Men who joined the regiment after this date received not only a brigade prefix, expressed as '25 Bde' or more usually '25B', but also a new service number from a series which commenced at 1. These numbers were common to the regiment as a whole, no differentiation being made in respect of either the 1st or 2nd Battalions.

In actual fact, the regiment did not implement this system until June 1873, by which time those men who had joined since 1st April had already been issued with battalion prefixes and numbers. The error was duly rectified and these men were re-allocated brigade prefixes and numbers in retrospect; several examples of such amendments are to be found in the Isandhlwana roll.

On 1st July 1881, under the Cardwell Act, the regiment became the South Wales Borderers, and a further series of service numbers, usually prefixed by 'SWB' and again commencing sequentially from 1, was introduced. These changes also included the introduction of a depot description book which applied to both battalions of the regiment. The information contained within this book relates not only to recruits and men taken on strength from other regiments, but also includes men who, having completed their term of service in the 24th Foot/25th Brigade, re-engaged for a further period in the South Wales Borderers. In the latter instances the original regimental or brigade prefix and number was retained until re-engagement, at which time a South Wales Borderers number was issued and relevant details concerning the man were then included in the description book. Men who had enlisted prior to 1st July 1881 but chose not to extend their service engagement were evidently regarded as serving in the South Wales Borderers, but not as having transferred to the documentary strength of the regiment, and consequently they retained their original regimental or brigade prefix and number.

The complications resulting from this system are perhaps better realised when attempting to identify the individual soldier in relation to the campaign medal(s) to which he was entitled. It is important to understand that the campaign medal for South Africa, as awarded to the 24th Regiment, is inscribed '1st Battalion' or '2nd Battalion, 24th Foot' and no known medal bears the inscription '25 Bde'. It is, therefore, possible to discover examples of medals named to men who have apparently identical service numbers, as is illustrated by the following :

1 Drummer T. Perkins, 1–24th Foot
1 Pte. A. Johnstone, 1–24th Foot

The campaign medals in respect of these men, both of whom were killed at Isandhlwana, would be inscribed as above, thereby giving no indication as to the prefixes (1/24 in the case of Perkins and 25B in respect of Johnstone), which differentiated the regimental and brigade numbers. The situation is rendered even more complicated in the instance where an apparently identical service number relates to men with the same name, as the following example serves to illustrate :

976 Pte. Thomas Jones, 2/24th Foot (killed 22/1/79).
Medal for South Africa.
976 Pte. Thomas Jones, 2nd Bn. South Wales Borderers.
Medal for Burma 1885–7.

A man killed in 1879 could not possibly have been eligible for a medal issued for service in 1885–7, and the natural conclusion is to assume that the Isandhlwana casualty roll is in error. The prefixes to the service numbers (2/24 in the first instance and SWB in the second) reveal two individual men; the first was killed at Isandhlwana, whilst the second man did not enlist until 2/1/84, subsequently serving in Burma for which he received the India General Service (1854) Medal with appropriately dated clasp.

A number of soldiers who had previously served in South Africa with the 2nd Battalion 24th Regiment/25th Brigade, also received the India General Service (1854) Medal with clasp for Burma 1885–7, 1887–9, and in some instances, both clasps. In those cases where the man concerned had re-engaged in the South Wales Borderers, as described above, his service number on the I.G.S. (1854) Medal would differ from the one described on the campaign medal for South Africa. Notes appropriate not only to these instances but also to numbers held whilst serving in other regiments or corps are contained in the individual biographical notes.

Due to the magnitude of the disaster at Isandhlwana and the resulting loss of various regimental documents on the field of battle, the production of an accurate casualty list has necessitated a considerable amount of research. The medal rolls provide little information beyond indicating the men who were dead, but do not specify the cause of death, i.e., killed in action, died of wounds, died of disease, etc. The casualty effects list provides the registration number of the documents in which the effects were enumerated and in some instances states the relationship of the claimant to the deceased soldier; however, this list cannot be regarded as being completely accurate since it includes the names of men who died from disease, and others who in reality were not dead. For example, a claim was submitted for the effects of 308 Private John Bye 1st Battalion, when in actual fact he was discharged to the Army Reserve on completion of his service.

It has been found necessary to incorporate within the Isandhlwana casualty roll the names of several individuals who were omitted from the original medal rolls. These include Paymaster White, 75 Private William Burn and 265 Boy Robert Richards, all of whom were killed whilst serving with the 1st Battalion. A further example of the errors contained in the medal rolls is to be found in the case of 1505 Private M. Roche (Roach), killed at Isandhlwana whilst serving with the 2nd Battalion. His name duly appears in the medal roll of the 2nd Battalion and also in that of the 1st Battalion, from which his medal was issued on 28/3/82. The foregoing examples are indicative of the type of errors and anomalies contained within the original source material. As previously stated, the relevant pay rolls provide the basic means of establishing the identity of those men killed in action, since their pay ceased from the date on which they became no longer effective.

The main source of biographical information in respect of men present, or thought to have been present, at the defence of Rorke's Drift, is to be found in the form of service documents. The service papers of men killed in action no longer exist, and similarly the documents relating to men with short service engagements are in many instances no longer available. In those cases where service papers are in existence, it then becomes a matter of decision regarding what is considered to be essential information which may be utilised, as against the minutiae which, although of interest, cannot be included by virtue of sheer volume.

In order to formulate a reasonable assessment of the men concerned, certain aspects of the biographical details should be regarded in the light of the times to which they relate. This applies in particular to the undoubtedly harsh punishments inflicted on the rank and file, often for seemingly minor breaches of military discipline. Men were frequently sentenced to long terms of imprisonment with hard labour, and despite the abolition in 1868 of flogging in peacetime, soldiers on active service continued to be subject to this form of punishment until the introduction of the Army Reform Act in 1881. It is not difficult to understand the reasons as to why some men deserted their regiment and others sought refuge in alcohol; on occasions the army in which they served must have appeared to represent a threat comparable to that of a potential enemy. The severity of the military disciplinary system is not without parallel in the civilian law of that time. For example, during Christmas 1876 a nine years old boy was convicted of stealing a loaf of bread and a few nuts. He was sentenced to 21 days imprisonment with hard labour and four years in a reformatory.

Perhaps the most significant factor emerging from the biographical information concerns the eventual fate of many of the soldiers who fought at Rorke's Drift. Sadly, three men were confined as inmates of lunatic asylums and a further two are known to have been victims of violent physical assaults, in one case at the hands of British soldiers. In addition to those men incapacitated as a result of wounds, a number were discharged from the army as being 'Unfit for further service', a term which often signified that they were equally incapable of contributing to their own support in civilian life.

The details contained in this work are considered to be sufficient in order to formulate an impression of the man to whom they relate.

ISANDHLWANA

1st Battalion

24th Regiment of Foot

List of Officers, Non-commissioned Officers and Men killed at the
battle of Isandhlwana, 22nd January 1879

Henry Burmester PULLEINE
(Brevet Lieutenant-Colonel)

Born on 12th December 1838 at Spennithorne, Yorkshire, he was the eldest son of the Reverend Robert Pulleine, rector of Kirkby Wiske, near Thirsk, Yorkshire, by his marriage with Susan, eldest daughter of H. Burmester of Wandsworth.

He was educated at Marlborough College, Wiltshire, and the Royal Military College, Sandhurst. On 16th November, 1855 he obtained an ensigncy, without purchase, in the 30th Regiment, which he joined at Fermoy in Ireland. On 4th June 1858 he was gazetted to a lieutenancy in the 2nd Battalion, 24th Regiment, which was then being raised. He served at Sheffield, Aldershot and afterwards in Mauritius, where he became a captain by purchase on 18th November, 1861. He held an appointment in the Commissariat Department for nearly four years and received high commendation for his work.

After two years spent at home on leave and at the depot at Buttevant and Sheffield, he rejoined the regiment at Rangoon and also served at Secunderabad. On 4th February, 1871 he purchased a majority in the 1st Battalion, 24th Regiment, then stationed at Malta, where for a period of four months he acted as deputy quartermaster-general and received further commendation for his work. He served with the battalion for three years at Gibraltar and then proceeded with it to South Africa, serving at Cape Town and King William's Town. On the 1st October, 1877 he received his brevet lieutenant-colonelcy.

As a result of the unrest in the Transkei and the subsequent war in Galekaland, he was called upon to raise two frontier corps, one of infantry known as 'Pulleine's Rangers' (afterwards the Transkei Rifles), and the other a cavalry force, which became the Frontier Light Horse. He served with his regiment in the Transkei for nearly three months and then, in September, 1878, in view of the impending hostilities with the Zulus, he returned to embark for Natal. On arrival there he was placed in command at the city of Durban and later succeeded Colonel Pearson as commandant at Pietermaritzburg, where for nearly two months he was responsible for the Remount Depot. When preparations were being made for war against the Zulus, he applied for, and was granted permission to rejoin his regiment, which he did on 17th January, 1879. He commanded the companies of the 24th Foot at the battle of Isandhlwana, and it was he who ordered Lieutenant Melvill to attempt to save the Queen's Colour of the 1st Battalion. Lieutenant-Colonel Pulleine was killed in action at Isandhlwana.

In 1866 he married Frances Katherine, daughter of Frederick Bell, J.P., of Fermoy, Ireland, and had a son and two daughters by his marriage. His son, Henry Percy Pulleine, served as a lieutenant in the 24th Regiment until his resignation from the army on 11th November 1896.

Medal for South Africa with clasp '1877-8-9'.

William DEGACHER
(Captain)

Born on 4th April, 1841, he was the third son of the late Walter Henry Degacher of St. Omer, France. He was educated at the Imperial College, St. Omer, and at Rugby.

On 31st May, 1859 he was gazetted (under the name of Hitchcock) as an ensign in the 2nd Battalion, 24th Regiment; becoming a lieutenant in the regiment on 19th August, 1862. He was promoted Captain on 2nd December, 1868 and also received his company on that date.

He served with his battalion at various home stations, in Mauritius, and at the Mediterranean stations. (In 1874 he took the name Degacher.) He served in South Africa, where he took part in the expedition to the Diamond Fields, under Sir Arthur Cunynghame, in 1876. On returning to Cape Town at the latter end of the year he proceeded home on leave.

Shortly after arriving in England, Captain Degacher formed an intention to retire from the service. In consequence, however, of the Kaffir war breaking out about this time, he volunteered for active service, and again embarked for South Africa.

In October, 1878 he rejoined his regiment which was then preparing for the forthcoming invasion of Zululand. Taking part in the subsequent advance of the Head-Quarter Column, he commanded the 1st Battalion, 24th Regiment at the crossing of the Buffalo and in the storming of Sirayo's stronghold in the Bashee Valley. His eldest brother, Lieutenant-Colonel Henry Degacher, C.B., was, at this time, in command of the 2nd Battalion, 24th Regiment. Captain Degacher subsequently advanced with the column to Isandhlwana, and in the disastrous encounter with the enemy on the 22nd January, was in command of the battalion, Lieutenant-Colonel Pulleine being in command of the troops. No account of the manner of his death exists; it is, however, assumed that he fell shortly after the three companies were driven in by the Zulus.

In March, 1877 he married Caroline, daughter of General Webber-Smith, C.B.

Medal for South Africa with clasp '1877-8-9'.

William Eccles MOSTYN
(Captain)

Born at Glasgow on 27th November, 1842, he was the only son of the late Reverend George Thornton Mostyn, M.A., formerly Incumbent of St. Thomas's, St. Helens, Lancashire, and afterwards of St. John's, Kilburn, by his marriage with Charlotte, daughter of the late William Eccles of Glasgow.

He was educated at Rugby, and on 29th July, 1862 he was gazetted as an ensign in the 24th Regiment. He was promoted to the rank of Lieutenant on 23rd March, 1866 and became a Captain on 31st October, 1871.

Captain Mostyn served with his battalion at various stations in Great Britain and Ireland and in Burma, India, Gibraltar, Malta and the Cape of Good Hope, where he acted for some time as Aide-de-Camp to General Cunynghame.

In November, 1878 he proceeded with his regiment to Natal, to join the force which, with a view to the impending invasion of Zululand, was then being concentrated on the frontier. On 9th January, 1879 his company marched from Piertermaritzburg to join the Head-Quarters which, six weeks earlier, had left the capital, and formed part of Glyn's column at Helpmakaar. The company reached Isandhlwana on 21st January, 1879. In the battle which ensued on the 22nd January, Captain Mostyn moved the men under his command out of camp to the support of another company of his battalion which, under Lieutenant Cavaye and 2nd Lieutenant Dyson, had engaged the enemy on a steep hill about a thousand yards distant to the left. A few minutes after his arrival on the hill, his company extended and entered into action, supported on the right by a small body of Native Infantry. Shortly afterwards, the enemy appeared in great force in the rear, and the two companies fell slowly back, keeping up firing. After descending the hill, which was rocky and precipitous, they formed in extended order at a distance of about four hundred yards from it, but the enemy, heavily reinforced, pressed on rapidly, and they continued to retire until within three hundred yards of the position occupied by the Native Contingent. Shortly afterwards, the Zulus broke through the lines and Captain Mostyn and his men were overwhelmed.

Medal for South Africa with clasp '1877–8–9'.

Reginald YOUNGHUSBAND
(Captain)

Born at Bath on 16th January, 1844, he was the fourth son of the late Thomas Younghusband, formerly Captain H.E.I.C.S., and Pascoa Georgina, only daughter of Joseph Barretto of Calcutta and Portland Place, London.

Gazetted to an ensigncy in the 2nd Battalion, 24th Regiment, on 20th August, 1862, he served in Mauritius; in Burma, where he accompanied the expedition to Mandalay in September, 1867; and in India. He returned with his regiment to England in 1872, and shortly afterwards was appointed Instructor of Musketry, an appointment which he held for four years. He was promoted to the rank of lieutenant on 29th August, 1866, and obtained his company on 14th March, 1876, having been promoted captain on 24th March, 1876.

Captain Younghusband was ordered to the Cape to join the 1st Battalion of his regiment. Early in 1878 he returned to England on leave, but embarked again for South Africa in July, to take part in the suppression of the Galeka outbreak. Shortly after his arrival at the Cape, his regiment was ordered to Natal to join the force then preparing for the impending invasion of Zululand.

Colonel Glyn's column, to which both battalions of the 24th Regiment were attached, crossed the Buffalo River on 11th January, 1879, and on the following day Captain Younghusband was engaged, with his company, in the reduction of Sirayo's stronghold. Moving through the Bashee Valley, the column encamped on 20th January at Isandhlwana. A bandsman of the 24th Regiment who escaped from the battlefield reported that he saw Captain Younghusband making a desperate stand at the last. With three men of his company, he turned a waggon into a rifle pit, and defended it as long as his ammunition lasted. A son of the chieftain Sirayo stated what had occurred in the neighbourhood of the waggons: " A very brave man was killed near one of them. I don't know whether he was an officer or not, for when I saw him after he was killed his coat had been taken off him, but he had a red stripe on his trousers and he had brown gaiters. He was a very tall man, and as we were rushing over the camps he jumped on to an empty waggon with a gun, and kept firing away, first on one side and then on another, so that no one got near him. We all saw him and watched him, for he was high up on the waggon, and we all said what a brave man that was! I think he was an officer. All those who tried to stab him were knocked over at once or bayoneted. He kept his ground for a very long time; then someone shot him."

Captain Younghusband married, in February, 1878, Evelyn, second surviving daughter of Richard Davies of the 'Vigia', Madeira, and Jerez de la Frontera, Spain.

Medal for South Africa with clasp '1879'.

George Vaughan WARDELL
(Captain)

Born on 21st February, 1840, at Toronto, Canada, he was the second son of Major Wardell, who served for forty-three years in the 66th Regiment, the 93rd Highlanders and the Royal Canadian Rifles. He was educated in Canada and England, passing the direct examination for a commission from Kensington School.

Gazetted to an Ensigncy in the 2nd Battalion, 24th Regiment, on 14th May, 1858, he joined the corps at Bury, and after serving at Sheffield and Aldershot, embarked with it for Mauritius in March, 1860. He became a Lieutenant by purchase on 23rd July, 1861, and acted for nearly two years as Deputy Assistant Commissary-General. In 1865 the battalion was sent to Burma, and he served there until 1867, when he came to England on leave, and was afterwards attached to the depot at Sheffield and Preston. Captain Wardell exchanged into the 1st Battalion, 24th Regiment, in 1870 and for three years he served at Malta and Gibraltar, having obtained his company on 10th January, 1872. He was for two years at the Brigade Depot at Brecon, and in May, 1875, he was placed in charge of the drafts then embarking to join the regiment at the Cape of Good Hope.

In 1876 he commanded a detachment at St. Helens, being at that place for just over a year, and received warm approval from the governor of the island for the way the men under his command had conducted themselves. He rejoined his regiment in 1877 and proceeded with it to King William's Town, and on the Galeka outbreak taking place, was again detached with a hundred men of the 24th, with about three hundred Burghers, Mounted Police and natives, to guard the drift across the Great Koi River at Impetu. It was at this place that he constructed a redoubt which he named Fort Warwick. After holding this place for three or four months, during which time he was more or less surrounded by the Kaffirs, his communications were at last cut and he had to be relieved in January, 1878, by a strong force under Colonel Lambert, 88th Regiment. For his services, Captain Wardell received commendation from Sir Arthur Cunynghame, who appointed him commandant of the Kei Road and Kabousie stations, with a force of five hundred colonial troops under him. Upon the arrival of Lord Chelmsford to take command, he was superseded by a field-officer of another regiment, and rejoined his own corps in the Transkei, where he served against the Galekas.

In 1878 Captain Wardell marched with his company from Durban to Helpmakaar, where he camped for one month. At the commencement of the Zulu War he was placed in command of two companies at Rorke's Drift and given the task of covering the parties engaged in constructing the pontoons, etc. His was the first company of the 24th Regiment to enter Zululand and his men were engaged in a skirmish with the enemy. On 20th January, 1879, he moved from his camp at the Bashee Valley to the new camp at Isandhlwana. During the battle on 22nd January he made a most desperate and gallant stand against the Zulus, and when the dead were buried five months later it was reported that the remains of Captain Wardell, together with two other officers who could not be recognised, were found in one spot with the bodies of sixty men of their regiment.

He married, in 1867, at Mauritius, Lucy Anne Charlotte, daughter of Captain Russell, R.N.

Medal for South Africa with clasp '1877–8–9'.

Edgar Oliphant ANSTEY
(Lieutenant)

Born on 18th March, 1851, at Highercombe, South Australia, he was the third son of G. A. Anstey of Harley Street, London. He was educated at Rugby, and after successfully completing the course at Sandhurst was gazetted Sub-Lieutenant on 9th March, 1872. On 9th March, 1873, he was promoted Lieutenant in the 1st Battalion, 24th Regiment, which he joined at Aldershot. He embarked with his regiment in May, 1874, for Gibraltar, and six months later proceeded from there to the Cape.

Lieutenant Anstey was engaged with his corps in the suppression of the Galeka outbreak, throughout which he performed distinguished service. He commanded his company in two actions, and for his conduct on both occasions was mentioned in despatches. He was subsequently ordered to hold Pullen's Farm, and was enabled to successfully fortify that position.

In November 1878 Lieutenant Anstey proceeded with the regiment to Natal, to join the force then being concentrated on the frontier with a view to the impending invasion of Zululand. On the 9th January, 1879, Captain Mostyn's company, to which Lieutenant Anstey was attached, marched from Pietermaritzburg to join the head-quarters which, six weeks earlier, had left the capital and formed part of Glyn's column at Helpmakaar. The company reached Isandhlwana on 21st January, 1879, and in the disastrous encounter with the enemy on the 22nd, Anstey was engaged under Captain Mostyn at the commencement of the engagement, on the hills to the left of the camp. No accurate record of his death exists, but it is believed that he fell towards the latter end of the engagement, in the last desperate rally made by the three companies of his battalion to the east of the camp.

Lieutenant Anstey's remains were subsequently recovered from the battlefield by his brother, Captain Anstey, R.E., who had them conveyed to England and interred in the family vault at Woking Cemetery.

Medal for South Africa with clasp '1877–8–9'.

Charles John ATKINSON
(Lieutenant)

Born on 27th May 1855, he was the eldest son of Adam Atkinson of Lorbottle, Northumberland, and Charlotte Eustatia, only daughter of John Collett, sometime M.P. for Cashel, Ireland.

He was educated at Eton and was successful in passing the examination for direct appointment into the army. On 28th February, 1874, he was gazetted Sub-Lieutenant in the 1st Battalion, 24th Regiment, and joining that corps at Aldershot he proceeded with it, in May, to Gibraltar; there he served until the following December, when he embarked with the battalion for the Cape. He was gazetted to a Lieutenantcy on the 11th March 1877.

After being quartered for two and a half years in South Africa, Lieutenant Atkinson saw active service, the regiment being ordered to the front on the outbreak of the Kaffir war of 1877–78. He served with his corps through the whole of that campaign, performing many important duties and assisting in the arduous task of clearing the country of the enemy. At the action at Quintena on the 7th February 1878, he commanded a company and greatly distinguished himself. He was mentioned by Major Upcher, the officer in command, for his conduct on that occasion, and also by General Sir A. Cunynghame in his despatch of the 28th March.

In November, 1878, Lieutenant Atkinson proceeded with his regiment to Natal to join the forces then preparing for the invasion of Zululand. He took part in the subsequent advance of Colonel Glyn's column and was present at the storming of Sirayo's stronghold in the Bashee Valley. He then proceeded with the column to Isandhlwana, and in the disastrous encounter with the enemy at that position, fell — it is believed, in the last desperate rally of the three companies to the left front of the camp.

Medal for South Africa with clasp '1877–8–9'.

Charles Walter CAVAYE
(Lieutenant)

Born on 29th May, 1849, he was the third son of General Cavaye, H.M.I.F., and Isabella, daughter of Major T. F. Hutchinson. He was educated at the New Academy, Edinburgh, and later at Edinburgh University, where he graduated M.A. in 1867. During 1871 he was at the Royal Military College, Sandhurst, and on 30th December of that year was gazetted Sub-Lieutenant in the 24th Regiment.

In March 1872 he joined the 1st Battalion, then serving in Gibraltar, and remained there until 1875 when the battalion embarked for the Cape of Good Hope. In 1876 he was with a detachment of the 1st/24th at St. Helena; he remained at that station until 1877 when he rejoined the head-quarters of the battalion. He was promoted Lieutenant on the 6th January 1874.

In November 1878 he joined the head-quarters column of the forces concentrating at Helpmakaar prior to the invasion of Zululand. Lieutenant Cavaye took part in the subsequent advance and was present at the action at Sirayo's stronghold in the Bashee Valley, and afterwards proceeded with the column to Isandhlwana. On the 22nd January, Lieutenant Cavaye had been sent with his company to an outpost position some thousand yards distant from, and to the left of, the camp. The company arrived at this position about 10 a.m. and immediately Lieutenant Cavaye detached a platoon, under the com-

-mand of Second Lieutenant Dyson, to cover a position some five hundred yards to the left of his own. Captain Mostyn and his company were sent to support Lieutenant Cavaye, which they did until both companies were forced back by the Zulus to a position some four hundred yards from Isandhlwana mountain, where they again formed in extended order. Shortly afterwards they were surrounded by countless hordes of the enemy and overwhelmed. It is believed that Lieutenant Cavaye was killed at this stage of the battle.

Medal for South Africa with clasp '1877–8–9'.

Nevill Josiah Aylmer COGHILL, V.C.
(Lieutenant, Staff-Officer and A.D.C.)

Born on 25th January 1852, at Dublin, he was the eldest son of Sir John Joscelyn Coghill, Bart., of Drum-condra, County Dublin. He was educated at Haileybury, and served for two years in the County of Dublin Militia. In 1871, he passed the examination for direct appointment to the army and, having passed through Sandhurst, was gazetted on the 26th February 1873 to the 24th Regiment as Sub-Lieutenant. He was promoted Lieutenant on 13th August 1875. Lieutenant Coghill joined the regiment in England and proceeded with it to Gibraltar, later going on to the Cape of Good Hope, where he was appointed Aide-de-Camp to General Sir Arthur Cunynghame. He accompanied the general on a tour of inspection through the colony and the adjacent country, including Natal, Griqualand, the Orange Free State and the Transvaal. Soon after returning to Cape Town, the Gaika and Galeka wars commenced and he served throughout both campaigns, still continuing as Aide-de-Camp to Sir Arthur Cunynghame. He returned to England with his general on the latter being replaced by General Thesiger, afterwards Lord Chelmsford.

With preparations being made for the impending Zulu War, Lieutenant Coghill returned to the Cape, and soon after his arrival was appointed Aide-de-Camp to Sir Bartle Frere, travelling with him to Pietermaritzburg, where he obtained leave of absence to join his regiment. He was then appointed extra Aide-de-Camp to Colonel Glyn, who commanded the column to which the 24th Regiment was attached. This appointment he continued to hold until his death.

Lieutenant Coghill advanced with the column into Zululand, and due to a severe injury of the knee he was present in the camp at Isandhlwana on the 22nd January 1879. During the ensuing battle he was seen firmly mounted on his horse and cutting his way through the encircling hordes of Zulus. He met up with Lieutenant Melvill, who was attempting to carry the Queen's colour of the 1st Battalion, 24th Regiment, to a place of safety, and both officers eventually managed to reach the Buffalo River, which only Coghill managed to cross. On reaching the Natal bank, he saw that Melvill was struggling in mid-stream, so he deliberately rode back into the river to render assistance.

Both officers were helped to the Natal bank by Lieutenant Higginson of the Native Contingent, who, being injured himself, rendered as much aid as possible before mounting his horse. The Zulus had by this time crossed the river, and although Melvill and Coghill resisted as much as they were able, both men were quickly overpowered and killed. On the 4th February 1879 the bodies of the two officers were discovered where they had fallen; they were subsequently buried there, a cairn of stones and a cross being erected to mark the place. The details of Lieutenant Coghill's gallant

deed appeared in a supplement to the London *Gazette* dated 1st May, 1879, stating that had he survived he would have been recommended for the Victoria Cross. A posthumous award of the decoration was made on the 15th January 1907.

Medal for South Africa with clasp '1877–8–9'.

James Patrick DALY
(Lieutenant)

Born in March 1855, he was educated at Oscott and at the Rev. E. Barney's establishment at Gosport. After leaving school, he served for two successive years with the Galway Militia.

On the 28th February 1874 he was gazetted to a Lieutenancy in the 1st Battalion, 24th Regiment, which he joined at Gibraltar, embarking later that year for the Cape of Good Hope.

Lieutenant Daly served throughout the Gaika and Galeka wars, seeing much service and performing many arduous duties. In November 1878 he joined the forces then preparing for the invasion of Zululand, and on the 9th January 1879 Captain Mostyn's company, to which he was attached, marched from Pietermaritzburg to Help-makaar. The company reached Isandhlwana on 21st January, and in the disastrous encounter with the enemy which took place on the following day he was engaged, under Captain Mostyn, at the commencement of the engagement, on the hills to the left of the camp. No accurate record of his death exists, but it is believed that he was killed towards the end of the engagement, in the rally made by the three companies of his battalion to the east of the camp.

Medal for South Africa with clasp '1877–8–9'.

George Frederick John HODSON
(Lieutenant)

Born on 26th November 1854 at Dublin, he was the second son of Sir George Hodson, Bart., of Holybrooke, Bray, County Wicklow, and of Green Park, Westmeath. He was educated at Haileybury College, Hertfordshire. On 28th February 1874 he was gazetted Sub-Lieutenant in the 1st Battalion, 24th Regiment, which he joined at Aldershot. He was promoted Lieutenant on 11th March 1877.

In May 1874 he embarked with his regiment for Gibraltar, and six months later proceeded to the Cape of Good Hope. Soon after arriving in South Africa, Lieutenant Hodson was appointed Aide-de-Camp to Sir Bartle Frere. He subsequently served as orderly officer to Colonel Glyn throughout the Gaika and Galeka campaign of 1877, during which his name was more than once mentioned in despatches. At the conclusion of the campaign he returned to his duties with Sir Bartle Frere, and held his appointment until November 1878 when his regiment was ordered to Natal in view of the impending invasion of Zululand.

Lieutenant Hodson took part with his regiment in the subsequent advance of the Head-Quarter column, in January 1879 into the enemy's country, and was present at the storming of Sirayo's stronghold in the Bashee Valley on the 13th January 1879. At Isandhlwana he was one of the first who fell, it is stated, in the stand made by the three companies to the east of the camp.

Medal for South Africa with clasp '1877–8–9'.

Teignmouth MELVILL, V.C.
(Lieutenant and Adjutant)

Born on 8th September 1842 at London, he was the younger son of Philip Melvill, late Secretary in the Military Department to the East India Company, by his marriage with Eliza, daughter of Colonel Sandys, of Lanarth, Helston. He was educated at Harrow, Cheltenham and Cambridge, where he graduated B.A. in February 1865. On 20th October 1865 he was gazetted to an Ensigncy in the 1st Battalion of the 24th Regiment. He joined his battalion in Ireland, afterwards proceeding with it to Malta and later to Gibraltar, where on 7th March 1873 he was appointed adjutant, having been promoted Lieutenant on 2nd December 1868. In January 1875 he went to the Cape, and during his service in South Africa he passed the examination for the Staff College, receiving orders to join that establishment. He embarked for England in January 1878.

Lieutenant Melvill, on hearing of the outbreak of fresh hostilities with the natives in Cape Colony, immediately volunteered to rejoin his regiment, and having been given permission, he set out, arriving at King William's Town at the end of February 1878. He served throughout the whole of the Galeka campaign, performing many important and difficult duties.

Prior to the commencement of the Zulu War, Lieutenant Melvill marched with his regiment to join the forces then assembling at Helpmakaar, and taking part in their subsequent advance into Zululand he was present at the storming of Sirayo's stronghold in the Bashee Valley on the 13th January 1879, afterwards proceeding to the camp at Isandhlwana. During the battle on 22nd January Lieutenant Melvill, who had remained in camp, received special orders from Lieutenant-Colonel Pulleine to endeavour to save the Queen's colour of the 1st Battalion. Accompanied by Lieutenant N. J. A. Coghill, Melvill rode off with the cased colour across his saddle. They were very closely pursued by the Zulus, who continually threw spears at them. Both officers reached the flooded Buffalo River, but only Coghill succeeded in crossing, Melvill being encumbered with the colour, having lost his horse, was clinging to a rock in the middle of the river. Lieutenant Coghill immediately went to the assistance of his comrade, and both men managed to reach the Natal bank of the river, although the colour had been swept from their grasp.

The Zulus, who had crossed the river, overtook Melvill and Coghill, and after a brief but gallant resistance both officers were killed. On the 4th February 1879 the bodies of the two officers were discovered where they had fallen. They were subsequently buried there, a cairn and stone cross being erected to their memory.

The details of Lieutenant Melvill's gallant deed appeared in a supplement to the London Gazette dated 1st May 1879, stating that had he survived he would have been recommended for the Victoria Cross. A posthumous award of the decoration was made on the 15th January 1907.

Lieutenant Melvill was married in February 1876 and left a widow and two sons.

Medal for South Africa with clasp '1877–8–9'.

Francis Pender PORTEOUS
(Lieutenant)

Born on 26th March 1847, he was the eldest son of James Porteous of Jamaica, and Emily, daughter of G. S. Kemble, Esq. He was educated at the Reverend A. Jessop Helston's in Cornwall, Mount Radford School (Dr. Roper's), Exeter, and Dr. Carter's in Jersey. Proceeding to Sandhurst, he passed the prescribed course and was gazetted to the 1st Battalion, 24th Regiment, as an Ensign on the 9th March 1866. He joined the regiment at the Curragh, Ireland, and subsequently saw service in Malta, Gibraltar and, in 1875, proceeded to the Cape of Good Hope.

On the 22nd December 1869 he obtained his Lieutenancy by purchase. In 1877 he was appointed Musketry Instructor of his battalion. Throughout the Kaffir War of 1878 he served as Garrison Adjutant at King William's Town.

In November 1878, in view of the impending hostilities with the Zulus, the regiment was ordered to Natal to join the Head-Quarters Column of the army of invasion, then concentrating at Helpmakaar. Taking part in the subsequent advance of that force, in January 1879, into the enemy's country, Lieutenant Porteous was present at the reduction of Sirayo's stronghold in the Bashee Valley, and afterwards proceeded with the column to Isandhlwana; in the disastrous encounter with the enemy which ensued at that position, he fell fighting gallantly at the head of a company of which he had been temporarily placed in command.

(Lieutenant Porteous is listed in the medal roll under the incorrect rank of 'Captain'.)

Medal for South Africa with clasp '1877–8–9'.

Edwards Hopton DYSON
(Second-Lieutenant)

Born on 23rd January 1858, the son of Major Edwards Dyson of Denne Hill, Canterbury, by his marriage with Caroline Agnes, daughter of John Stuart Jerdan of London. He was educated in France, Germany and at Wimbledon School. He subsequently entered the Royal Military College at Sandhurst and on passing out was gazetted on the 1st May 1878 to a Second-Lieutenancy in the 1st Battalion, 24th Regiment, and embarking immediately he joined the battalion at King William's Town.

In November 1878 he proceeded to Helpmakaar to join the forces then assembling for the forthcoming invasion of Zululand, and taking part in the advance of the column he was present at the storming of Sirayo's stronghold in the Bashee Valley, afterwards marching to the camp at Isandhlwana.

During the battle on the 22nd January 1879, Second-Lieutenant Dyson accompanied Captain Cavaye and his company to a position about one thousand yards to the north of the camp. On reaching the position he was given the command of a platoon which was stationed on the left flank of Captain Mostyn's company. It is reported that his platoon rejoined the main body without any loss of life, and the following extract from a private letter written to his father gives some clue to the manner in which he met his death :

"The last person who saw your son and escaped, that I can find, was Captain Essex, 75th Regiment, acting Transport Officer. He tells me that just before the Zulu horns got round our flanks and the last overwhelming rush was made, Dyson was with one section of his company which was in skirmishing order to the left-front of the camp. He gave him orders to retire, and I believe, from another witness, that he and all his company rejoined the main body without loss. The five companies were then together in line, giving volley after volley into dense masses of Zulus at only 150 yards range. The men were laughing and chatting, and thought they were giving the black an awful hammering, when suddenly the enemy came down in irresistible numbers from the rear; the left and right flanks came in with a rush, and in a few minutes all was over."

Second-Lieutenant Dyson was killed on the day before his twenty-first birthday.

The medal roll gives his rank incorrectly as 'Lieutenant'.

Medal for South Africa with clasp '1879'.

Francis Freeman WHITE
(Honorary Major-Paymaster)

Born on 5th February 1829, he was the second son of Benjamin Finch White of Rath Cahill, King's County, Ireland. He was educated by the Reverend H. Tyrrel, curate of Shinrone, King's County.

On the 17th February 1850 he transferred his Ensigncy from the 73rd Regiment to the 24th Regiment, purchasing his Lieutenantcy on 5th May 1854. He was appointed Paymaster on 11th July 1856, promoted Honorary Captain on 11th July 1861, and Honorary Major on 11th July 1866.

Shortly after joining the depot at Chatham in April 1850, he embarked for India to join the head-quarters of the regiment, then stationed in Bengal. During the Indian Mutiny he served with his own regiment, performing many important duties, and subsequently received the Indian Mutiny Medal, without clasp. In 1859 he returned to England, until 1866, when he again proceeded abroad with his regiment, being stationed in Malta and Gibraltar, and then in the latter part of 1874 embarking for the Cape.

He served throughout the Gaika and Galeka campaign, and in November 1878 joined the forces then assembling in readiness for the forthcoming war against the Zulus. Major White took part in the advance into Zululand and was present at the storming of Sirayo's stronghold in the Bashee Valley, afterwards proceeding to Isandhlwana. Little is known of his activities during the battle on the 22nd January 1879; however, the burial party found his body " To the left of the 2nd Battalion, 24th camp."

Major White was the oldest officer in his battalion and had served with it continuously from February 1850 to the day of his death.

He was married in 1874 to Agnes, daughter of Captain Tracey, R.A.

Major White is not named in the original medal roll, but it is presumed that he was entitled to the medal for South Africa with clasp '1877–8–9'.

James PULLEN
(Quartermaster)

Nothing is known about this officer prior to his enlistment as a private soldier in the 24th Regiment in the year 1851. He served for nineteen years in all parts of the globe, and whilst stationed in Malta in 1870 was appointed Colour-Sergeant, and in 1873, when at Gibraltar, was appointed Sergeant Instructor of Musketry.

In 1874 he proceeded with the regiment to the Cape of Good Hope, serving at various stations in the colony. During a period from May to December 1876 he acted as Sergeant-Major to a detachment of his regiment which formed part of the expedition to Griqualand West.

On the 21st September 1877 he was promoted to Quarter-master and served with his battalion in that capacity throughout the Kaffir wars of 1877–1878.

At the commencement of the hostilities against the Zulus, he advanced with his battalion into Zululand, taking part in the reduction of Sirayo's stronghold in the Bashee Valley, later proceeding to the camp at Isandhlwana.

During the battle on 22nd January 1879, Quartermaster Pullen was engaged in supplying ammunition from the battalion ammunition wagon. When the Zulus broke through the defence lines he is reputed to have jumped from the wagon, rallied some twenty men about him, and with them attempted to hold back the tip of the Zulu left horn. It is presumed that he was killed at this stage of the battle.

Medal for South Africa with clasp '1877–8–9'.

Staff

1–24/671 Sergeant-
Major GAPP Frederick
Attested circa 1861. Posted to 1/24th from Depot on 25/11/74. Promoted Sergeant-Major on 31/3/75. Wife (Maria) placed on married establishment on 31/12/74. Effects claimed by next of kin. Medal and clasp '1877–8–9'.

1–24/557 Q.M.S. LEITCH Thomas
Attested on 18/10/60, aged 19 years 6 months. Re-engaged, as a Colour-Sergeant, at Malta on 25/7/70. Wife (Catherine) placed on married establishment on 23/2/67. Children born circa August 1870 and September 1872. Effects claimed by next of kin. Medal and clasp '1877–8–9'.

1–24/1011 Sgt. Inst.
of Musketry CHAMBERS George
Attested at Cork on 6/7/64, aged 18 years 6 months. Promoted Corporal 13/9/67, appointed Sergeant Instructor of Musketry 1/7/77. Made an allowance of 15/6d to Miss J. Kedward, Charles St., Brecon. (There is a memorial to him in Brecon.) Effects claimed by next of kin. Medal and clasp '1879'.

1–24/400 Armourer
Sergeant HAYWARD Henry
Posted to 1/24th from Depot on 12/8/77. Effects claimed by his mother. Medal and clasp '1877–8–9'.

1–24/896 Pay Sgt. MEAD George
Attested on 29/10/63, aged 17 years 3 months. Appointed Pay Sergeant on 16/2/76. Effects claimed by next of kin. Medal and clasp '1877–8–9'.

1–24/843 Drum-
Major TAYLOR Robert
Attested on 11/4/63, aged 14 years. Re-engaged on 23/8/74. Appointed Lance-Corporal 23/8/76. Appointed Drum-Major on 1/5/77. Wife (Maria) placed on married establishment on 1/8/74. Effects claimed by next of kin. Medal and clasp '1877–8–9'.

1–24/1850 Ord. Room
Clerk FITZGERALD Gerald
Posted to service companies on 15/4/72. Promoted Corporal 14/7/74, Sergeant (Orderly Room Clerk) 5/8/74. Effects claimed by next of kin. Medal and clasp '1877–8–9'.

1–24/1510 Sgt. Cook FIELD Alfred
Attested on 18/2/68, aged 18 years. Appointed Master Cook on 6/6/74. Re-engaged at King William's Town on 22/2/78. Wife (Jane Maria) placed on married establishment on 19/12/76. Effects claimed by next of kin. Medal and clasp '1877–8–9'.

1–24/539 Sgt. Tailor SMEDLEY John
Attested on 21/11/60, aged 21 years. Re-engaged at Malta on 26/9/67. Effects claimed by next of kin. Medal and clasp '1877–8–9'.

———— Canteen
Steward SEATON William P.
Formerly Sergeant-Major 24th Foot (No. 601). Served with the regiment for many years prior to being discharged to pension on 11/11/73. His wife was with the regiment from 1862. They had two children born in 1863 and 1871. Appointed Canteen Steward on discharge. Medal and clasp '1877–8–9'.

Colour Sergeants

1–24/1125 Col. Sgt. BALLARD James G.
Attested on 17/2/65, aged 17 years 8 months. Re-engaged, as a Sergeant, at Gibraltar on 14/5/74. Appointed Colour-Sergeant on 23/5/74. Effects claimed by his widow. Medal and clasp '1877–8–9'.

1–24/1118 Col. Sgt. BROWN Thomas P.
Attested on 16/12/64, aged 18 years. Promoted Corporal 25/9/68. Re-engaged at Gibraltar on 9/4/72. Promoted Sergeant 26/7/72, appointed Colour-Sergeant 25/7/75. Effects claimed by his mother. Medal and clasp '1877–8–9'. Medal returned to Mint on 17/9/83.

1–24/1289 Col. Sgt. EDWARDS William
Attested on 28/8/66, aged 18 years. Re-engaged at Cape Town on 15/7/76. Appointed Colour-Sergeant 31/3/75. Medal and clasp '1877–8–9'.

1–24/1887 Col. Sgt. WHITFIELD William
Posted from Depot to Gibraltar on 15/4/72. Promoted Corporal 19/10/73, Sergeant 1/10/74, appointed Colour-Sergeant 9/8/76. Effects claimed by next of kin. Medal and clasp '1877–8–9'.

1–24/617 Col. Sgt. WOLFE Frederick H.
Attested on 16/3/60, aged 15 years. Re-engaged at Malta on 19/5/71. Served in 'H' Company at St. Helena in 1876/77. Effects claimed by next of kin. Medal and clasp '1877–8–9'.

Sergeants

1–24/1699 Sergeant AINSWORTH Peter
Attested at Rugby on 24/6/69, aged 18 years. Previously served in 2nd Stafford Militia. Promoted Corporal 15/9/72, Sergeant 17/10/74. Served in 'H' Company at St. Helena in 1876/77. Effects claimed by his mother, brother and sisters. Medal and clasp '1877–8–9'.

1–24/1895 Sergeant BENNETT George
Posted to Gibraltar in October 1872. Promoted Corporal 17/4/74, Sergeant 31/3/75. Effects claimed by his father. Medal and clasp '1877–8–9'.

1–24/909 Sergeant BRADLEY Daniel
Attested on 23/11/63, aged 19 years. Re-engaged at Malta on 5/8/70. Promoted Corporal 6/1/71. Sent to hospital and probably to England, returning to service companies, as a Sergeant, on 15/5/76. Effects claimed by next of kin. Medal and clasp '1877–8–9'.

1–24/954 Sergeant CLARKSON John
Attested on 21/4/64, aged 18 years. Re-engaged at Malta on 21/3/71. Promoted Corporal in April 1873, Sergeant on 1/10/74. Effects claimed by his father. Medal and clasp '1877–8–9'.

1–24/1019 Sergeant COHOLAN William
Attested on 5/7/64, aged 18 years. Re-engaged at Malta on 9/3/71. Promoted Corporal 17/4/75, appointed Lance-Sergeant 27/2/77, promoted Sergeant 31/7/77. claimed by next of kin. Medal and clasp '1877–8–9'.

1–24/1313 Sergeant COOPER Thomas
Attested on 7/11/66, aged 18 years. Re-engaged, as a Corporal, on 23/12/73. Promoted Sergeant 13/8/74. Effects claimed by his father. Medal and clasp '1877–8–9'.

1–24/1881 Sergeant EDWARDS John
To service companies on 15/4/72. Promoted Corporal 10/7/73, Sergeant 9/8/76. Effects claimed by his mother. Medal and clasp '1877–8–9'.

1–24/1849 Sergeant FAY Thomas
Attested on 19/7/66, aged 19 years. Promoted Corporal 26/8/73. Re-engaged at Gibraltar on 3/1/74. Promoted Sergeant 6/4/77. Wife (Sarah Jane) placed on married establishment on 2/2/74. Child born circa August 1874. Effects claimed by next of kin. Medal and clasp '1877–8–9'.

1–24/315 Sergeant FOWDEN James
Promoted Corporal in 1875, Sergeant 9/8/76. Effects claimed by his brother and sisters. Medal and clasp '1877–8–9'.

1–24/570   Sergeant
(Band)   GAMBLE David
Attested on 30/10/60, aged 14 years 9 months. Re-engaged, as a Sergeant, at Gibraltar on 15/7/73. Wife (Martha) placed on married establishment on 14/10/73. Child born circa December 1875. He managed to escape from the camp, but being on foot he was overtaken and killed by the Zulus. (Statements by 139 Private John Williams and Mr. Brickhill.) Effects claimed by next of kin. Medal and clasp '1877–8–9'.

1–24/968   Sergeant   GILES   Edward
Attested on 19/5/64, aged 19 years. Re-engaged, as a Sergeant, at Gibraltar on 23/3/74. Wife (Anne) placed on married establishment 18/11/71. Effects claimed by next of kin. Medal and clasp '1877–8–9'.

1–24/1754 Sergeant   GREATOREX
Attested on 17/8/70, aged 20 years 4 months. Promoted Sergeant 1/10/74. Served in 'H' Company at St. Helena in 1876/77. Re-engaged at King William's Town on 18/9/78. Effects claimed by his mother. Medal and clasp '1877–8–9'.

1–24/1806 Sergeant   HEPPENSTALL   Christopher
To service companies on 31/1/72. Promoted Corporal on 27/12/73, Sergeant 1/10/75. Effects claimed by his widow, mother, brother and sisters. Medal and clasp '1877–8–9'.

1–24/824   Sergeant   HORNIBROOK   Michael
Attested on 16/1/63, aged 21 years. Re-engaged at Malta, as a Corporal, on 6/10/69. Wife placed on married establishment on 26/10/64. She died on 5/3/76 leaving four children. He re-married (Matilda) and a child was born in 1878. Effects claimed by his brother. Medal and clasp '1879'.

1–24/581   Sergeant   PARSONS   William
Posted to service companies on 4/2/70. Promoted Corporal 7/4/73, Sergeant 1/10/74. Wife (Jane Maria) placed on married establishment on 19/12/76. Effects claimed by his brother. Medal and clasp '1879'.

1–24/1045 Sergeant   PIALL   Alfred
Attested on 5/9/65, aged 15 years. Promoted Corporal 1/10/74. Re-engaged at Cape Town on 16/3/75. Appointed Lance-Sergeant 8/8/76, promoted Sergeant 16/5/77. Served in 'H' Company at St. Helena during 1876/77. Effects claimed by next of kin. Medal and clasp '1877–8–9'.

1–24/1260 Sergeant   REARDON   John
Attested at Curragh on 11/4/66, aged 14 years 6 months. Appointed Drummer circa 1870. Promoted Corporal 24/9/72, appointed Lance-Sergeant 30/9/78. Brother of Drummer Timothy Reardon who was also killed at Isandhlwana. Effects claimed by another brother. Medal and clasp '1877–8–9'.

1–24/1370 Sergeant   SMITH   Joseph
Attested on 13/12/66. Re-engaged, as a Corporal, at Gibraltar, on 20/2/74. Promoted Sergeant on 19/9/74. Wife (Amelia) placed on married establishment on 8/4/74. Children born circa May 1874 and December 1875. Effects claimed by next of kin. Medal and clasp '1877–8–9'.

1–24/565   Sergeant   UPTON   George
Attested on 23/10/60, aged 19 years. Re-engaged at Malta as a Sergeant on 2/10/69. Effects claimed by his widow and child. Medal and clasp '1877–8–9'.

Lance-Sergeant

25B/232   Lance-
Sergeant   MILNER   John
Attested at Liverpool on 28/5/74, aged 18 years 3 months. Effects claimed by his father. Medal and clasp '1879'.

Corporals

25B/126   Corporal   BALL   Nicholas
Attested at Liverpool on 13/4/74, aged 20 years. Effects claimed by his mother and sisters. Medal and clasp '1877–8–9'.

25B/421   Corporal   BELL   Peter
Attested at Liverpool on 28/7/74, aged 23 years 2 months. Effects claimed by next of kin. Medal and clasp '1877–8–9'.

1–24/1415 Corporal   BELLHOUSE   John
Attested on 12/1/67, aged 18 years. Re-engaged at Cape Town on 7/6/76. Promoted Corporal 23/8/76. Effects claimed by next of kin. Medal and clasp '1879'.

1–24/1391 Corporal   BOARD   Alfred C.
Attested on 9/1/67, aged 19 years. Promoted Corporal 21/12/71, reduced to Private 26/8/73. Re-engaged at Cape Town in January 1877. Appointed Lance-Corporal 26/9/77, Corporal 14/9/77. Awarded good shooting prize in 1878. Effects claimed by his mother. Medal and clasp '1877–8–9'

25B/125   Corporal   DAVIES   Richard Simpson
Attested at Manchester on 10/4/74, aged 24 years 10 months. Effects claimed by his brother and sister. Medal and clasp '1877–8–9'.

25B/28   Corporal   EVERETT   Edward R.
Attested circa April 1873. Posted to 2/24th (2–24/2473). Given new Brigade number and posted to 1/24th in October 1873. Promoted Corporal in 1876. Effects claimed by his mother. Medal and clasp '1877–8–9'.

25B/23 Corporal FRANKS John
Attested circa April 1873. Posted to 2/24th (2-24/2479). Given new Brigade number and posted to 1/24th in October 1873. Appointed Lance-Corporal 10/5/77, promoted Corporal 26/9/77. Effects claimed by his mother, brothers and sisters. Medal and clasp '1877-8-9'.

1-24/1886 Corporal KNIGHT John
To service companies on 15/4/72. Promoted Corporal 26/10/75. Effects claimed by next of kin. Medal and clasp '1877-8-9'.

25B/415 Corporal LAWLER James
Attested at Liverpool on 24/7/74, aged 20 years. Effects claimed by his brother and sister. Medal and clasp '1877-8-9'.

25B/524 Corporal MARKHAM Patrick
Attested at Ennis on 2/12/74, aged 18 years 8 months. Effects claimed by his mother and half-sisters. Medal and clasp '1877-8-9'.

1-24/1616 Corporal MILLER Matthew
To service companies on 21/7/69. Promoted Corporal 1/3/70. Effects claimed by his father. Medal and clasp '1879'.

1-24/1736 Corporal (Pioneer) RICHARDSON Henry
Posted from Depot on 4/2/71. He had managed to obtain a horse on which to escape but being wounded in the arm he fell and could not remount. (Statement by Pte. J. Bickley.) Effects claimed by next of kin. Medal and clasp '1877-8-9'.

1-24/855 Corporal ROWDEN John
Attested on 3/10/63, aged 24 years. Re-engaged at Malta on 5/8/70. Appointed Lance-Corporal 8/10/77, promoted Corporal 9/4/78. Effects claimed by his brother and sisters. Medal and clasp '1877-8-9'.

1-24/1538 Corporal TARBUCK John
Attested at Westminster on 8/5/68, aged 18 years. Effects claimed by next of kin. Medal and clasp '1877-8-9'.

25B/193 Corporal WILLIAMS Robert
Attested at Wrexham on 16/5/74, aged 19 years 6 months. Effects claimed by his mother, brother and sister. Medal and clasp '1879'.

Drummers

1-24/2003 Drummer ADAMS William H.
Attested at Gibraltar on 10/5/73, aged 14 years 2 months. Effects claimed by his brother. Medal and clasp '1877-8-9'.

25B/268 Drummer ANDREWS Charles
Attested at Brecon on 6/6/74, aged 19 years. Effects claimed by his mother and brother. Medal and clasp '1877-8-9'.

1-24/1786 Drummer DIBDEN George
To Malta on 4/2/71. Appointed Drummer 2/4/74. Served in 'H' Company at St. Helena during 1876/77. Effects claimed by his father. Medal and clasp '1877-8-9'.

25B/2 Drummer ORLOPP John Frederick
Born on 14/4/59, he lived in John St., Brecon. Attested at Brecon on 12/7/73, aged 14 years 3 months. Appointed Drummer on 6/7/74. Posted to 1/24th, as a Boy, from Depot on 6/10/73. Effects claimed by his next of kin. Medal and clasp '1877-8-9'.

1-24/1226 Drummer OSMOND Charles
Attested on 28/11/65, aged 18 years. Re-engaged at Gibraltar on 18/2/74. Effects claimed by his father. Medal and clasp '1877-8-9'.

1-24/1 Drummer PERKINS Thomas
Posted to 1/24th from Depot on 25/11/75. In view of his service number he may have served at the Depot for several years as a Boy. Effects claimed by next of kin. Medal and clasp '1877-8-9'.

25B/318 Drummer REARDON Timothy
Attested at Cork on 24/6/74, aged 14 years 3 months. Brother of Sergeant John Reardon who was also killed at Isandhlwana. Effects claimed by another brother. Medal and clasp '1879'.

25B/114 Drummer STANSFIELD Michael
Attested at Manchester on 6/4/74, aged 18 years 11 months. The medal roll gives his rank as Private; however, he received pay as a Drummer. Effects claimed by next of kin. Medal and clasp '1877-8-9'.

1-24/1787 Drummer THOMPSON John
Posted to Service Companies on 4/2/71. Appointed Drummer on 1/4/73. Effects claimed by next of kin. Medal and clasp '1877-8-9'.

1-24/1237 Drummer TROTTMAN Daniel
Attested on 29/12/65, aged 16 years. Sentenced to 84 days imprisonment in April 1876. Re-engaged at King William's Town on 25/8/77. Effects claimed by next of kin. Entry on roll reads 'Wife deserted her husband and his child'. Medal and clasp '1877-8-9'.

1-24/2004 Drummer WOLFENDALE Alfred
Attested at Gibraltar on 31/5/73, aged 14 years. Effects claimed by next of kin. Medal and clasp '1877-8-9'.

1-24/1399 Drummer WOLFENDALE James
Named as 'Wolfenden' in some muster rolls. Attested, as a Boy, on 22/12/66. Appointed Drummer on 1/4/69. Effects claimed by next of kin. Medal and clasp '1877-8-9'.

Privates

1–24/1442 Private   ABBOTT Richard
Attested at Westminster on 3/7/67, aged 17 years. Promoted Corporal on 19/4/71. Reduced to Private on 7/12/71. Wife (Elizabeth) with Regiment from 25/9/76. Child born circa January 1877. Effects claimed by next of kin. Medal and clasp '1877–8–9'.

1–24/476 Private   ALLINGHAM Thomas
Attested on 26/8/59, aged 17 years 6 months. Re-engaged at Malta on 27/3/69. Effects claimed by next of kin. Medal and clasp '1877–8–9'.

1–24/937 Private   AMOS Edward
Attested on 26/3/64, aged 18 years. Re-engaged at Malta on 31/12/71. Effects claimed by his brother and sister. Medal and clasp '1877–8–9'.

1–24/1230 Private   ATKINS Alfred
Attested on 2/12/65, aged 20 years. Re-engaged at Gibraltar on 16/8/73. Effects claimed by his mother, brother and sister. The medal roll gives his number incorrectly as '1237'. Medal and clasp '1877–8–9'.

25B/710 Private   BAILEY Joseph
Attested at Brecon on 5/1/76, aged 18 years 1 month. Effects claimed by next of kin. Medal and clasp '1879'.

1–24/1496 Private   BAKER Elijah
Transferred from 1/15th Regiment (1357) on 1/2/68. Effects claimed by his father. Medal and clasp '1877–8–9'.

25B/466 Private   BARRY John
Attested at Oswestry on 24/11/74, aged 19 years 7 months. Effects claimed by his father. Medal and clasp '1877–8–9'.

25B/727 Private   BARRY John
Attested in January 1876. Posted to 2/24th prior to being transferred to 1/24th on 15/5/76. Effects claimed by his brothers. Medal and clasp '1877–8–9'.

25B/300 Private   BARSLEY Elias
Attested at Ashton on 22/6/74, aged 24 years 4 months. Effects claimed by next of kin. Medal and clasp '1877–8–9'.

1–24/1476 Private   BARTLES John
Attested on 10/9/67, aged 19 years 6 months. Re-engaged at Cape of Good Hope on 22/10/75. Served in 'H' Company at St. Helena during 1876/77. Effects claimed by his father. Medal and clasp '1877–8–9'.

25B/451 Private   BASTARD Claude
Attested at Newport on 17/10/74, aged 19 years 2 months. Effects claimed by next of kin. Medal and clasp '1879'.

25B/501 Private   BEADON Robert
Born on 27/5/60. Attested in November 1874 as a Boy. Posted to 2/24th prior to being transferred to 1/24th on 15/5/75. Effects claim by next of kin. Medal and clasp '1877–8–9'.

25B/349 Private   BENHAM John
Attested at Newbury on 2/7/74, aged 20 years. Effects claimed by his mother, brothers and sister. Medal and clasp '1877–8–9'.

1–24/1469 Private   BENNETT Alfred
Attested at Birmingham on 10/9/67, aged 18 years. Effects claimed by next of kin. Medal and clasp '1877–8–9'.

25B/647 Private   BENNETT Richard
Attested on 10/10/75. Posted to 2/24th on 6/1/76, transferred to 1/24th on 15/5/76. Effects claimed by next of kin. Medal and clasp '1877–8–9'.

25B/643 Private   BENSON Robert
Attested on 2/10/75. Posted to 2/24th on 6/1/76, transferred to 1/24th on 15/5/76. Effects claimed by next of kin. Medal and clasp '1877–8–9'.

1–24/1656 Private   BETTERTON Noah
Transferred from 2/2nd Regiment (2–2/1809) on 1/1/69. Effects claimed by next of kin. Medal and clasp '1877–8–9'.

25B/635 Private   BIRCH Joseph
Attested on 27/8/75. Posted to 2/24th on 6/1/76, transferred to 1/24th on 15/5/76. Effects claimed by his father. Medal and clasp '1877–8–9'.

25B/154 Private   BISHOP John
Attested at Liverpool on 30/4/74, aged 18 years 6 months. Effects claimed by next of kin. Medal and clasp '1877–8–9'.

1–24/1681 Private   BLACKHURST Robert
Attested at Preston on 5/6/69, aged 18 years. Effects claimed by his mother. Medal and clasp '1877–8–9'.

1–24/1474 Private   BLOWER James
To service companies on 27/4/69. Promoted Corporal 15/1/74, Sergeant 27/1/77. Served in 'H' Company at St. Helena during 1876/77. Reduced to Private on 13/1/78. Effects claimed by next of kin. Medal and clasp '1879'.

25B/221 Private   BODMAN Frederick
Attested at Devizes on 26/5/74, aged 19 years 8 months. Effects claimed by his brothers. Medal and clasp '1877–8–9'.

25B/64 Private   BOULTON Samuel
Attested at Ashton on 27/2/74, aged 20 years 2 months. Effects claimed by his mother. Medal and clasp '1879'.

25B/106 Private   BOYLAN John
Attested at Ashton on 30/3/74, aged 20 years. Effects claimed by his brother and sisters. Medal and clasp '1877–8–9'.

1–24/950 Private BRAY James
Attested on 29/4/64, aged 19 years. Re-engaged at Malta on 24/3/71. Effects claimed by his mother. Medal and clasp '1877–8–9'.

25B/487 Private BREESE John
Attested at Welshpool on 25/11/74, aged 18 years 10 months. Effects claimed by next of kin. Medal and clasp '1877–8–9'.

25B/43 Private BREW John Wilson
Born on 3/5/59. Attested at Gibraltar, as a Boy, on 2/10/73. Effects claimed by his father. Medal and clasp '1879'.

25B/718 Private BRODERICK Jeremiah
Attested at Newport on 13/1/76, aged 19 years. Effects claimed by next of kin. The medal roll shows him as being entitled to the clasp '1877–8–9'. The actual medal bears a clasp with the date '1879'.

25B/628 Private BROWN Joseph
Attested at Cape Town on 31/5/75, aged 19 years 10 months. Served in 'H' Company at St. Helena during 1876/77. Effects claimed by his father. Medal and clasp '1879'.

25B/320 Private BROWN William
Attested at Liverpool on 30/6/74, aged 22 years. Effects claimed by his father. Medal and clasp '1879'.

25B/452 Private BUGBY Frederick
Named as 'Bugley' in muster roll. Attested at Northampton on 17/10/74, aged 18 years. Effects claimed by his father. Medal and clasp '1879'.

1–24/1875 Private BULL James
To service companies on 15/4/72. Effects claimed by next of kin. Medal and clasp '1877–8–9'.

25B/55 Private BURKE Timothy
Attested at Newport on 26/1/74, aged 19 years. Effects claimed by next of kin. Medal and clasp '1877–8–9'.

25B/176 Private BURKE William
Attested at Brecon on 14/5/74, aged 24 years. Effects claimed by next of kin. Medal and clasp '1877–8–9'.

25B/886 Private BURKE William
Attested at Brecon on 11/11/76. Effects claimed by next of kin. Medal and clasp '1877–8–9'.

25B/75 Private BURNS William
Attested at Liverpool on 6/3/74, aged 21 years 1 month. Effects claimed by his father. His name does not appear in the medal roll, but he is named in the effects list where his rank is given as Corporal. It is presumed that he was entitled to the clasp '1877–8–9'.

1–24/1461 Private BUSBY Thomas
Attested on 31/8/67, aged 20 years 1 month. Re-engaged at the Cape of Good Hope on 23/12/75. Served in 'H' Company at St. Helena during 1876/77. Effects claimed by his mother. Medal and clasp '1877–8–9'.

1–24/1908 Private BUTLER William James
Posted from Depot to Gibraltar in October 1872. Effects claimed by his father. Medal and clasp '1877–8–9'.

25B/494 Private CAHILL Joseph
Named as 'Callahan' in muster roll. Attested at Liverpool on 30/11/74, aged 20 years. Effects claimed by next of kin. Medal and clasp '1877–8–9'.

1–25/825 Private CAMP James
Attested on 13/1/63, aged 18 years. Re-engaged at Malta on 8/4/70. Effects claimed by next of kin. Medal and clasp '1877–8–9'.

25B/840 Private CAMPBELL Michael
Deserted shortly after enlisting and was sentenced to 336 days imprisonment in June 1876. In October 1878 he was sentenced to 252 days imprisonment, but this may have been remitted on commencement of the Zulu War. Effects claimed by next of kin. Medal and clasp '1879'.

25B/713 Private CANTILLON James
Attested on 11/1/76. Posted to 2/24th on 28/1/76, transferred to 1/24th on 15/5/76. Effects claimed by his father. Medal and clasp '1877–8–9'.

25B/468 Private CARPENTER William Henry
Attested at Newport on 5/11/74, aged 19 years. Effects claimed by his mother, brothers and sisters. Number in medal roll given incorrectly as '648'. Medal and clasp '1877–8–9'.

25B/337 Private CARROL Peter
Attested at Manchester on 3/7/74, aged 19 years 2 months. Effects claimed by next of kin. Medal and clasp '1879'.

25B/507 Private CASEY James
Shown as 'Case' in effects roll. Attested at Limerick on 24/11/74, aged 23 years. Effects claimed by his father. Medal and clasp '1877–8–9'.

25B/204 Private CEILEY Edward
Shown as 'Ceily' in medal roll. Attested at Brecon on 26/5/74, aged 19 years 4 months. Effects claimed by next of kin. Medal and clasp '1877–8–9'.

1–24/406 Private CHADWICK William
Attested on 12/9/59, aged 15 years. Re-engaged at Malta on 12/2/70. Effects claimed by his brothers and sisters. Medal and clasp '1877–8–9'.

1–24/2001 Private   CHALMERS William
Transferred from 71st Regiment on 1/4/73. Awarded a good shooting prize in 1873. Wife (Elizabeth) placed on married establishment on 20/8/74. Effects claimed by next of kin. Medal and clasp '1877–8–9'.

25B/389 Private   CHATTERTON James
Attested at Manchester on 16/7/74, aged 21 years. Effects claimed by his mother. Medal and clasp '1877–8–9'.

1–24/206 Private   CHEPMAN William
(Correct name was Chapman). Born at Tonbridge; trade – labourer. Attested on 18/2/58, aged 18 years 4 months. Re-engaged at Malta on 5/5/68. Effects claimed by his mother. Medal and clasp '1877–8–9'.

1–24/1177 Private   CHRISTIAN John
Attested on 7/6/65, aged 18 years. Re-engaged at Cape of Good Hope on 13/3/75. Effects claimed by his brother. Medal and clasp '1879'.

25B/1545 Private   CLARKE Alfred
Attested circa February 1878. Effects claimed by next of kin. Medal and clasp '1877–8–9'.

1–24/1801 Private   CLARKE Michael
Attested on 20/11/65, aged 18 years. Re-engaged at Gibraltar, as a Corporal, on 27/9/73. Reduced to Private on 20/10/73. Served in 'H' Company at St. Helena during 1876/77. Effects claimed by next of kin. Medal and clasp '1877–8–9'.

25B/226 Private   CLEMENTS William Henry
Attested at Swindon on 28/5/74, aged 18 years 9 months. Effects claimed by his sister. Medal and clasp '1877–8–9'.

25B/724 Private   CLUTTERBUCK William
Attested on 27/1/76. Effects claimed by his father. Medal and clasp '1877–8–9'.

25B/334 Private   COLE Albert
Attested at Swindon on 2/7/74, aged 22 years. Effects claimed by next of kin. Medal and clasp '1879'.

25B/749 Private   COLEMAN James
Attested at Brecon on 5/2/76, aged 18 years. Effects claimed by his brother. Medal and clasp '1877–8–9'.

25B/359 Private   COLLINS Daniel
Attested at Cardiff on 8/7/74, aged 19 years. Effects claimed by his mother and sisters. Medal and clasp '1879'.

25B/245 Private   COLLINS Thomas
Attested at Manchester on 3/6/74, aged 24 years. Effects claimed by next of kin. Medal and clasp '1879'.

1–24/205 Private   COLSTON Thomas
Reached Service Companies 2/8/77 with a renumbering of 25B/712, which is given on the list of effects. His 1/24 number suggests he was an old soldier. Effects claimed by his brother or sister. Medal and clasp '1877–8–9'.

1–24/1424 Private   CONBOYE George
To service companies on 4/1/70. Effects claimed by his father. Medal and clasp '1879'.

25B/722 Private   CONNOLLY Cornelius
Attested at Brecon on 22/1/76, aged 21 years 2 months. He was the brother of Private John Connolly, who was also killed at Isandhlwana. Effects claimed by his father. Medal and clasp '1879'.

25B/199 Private   CONNOLLY John
Attested at Newport on 21/5/74, aged 18 years 9 months. He was the brother of Private Cornelius Connolly, who was also killed at Isandhlwana. Effects claimed by his father. Medal and clasp '1877–8–9'.

25B/290 Private   CONNORS Samuel
Attested at Cardiff on 15/6/74, aged 18 years. Effects claimed by next of kin. Medal and clasp '1877–8–9'.

25B/112 Private   COOK James
Attested at Manchester on 4/4/74, aged 20 years. Effects claimed by his brother and sister. Medal and clasp '1877–8–9'.

25B/18 Private   COOPER Henry
Attested circa April 1873. Posted to 2/24th (2–24/2458). Given new brigade number and transferred to 1/24th in October 1873. Served in 'H' Company at St. Helena during 1876/77. Effects claimed by his father. Medal and clasp '1877–8–9'.

1–24/1690 Private   COUGHLAN Richard
To service companies on 4/1/70. Effects claimed by next of kin. Medal and clasp '1879' issued on 3/11/81.

25B/505 Private   COX James
Attested at Leeds on 2/12/74, aged 18 years. Effects claimed by his mother. Medal and clasp '1877–8–9'.

1–24/290 Private   COX Thomas
Attested on 2/3/58, aged 18 years 2 months. Re-engaged at Sheffield on 5/5/68 to complete 21 years service. Effects claimed by his father. Medal and clasp '1877–8–9'.

1–24/797 Private   CULLEN Martin
Attested on 22/11/60, aged 18 years. Re-engaged at Malta on 6/4/69. Effects claimed by his father. Medal and clasp '1877–8–9'.

25B/101 Private   CULLENAN Jeremiah
Named as 'Callahan' in the muster roll. Attested at Pontypool on 26/3/73, aged 24 years. Effects claimed by next of kin. Medal and clasp '1877–8–9'.

25B/650 Private DAVIES Aaron
Shown as 'Davis' in medal roll. Attested at Monmouth on 15/9/75, aged 22 years. Effects claimed by next of kin. Medal and clasp '1877–8–9'.

25B/1042 Private DAVIES William
Shown as 'Davis' in medal roll. Attested at Brecon on 11/1/77. Effects claimed by William Hiley. Medal and clasp '1877–8–9'.

25B/1099 Private DAVIS Edward
Attested at Monmouth on 20/1/77. Effects claimed by next of kin. Medal and clasp '1879'.

25B/184 Private DIGGLE Mark
Attested at Burnley on 14/5/74, aged 22 years. Effects claimed by next of kin. Medal and clasp '1877–8–9'.

25B/115 Private DIGGLE Thomas
To service companies on 25/11/74. Served in 'H' Company at St. Helena during 1976/77. Effects claimed by next of kin. Medal and clasp '1877–8–9'.

25B/395 Private DOBBIN John
Attested at Liverpool on 20/7/74, aged 25 years. Effects claimed by next of kin. Medal and clasp '1877–8–9'.

25B/550 Private DOBBS William
Attested at Monmouth on 1/2/75, aged 21 years. Effects claimed by his mother, brothers and sisters. Medal and clasp '1877–8–9'.

1–24/1790 Private DONOHOE Christopher
To service companies on 31/1/72. Effects claimed by his mother. Medal and clasp '1879'.

25B/242 Private DORAN Michael
Attested at Manchester on 1/6/74, aged 18 years 7 months. Effects claimed by his mother, brother and sisters. Medal and clasp '1877–8–9'.

1–24/1845 Private DORMAN John
To service companies on 15/4/72. Effects claimed by next of kin. Medal and clasp '1879'.

25B/674 Private DOWDE Patrick
Attested at Tredegar on 15/11/75, aged 20 years. Effects claimed by next of kin. Medal and clasp '1879'.

25B/235 Private DREDGE William Robert
Attested at Salisbury on 29/5/74, aged 18 years 3 months. Effects claimed by his brothers and sisters. Medal and clasp '1877–8–9'.

25B/438 Private DUCK Thomas
Attested at Newport on 24/9/74, aged 18 years. Effects claimed by his father. Medal and clasp '1877–8–9'.

1–24/1677 Private DUCKWORTH George
Attested at Preston on 4/6/69, aged 24 years. Effects claimed by his mother-in-law, who stated that she 'looked after his child for six months'. Medal and clasp '1877–8–9'.

25B/185 Private DUFFY John
Attested at Burnley on 14/5/74, aged 18 years 2 months. Effects claimed by his father. Medal and clasp '1877–8–9'.

1–24/1327 Private DUGMORE Edward
Attested on 27/11/66, aged 22 years. Re-engaged at Gibraltar on 29/11/73 to complete 21 years service. Effects claimed by his father. Medal and clasp '1877–8–9'.

1–24/446 Private DUNN Francis
Attested on 6/3/58, aged 18 years. Re-engaged at Malta on 17/10/68 to complete 21 years service. Effects claimed by his brother. Medal and clasp '1877–8–9'.

25B/215 Private DYER John
Attested at Liverpool on 23/5/74, aged 19 years 5 months. Effects claimed by next of kin. Medal and clasp '1877–8–9'.

25B/562 Private EDWARDS John
Attested at Cape Town on 19/1/75, aged 21 years. Effects claimed by next of kin. Medal and clasp '1877–8–9'.

1–24/1799 Private EDWARDS William J.
Posted to service companies on 31/1/72. Wife (Jane Caroline) placed on married establishment on 6/5/73. Child born circa December 1875. Effects claimed by next of kin. Medal and clasp '1877–8–9'.

25B/66 Private EGAN Thomas
Attested at Ashton on 28/2/74, aged 19 years 3 months. Effects claimed by next of kin. Medal and clasp '1877–8–9'.

1–24/1582 Private EGAN William
Attested at Sheffield on 30/6/68, aged 21 years. Effects claimed by his father. Medal and clasp '1877–8–9'.

25B/211 Private ELDERINGTON William
Named as 'Eldrington' in medal roll. Attested at Liverpool on 23/5/74, aged 23 years. Effects claimed by next of kin. Medal and clasp '1877–8–9'.

1–24/1318 Private ELDERTON George
Attested on 14/11/66, aged 18 years. Re-engaged at Gibraltar on 24/7/73. Served in 'H' Company at St. Helena during 1876/77. Effects claimed by his mother, brothers and sisters. Medal and clasp '1879'.

25B/312 Private ELLIS Owen
Attested at Caernarvon on 26/6/74, aged 22 years. (For his letters, see 'The Red Soldier'.) Effects claimed by next of kin. Medal and clasp '1877–8–9'.

25B/163 Private   ELLISON Henry
Attested at Manchester on 4/5/74, aged 23 years 8 months. Effects claimed by next of kin. Medal and clasp '1877–8–9'.

25B/450 Private   ELLSMORE James
Attested at Newport on 16/10/74, aged 18 years. Effects claimed by next of kin. Medal and clasp '1877–8–9'.

25B/556 Private   EVANS David
Attested at Brecon on 16/3/75, aged 19 years. Effects claimed by next of kin. Medal and clasp '1877–8–9'.

25B/109 Private   EVANS John William
Attested at Cardiff on 31/3/74, aged 25 years. Effects claimed by his mother. Medal and clasp '1879'.

25B/518 Private   EVRY Thomas
Attested at Cork on 1/12/74, aged 19 years. Effects claimed by next of kin. Medal and clasp '1877–8–9'.

25B/21 Private   FAIRCLOTH John
Attested circa April 1873. Posted to 2/24th (2–24/2482). Given new brigade number and transferred to 1/24th in October 1873. Effects claimed by next of kin. Medal and clasp '1879'.

25B/178 Private   FARMER William
Attested at Liverpool on 11/5/74, aged 19 years 1 month. Effects claimed by his father. Medal and clasp '1877–8–9'.

25B/403 Private   FAY George Henry
Attested at Manchester on 18/7/74, aged 22 years. Effects claimed by his widow, mother, brother and sisters. Medal and clasp '1877–8–9'.

25B/354 Private   FERRIS Michael
Attested at Cardiff on 4/7/74, aged 23 years. Effects claimed by his father. Medal and clasp '1877–8–9'.

25B/73 Private   FITZGERALD Thomas
Attested at Manchester on 9/3/74, aged 20 years 10 months. Effects claimed by next of kin. Medal and clasp '1877–8–9'.

1–24/1897 Private   FLINT Edward
To service companies at Gibraltar in October 1872. Effects claimed by his father. Medal and clasp '1877–8–9'.

1–24/1752 Private   FLOOD William
To service companies on 4/2/71. Effects claimed by next of kin. Medal and clasp '1877–8–9'.

25B/459 Private   FORTUNE James
The medal roll gives his number incorrectly as '1459'. Attested at Chippenham on 26/10/74, aged 18 years 1 month. Effects claimed by his mother. Medal and clasp '1877–8–9'.

1–24/862 Private   FREEMAN William
Attested on 8/8/63, aged 20 years. Re-engaged at Malta on 12/4/70. Effects claimed by his mother and brother. Medal and clasp '1877–8–9'.

1–24/1305 Private   GILDER Thomas
Attested on 19/10/66, aged 19 years. Re-engaged at Cape Town on 22/11/76. Effects claimed by his brothers and sister. Medal and clasp '1877–8–9'.

25B/22 Private   GILLAN John
Attested circa April 1873. Posted to 2/24th (2–24/2480). Given new brigade number and transferred to 1/24th in October 1873. Served in 'H' Company at St. Helena during 1876/77. Effects claimed by his sisters. Medal and clasp '1877–8–9'.

25B/830 Private   GINGELL Charles
Attested at Monmouth on 19/5/76, aged 19 years. Effects claimed by next of kin. Medal and clasp '1877–8–9'.

25B/408 Private   GLASS George
Attested at Liverpool on 28/7/74, aged 18 years 4 months. Effects claimed by his father. Medal and clasp '1877–8–9'.

1–24/1794 Private   GOATHAM Ashley
Reached service companies January 1872. Shown as 'Ashby Gotham' in earlier muster rolls. Effects claimed by his father. Medal and clasp '1877–8–9'.

1–24/863 Private   GODDARD Charles
Attested on 31/7/63, aged 18 years 10 months. Re-engaged at Gibraltar on 11/5/72. Effects claimed by next of kin. Medal and clasp '1877–8–9'.

1–24/1872 Private   GOODCHILD George
Posted to Gibraltar in October 1872. Effects claimed by his father. Medal and clasp '1877–8–9'.

1–24/1750 Private   GOSS Thomas
Posted to service companies on 4/2/71. Effects claimed by his mother. Medal and clasp '1877–8–9'.

1–24/1854 Private   GREEN William
Attested on 15/7/68, aged 18 years. Re-engaged at King William's Town on 14/9/78. Served in 'H' Company at St. Helena during 1876/77. Effects claimed by his father. Medal and clasp '1877–8–9'.

1–24/1423 Private   GREGG William
Transferred from 2/24th (2–24/1818) to 1/24th, as a Boy, on 31/1/67. Effects claimed by next of kin. Medal and clasp '1879'.

1–24/514   Private   GREGSON William
Attested on 20/1/60, aged 20 years. Re-engaged at Malta on 19/12/67. Wife (Fanny) placed on married establishment on 14/6/73. Children born circa Feb. 1869, Oct. 1871 and Oct. 1875. Effects claimed by next of kin. Medal and clasp '1879'.

25B/535   Private   GRIFFITHS George
Attested at Brecon on 21/12/74, aged 21 years. Effects claimed by his mother, brothers and sister. Medal and clasp '1877–8–9'.

1–24/667   Private   HADDEN George
Attested on 6/1/60, aged 18 years. Re-engaged at Malta on 30/3/69 to complete 21 years service. Effects claimed by his widow and child. Medal and clasp '1877–8–9'.

25B/153   Private   HALE Isaac
Attested at Monmouth on 30/4/74, aged 19 years. Effects claimed by next of kin. Medal and clasp '1877–8–9'.

25B/633   Private   HALL John
Attested at Newport on 18/8/75, aged 18 years 1 month. Effects claimed by next of kin. Medal and clasp '1877–8–9'.

25B/11   Private   HANNAFORD Jacob
Attested circa April 1873. Posted to 2/24th (2–24/2397). Given new brigade number and transferred to 1/24th in October 1873. Effects claimed by his brother. Medal and clasp '1879'.

1–24/1459   Private   HARKIN Thomas
Attested on 29/8/67, aged 21 years. Re-engaged at Cape Town on 19/12/76. Effects claimed by his father. Medal and clasp '1877–8–9'.

1–24/678   Private   HARMAN John
Effects claimed by next of kin. Medal and clasp '1879'.

25B/565   Private   HARNEY Daniel
Attested at Monmouth on 29/3/75, aged 21 years. Effects claimed by his mother. Medal and clasp '1877–8–9'.

1–24/787   Private   HARRINGTON Denis
Attested on 11/1/62, aged 21 years. Re-engaged at Malta on 27/3/68 to complete 21 years service. Effects claimed by next of kin. Medal and clasp '1877–8–9'.

————   Boy   HARRINGTON Thomas
Effects claimed by next of kin. Medal and clasp '1879'.

25B/234   Private   HARRIS Thomas H.
Attested at Devizes on 30/5/74, aged 18 years 6 months. Effects claimed by his father. Medal and clasp '1879'.

25B/392   Private   HARRIS William
Attested at Manchester on 23/7/74, aged 24 years 5 months. Effects claimed by next of kin. Medal and clasp '1877–8–9'.

25B/400   Private   HAYDEN William
Attested at Liverpool on 22/7/74, aged 18 years. Effects claimed by next of kin. Medal and clasp '1879'.

25B/542   Private   HAYNES John
Born on 13/7/60. Attested circa January 1875, as a Boy. Effects claimed by next of kin. Medal and clasp '1877–8–9'.

25B/30   Private   HEDGES James
Attested circa April 1873. Posted to 2/24th (2–24/2471). Given new brigade number and transferred to 1/24th in October 1873. Effects claimed by next of kin. Medal and clasp '1877–8–9'.

25B/696   Private   HEMMINGS Charles
Attested on 15/12/75. Joined 1/24th in South Africa on 2/8/77. Effects claimed by his mother. Medal and clasp '1879'.

1–24/7   Private   HEWITT John
His wife (Mary Ann) was placed on the married establishment on 11/10/73. They had three children born circa January 1869, March 1871 and August 1873. Effects claimed by his widow and brother. Medal and clasp '1877–8–9'.

1–24/1295   Private   HIBBARD James
Number given as 1294 and shown as Hibbert in some musters. Attested at London on 6/9/66, aged 18 years. Effects claimed by his cousin. Medal and clasp '1877–8–9'.

25B/747   Private   HICKEN William H.
Attested on 5/1/76. Joined 1/24th in South Africa on 2/8/77. Effects claimed by next of kin. Medal and clasp '1877–8–9'.

1–24/1856   Private   HICKS Thomas
To service companies on 15/4/72. Effects claimed by his father. Medal and clasp '1877–8–9'.

25B/720   Private   HIGGINS Thomas
Attested on 21/1/76. Joined 1/24th in South Africa on 2/8/77. Effects claimed by his father. Medal and clasp '1879'.

1–24/1857   Private   HIND James
To service companies on 15/4/72. Effects claimed by next of kin. Medal and clasp '1877–8–9'.

25B/776   Private   HITCHEN John
Attested at Brecon on 9/3/76, aged 24 years. Effects claimed by next of kin. Medal and clasp '1879'.

1–24/1757   Private   HOLDEN William
To service companies on 4/2/71. Effects claimed by his brothers and sisters. Medal and clasp '1879'.

1–24/1780   Private   HOLLAND John
Posted to Malta on 4/2/71. Effects claimed by next of kin. Medal and clasp '1879'.

1–24/833 Private HORGAN David
Attested on 16/2/63, aged 18 years. Re-engaged at Malta, as a Corporal, on 13/1/70. Promoted Sergeant 1/4/72. Reduced to Private 9/8/72. Effects claimed by next of kin. Medal and clasp '1879'.

1–24/1673 Private HORN John
Attested on 5/6/69, aged 18 years. Re-engaged at King William's Town on 18/9/78. Served in 'H' Company at St. Helena during 1876/77. Effects claimed by next of kin. Medal and clasp '1877–8–9'.

1–24/1501 Private HORNBUCKLE Charles
Attested on 17/2/68, aged 22 years. Re-engaged at Cape Town on 3/3/75. Served in 'H' Company at St. Helena during 1876/77. Effects claimed by his father. Medal and clasp '1877–8–9'.

1–24/1444 Private HOUGH William
(Col. Glyn's cook.) Born at Manchester, Lancashire; trade – striker. Attested at Litchfield on 13/8/67, aged 19 years. Served in 'H' Company at St. Helena during 1876/77. Information concerning the activities of Private Soldiers during the battle is necessarily scant. William Hough and his participation in the battle has been narrated to some extent by Private Williams, a survivor of the action. It has been conjectured that Hough may possibly have escaped also had he but remained with Williams. (See account by 139 Private John Williams.) Effects claimed by his mother. Medal and clasp '1877–8–9'.

25B/533 Private HUGHES Edwin
The medal roll gives his number incorrectly as '553'. Attested at Wrexham on 5/12/74, aged 19 years. Effects claimed by his mother, brothers and sisters. Medal and clasp '1877–8–9'.

25B/237 Private HUGHES John
Attested at Chippenham on 30/5/74, aged 24 years. Effects claimed by his brother. Medal and clasp '1877–8–9'.

25B/404 Private HUGHES John
Attested at Cardiff on 20/7/74, aged 21 years. Effects claimed by his brother. Medal and clasp '1877–8–9'.

25B/324 Private HUGHES Owen
Attested at Caernarvon on 30/6/74, aged 19 years. Effects claimed by his father. Medal and clasp '1879'.

25B/206 Private HUGHES Thomas
Attested at Caernarvon on 19/5/74, aged 19 years. Effects claimed by next of kin. Medal and clasp '1877–8–9'.

1–24/1892 Private IGGULDEN Alfred
To service companies on 15/4/72. Effects claimed by his mother and father. Medal and clasp '1877–8–9'.

1–24/1822 Private ILSLEY Frederick George
Posted to service companies on 15/4/72. Effects claimed by his sister. Medal and clasp '1877–8–9'.

25B/536 Private IVATTS Ernest
Attested at Abergavenny on 21/12/74, aged 18 years 3 months. Effects claimed by next of kin. Medal and clasp '1877–8–9'.

1–24/1083 Private JENKINS Watkin
Attested at Brecon on 30/6/72, aged 19 years 1 month. He is named as a survivor in the 'Chard' roll for Rorke's Drift, but Bourne lists him as 'killed in action'. He has also been mis-named at 'Matthew' in several instances. It would appear that he has been confused with 841 Pte. James Jenkins, also named in the 'Chard' roll, who was killed in action at Rorke's Drift. Effects claimed by next of kin. Medal and clasp '1879'.

1–24/1767 Private JENKINS William
Born at Marylebone, London; trade – labourer. Posted to service companies on 4/2/71. Wife (Elizabeth) on married establishment on 11/2/77. Effects claimed by widow. Medal and clasp '1879'.

25B/553 Private JOHNSON George
Transferred from 31st Regiment on 1/11/74. Promoted Corporal 10/4/75. Reduced to Private 14/9/75. Effects claimed by his brother, half-brother, sisters and half-sisters. Medal and clasp '1877–8–9'.

1–24/1774 Private JOHNSON Henry
Posted to service companies on 4/1/71. Effects claimed by his father. Medal and clasp '1877–8–9'.

25B/287 Private JOHNSON Joseph
Attested at Liverpool on 16/6/74, aged 21 years. Effects claimed by his mother. Medal and clasp '1879'.

1–24/1449 Private JOHNSON William
Attested on 15/8/67, aged 18 years. Re-engaged at King William's Town on 23/9/78. Effects claimed by his mother, brothers and sisters. Medal and clasp '1877–8–9'.

1–24/1465 Private JOHNSTON George
To service companies on 27/4/68. Promoted Corporal but reduced to Private on 26/1/74. No trace of effects having been claimed. Medal and clasp '1877–8–9'.

1–24/633 Private JOHNSTON James
Attested on 13/12/60, aged 18 years 4 months. Re-engaged at Malta on 12/6/68. Effects claimed by next of kin. Medal and clasp '1877–8–9'.

25B/381 Private JOHNSTON John
Attested at Manchester on 15/7/74, aged 18 years 1 month. Effects claimed by next of kin. Medal and clasp '1877–8–9'.

25B/1 Private JOHNSTONE Alexander
Attested at Brecon on 12/7/73, aged 15 years 1 month. He lived in John St., Brecon. Effects claimed by his father. Medal and clasp '1879'.

25B/350 Private JONES Evan
Attested at Caernarvon on 4/7/74, aged 22 years. Effects claimed by his father. Medal and clasp '1877-8-9'. (In 'Medal Rolls (1793-1889) of the 24th Foot' the above-named was given as 'Enlisted at Monmouth on 6/7/74, aged 19 years 9 months'. This information was extracted from a muster roll which has since been found to be in error. The details as given above are correct.)

25B/360 Private JONES John
Attested at Cardiff on 8/7/74, aged 24 years. Effects claimed by his brothers. Medal and clasp '1879'.

25B/428 Private JONES John
Attested at Brecon on 29/8/74, aged 19 years 6 months. Effects claimed by his father. Medal and clasp '1877-8-9'.

25B/259 Private JONES Thomas
Attested at Monmouth on 5/6/74, aged 23 years. Effects claimed by his father. Medal and clasp '1877-8-9'.

25B/341 Private JONES William
Attested at Monmouth on 6/7/74, aged 19 years 9 months. Effects claimed by his father. Medal and clasp '1877-8-9'.

1-24/1682 Private JONES William
Posted to service companies on 4/1/70. Effects claimed by his wife. Medal and clasp '1879'.

25B/88 Private KEANE John
Attested at Manchester on 18/3/74, aged 18 years 6 months. Effects claimed by his mother, brother and sister. Medal and clasp '1879'.

1-24/1259 Private KEEGAN James
Attested, as a Boy, in April 1866. Appointed Drummer 1/2/69. Reduced to Private 9/3/74. Deserted at King William's Town on 4/4/76, rejoined on 8/5/76. Sentenced to 28 days imprisonment. Tried on 10/11/76 and sentenced to 252 days imprisonment. Effects claimed by his father. Medal and clasp '1877-8-9'.

25B/432 Private KELLY Andrew
Attested at Newport on 31/8/74, aged 19 years. Effects claimed by his father. Medal and clasp '1877-8-9'.

1-24/645 Private KELLY Fenton
Attested on 6/10/75. Effects claimed by his father. Medal and clasp '1879'.

25B/520 Private KELLY James
Attested at Wexford on 5/12/74, aged 21 years 5 months. Effects claimed by next of kin. Medal and clasp '1879'.

25B/789 Private KELLY John F.
Attested at Brecon on 15/3/76, aged 19 years. Effects claimed by his father. Medal and clasp '1877-8-9'.

1-24/1890 Private KEMPSELL Nelson
Posted to service companies on 15/4/72. Effects claimed by his father. Medal and clasp '1877-8-9'.

1-24/883 Private KEMPSTER John
Attested on 20/9/63, aged 22 years. Re-engaged at Malta on 25/6/70. Effects claimed by his sister. Medal and clasp '1877-8-9'.

1-24/1155 Private KNIGHT James
Attested on 21/4/65, aged 19 years. Re-engaged at Gibraltar on 9/8/73. Promoted Corporal on 12/5/74, but later reduced to Private. Served in 'H' Company at St. Helena during 1876/77. Effects claimed by next of kin. Medal and clasp '1879'.

25B/275 Private LAMB John
Attested at Liverpool on 10/6/74, aged 20 years. Effects claimed by his widow. Medal and clasp '1877-8-9'.

25B/707 Private LAMBERT Thomas
Attested at Newport on 31/12/75, aged 20 years. Effects claimed by his mother. Medal and clasp '1879'.

25B/1541 Private LAWRENCE John
Attested circa February 1878. Shown as 'George' in some muster rolls. Effects claimed by next of kin. Medal and clasp '1877-8-9'.

25B/131 Private LEACH Robert
Attested at Liverpool on 13/4/74, aged 19 years 11 months. Effects claimed by his brothers and sisters. Medal and clasp '1877-8-9'.

25B/326 Private LEAVER Thomas
Attested circa June 1874. Posted to 1/24th on 16/10/74. Effects claimed by his sisters. Medal and clasp '1879'.

25B/882 Private LEE John
Attested at Brecon on 7/11/76. Effects claimed by his father. Medal and clasp '1879'.

25B/72 Private LEWIS Henry
Attested at Brecon on 6/3/74, aged 22 years 2 months. Effects claimed by next of kin. Medal and clasp '1879'.

25B/478 Private LEWIS Richard
Attested at Brecon on 21/11/74, aged 18 years. Effects claimed by his mother. Medal and clasp '1879'.

1–24/1277 Private   LING James
        Attested on 16/7/66, aged 21 years. Re-engaged at Gibraltar on 20/8/74. Effects claimed by his father. Medal and clasp '1877–8–9'.

25B/531 Private   LINNANE John
        Attested at Ennis on 7/12/74, aged 20 years. Effects claimed by next of kin. Medal and clasp '1877–8–9'.

25B/133 Private   LIPPETT Stephen
        Attested at Monmouth on 17/4/74, aged 20 years 3 months. Effects claimed by next of kin. Medal and clasp '1877–8–9'.

1–24/710 Private   LISBECK George
        Attested on 31/7/58, aged 18 years. Effects claimed by next of kin. Medal and clasp '1877–8–9'.

1–24/1862 Private   LLOYD George
        To service companies on 15/4/72. Served in 'H' Company at St. Helena during 1876/77. Effects claimed by next of kin. Medal and clasp '1879'.

25B/296 Private   LOCKETT William
        Attested at Manchester on 17/6/74, aged 23 years 6 months. Effects claimed by his father. Medal and clasp '1877–8–9'.

25B/521 Private   LOVELL Charles
        Attested at Northampton on 9/12/74, aged 18 years. Effects claimed by next of kin. Medal and clasp '1879'.

1–24/1649 Private   LOWE Charles Samuel
        Attested as a Boy at 14th Brigade Depot on 25/3/69. Effects claimed by his grandmother. He was the brother of Pte. Richard Lowe who was also killed at Isandhlwana. Medal and clasp '1877–8–9'.

1–24/1841 Private   LOWE Richard
        To service companies on 15/4/72. Effects claimed by his grandmother. He was the brother of Pte. Charles Lowe who was also killed at Isandhlwana. Medal and clasp '1877–8–9'.

25B/268 Private   LYCETT James
        Attested at Liverpool on 2/6/74, aged 20 years 1 month. Effects claimed by next of kin. Medal and clasp '1877–8–9'.

1–24/258 Private   LYONS John
        Attested on 21/11/57, aged 19 years. Re-engaged at Malta on 26/6/67. Effects claimed by his sister. Medal and clasp '1877–8–9'.

25B/663 Private   McDONALD Miles
        Taken into the 1st/24th as a deserter from the 86th Regiment (No. 1532). Tried on 13/9/75 and sentenced to 84 days imprisonment. He served in the Mounted Infantry at Isandhlwana and, as in the case of 1444 Pte. William Hough, some brief details concerning him are known. In 1907 Smith-Dorrien wrote a narrative of the battle at the request of the officers of the 24th Regiment. He says: 'I then came to Fugitives Drift – I found there a man in a red coat badly assegaied in the arm and unable to move. He was, I believe, a Mounted Infantryman of the 24th named MacDonald, but of his name I cannot be sure. I managed to make a tourniquet with a handkerchief to stop the bleeding, and got him half-way down, when a shout behind said, "Get on, man, the Zulus are on top of you." I turned round and saw Major Smith, R.A., as white as a sheet and bleeding profusely, and in a second we were surrounded, and assegais accounted for poor Smith, my wounded M.I. friend and my horse.' Effects claimed by his brothers. Medal and clasp '1879'.

25B/1393 McFARLANE Matthew
        Attested on 2/8/77. Effects claimed by next of kin. Medal and clasp '1877–8–9'.

25B/330 Private   McHALE John
        Attested on 16/10/74. Tried by Civil Power in January 1875 and sentenced to 1 month imprisonment. Effects claimed by next of kin. Medal and clasp '1877–8–9'.

1–24/1378 Private   MACK Hugh Anthony
        Attested on 26/12/66, aged 18 years. Re-engaged at Gibraltar on 11/9/73. Effects claimed by his father. Medal and clasp '1877–8–9'.

25B/630 Private   MACKENZIE John J.
        Attested at Cape Town on 9/6/75, aged 21 years 5 months. Effects claimed by next of kin. Medal and clasp '1877–8–9'.

25B/47 Private   MAER George Richard
        Attested at Newport on 2/12/73, aged 20 years. Effects claimed by his father. Medal and clasp '1877–8–9'.

25B/590 Private   MAHONEY Charles
        (Attached to Rocket Battery.) Attested at Cardiff on 5/5/75, aged 19 years. Effects claimed by his father. Medal and clasp '1879'.

25B/137 Private   MALONEY Martin
        Attested at Brecon on 20/4/74, aged 22 years. Effects claimed by next of kin. Medal and clasp '1877–8–9'.

1–24/992 Private   MANN William
        Attested on 17/6/64, aged 19 years. Re-engaged at Malta on 24/3/71. Effects claimed by next of kin. Medal and clasp '1879'.

25B/916 Private   MARLEY Luke
        Attested at Monmouth on 22/11/76. Effects claimed by next of kin. Medal and clasp '1879'.

1-24/1348 Private   MARNEY Cornelius
Shown in some musters as 'Mahoney'. Attested on 3/12/66, aged 18 years. Re-engaged at Cape Town on 22/11/76. Effects claimed by his brother. Medal and clasp '1879'.

1-24/1758 Private   MARTIN David
Attested on 23/8/70, aged 21 years. Re-engaged at King William's Town on 20/9/78. Effects claimed by his mother. Medal and clasp '1877-8-9'.

25B/293 Private   MEREDITH John H.
Attested at Manchester on 17/6/74, aged 19 years. Effects claimed by his father. Medal and clasp '1879'.

1-24/1509 Private   MILLEN Charles
Attested on 19/2/68, aged 21 years. Re-engaged at King William's Town on 18/9/78. Served in 'H' Company at St. Helena during 1876/77. Effects claimed by his father. Medal and clasp '1879'.

1-24/508 Private   MILLER Patrick
Attested on 7/12/59, aged 24 years. Re-engaged at Malta on 9/10/67. Wife (Frances) on married establishment on 3/7/62. Five children born between 1862 and 1875. Served in 'H' Company at St. Helena during 1876/77. Effects claimed by next of kin. Medal and clasp '1877-8-9'.

1-24/1398 Private   MOORE Richard
Attested on 22/12/66, aged 16 years 5 months. Re-engaged at Cape Town on 20/6/77. Effects claimed by next of kin. Medal and clasp '1877-8-9'.

25B/803 Private   MORGAN John
Attested at Tredegar on 27/3/76, aged 18 years 6 months. Effects claimed by his mother. Medal and clasp '1877-8-9'.

25B/490 Private   MORGAN William
Attested at Shrewsbury on 26/11/74, aged 18 years 1 month. Effects claimed by next of kin. Medal and clasp '1877-8-9'.

25B/610 Private   MORRIS George
Attested at Brecon on 21/6/75, aged 21 years. Effects, including £9-13-2d, claimed by his mother (Jane Morris). Medal and clasp '1879'.

1-24730 Private   MORSE Richard
Attested on 23/11/68, aged 22 years 5 months. Re-engaged at Malta on 30/3/69. Effects claimed by next of kin. Medal and clasp '1877-8-9'.

25B/63 Private   MURPHY John
Attested at Brecon on 27/2/74, aged 20 years. Effects claimed by next of kin. Medal and clasp '1877-8-9'.

25B/862 Private   MURPHY Patrick
Attested at Brecon on 18/10/76. Effects claimed by his mother. Medal and clasp '1879'.

1-24/594 Private   MURRAY John
Attested on 12/12/60, aged 18 years. Re-engaged at Malta on 3/4/69. Effects claimed by next of kin. Medal and clasp '1877-8-9'.

25B/399 Private   NASH Patrick
Posted to service companies on 16/10/74. Effects claimed by next of kin. Medal and clasp '1877-8-9'.

1-24/1928 Private   NEWBERRY Alfred
To the 25 Bde., when it was formed, and returned to 1/24th on 15/11/74. Effects claimed by his father. He was the brother of Pte. Thomas Newberry who was also killed at Isandhlwana. Medal and clasp '1877-8-9'.

1-24/1906 Private   NEWBERRY Thomas
To the 25 Bde. when it was formed, and returned to 1/24th on 15/11/74. Promoted to Cpl. 5/7/76. Later reduced to Private. Effects claimed by his father. He was the brother of Pte. Alfred Newberry who was also killed at Isandhlwana. Medal and clasp '1879'.

25B/648 Private   NICHOLAS Walter
Attested at Newport on 4/10/75, aged 18 years. Effects claimed by next of kin. Medal and clasp '1879'.

1-24/1839 Private   NYE William E.
Reached Service Companies January 1872. Effects claimed by his widow. Medal and clasp '1877-8-9'.

1-24/1245 Private   OAKLEY William
Attested on 15/1/66, aged 19 years. Re-engaged at Gibraltar on 25/2/73. Effects claimed by his father. Medal and clasp '1877-8-9'.

25B/754 Private   ODEY George
Attested at Monmouth on 9/2/76, aged 19 years. Medal and clasp '1877-8-9'.

1-24/1417 Private   OGDEN James
Attested on 24/1/67, aged 19 years. Re-engaged at Gibraltar on 13/8/74. Effects claimed by his father. Medal and clasp '1877-8-9'.

1-24/1478 Private   PADMORE James
Attested on 18/9/67, aged 17 years. Promoted Corporal. Reduced to Private on 7/4/73. Re-engaged at King William's Town on 18/9/78. Effects claimed by next of kin. Medal and clasp '1877-8-9'.

1-24/980 Private   PAINTER Thomas
Attested on 6/6/64, aged 19 years. Re-engaged at Malta on 30/11/71. Effects claimed by next of kin. Medal and clasp '1877-8-9'.

25B/471 Private   PARRY Robert
Attested at Cork on 6/11/74, aged 21 years. Effects claimed by his brothers and sisters. Medal and clasp '1877-8-9'.

25B/12   Private   PATTERSON Henry H.
            Attested circa April 1873. Posted to 2/24th (2–24/2475), given new brigade number and transferred to 1/24th in October 1873. Effects claimed by next of kin. Medal and clasp '1879'.

25B/310   Private   PETERS John
            Attested at Newport on 26/6/74, aged 24 years 5 months. Effects claimed by next of kin. Medal and clasp '1877–8–9'.

1–24/845   Private   PHILLIPS James Nicholas
            Attested on 21/5/63, aged 19 years. Re-engaged at Malta on 8/6/70. Effects claimed by his father. Medal and clasp '1877–8–9'.

1–24/237   Private   PHILLIPS John
            Attested on 1/9/57, aged 18 years. Re-engaged at York on 11/3/67. Effects claimed by his father. Medal and clasp '1877–8–9'.

25B/87   Private   PICKARD Jabez Reid
            Attested at Ashton on 17/3/74, aged 22 years. Served in 'H' Company at St. Helena during 1876/77. Effects claimed by his mother and half-sister. Medal and clasp '1877–8–9'.

1–24/374   Private   PLANT Samuel
            With regiment from July 1859. Wife (Mary) on married establishment from 3/7/62. Served in 'H' Company at St. Helena during 1876/77. Effects claimed by his widow. Medal and clasp '1877–8–9'.

25B/181   Private   PLUNKETT James
            Attested at Burnley on 13/5/74, aged 20 years. Effects claimed by his half-brother and half-sister. Medal and clasp '1879'.

1–24/1368   Private   POLLEN Augustus
            Attested on 11/12/66, aged 22 years. Re-engaged at Gibraltar on 19/9/73. Effects claimed by his brother. Medal and clasp '1877–8–9'.

1–24/1793   Private   POPE William
            To service companies in January 1872. Served in 'H' Company at St. Helena during 1876/77. Effects claimed by his mother. Medal and clasp '1877–8–9'.

25B/222   Private   POTTOW Uriah
            Attested at Devizes on 27/5/74, aged 18 years. Effects claimed by next of kin. Medal and clasp '1879'.

25B/739   Private   POWELL Henry
            Attested at Tredegar on 31/1/76, aged 19 years 6 months. Effects claimed by next of kin. Medal and clasp '1877–8–9'.

25B/950   Private   PROCTOR John
            Attested at Cape Town on 20/10/76, aged 19 years. Effects claimed by next of kin. Medal and clasp '1879'.

25B/597   Private   PROSSER George
            Attested at Monmouth on 29/5/75, aged 19 years. No trace of effects having been claimed. Medal and clasp '1879'.

25B/797   Private   PROSSER John
            Number in effects roll given incorrectly as '799'. Attested at Monmouth on 23/3/76, aged 18 years 4 months. Effects claimed by his mother and brother. Medal and clasp '1877–8–9'.

25B/182   Private   PUGH Walter
            Attested at Newport on 13/5/74, aged 19 years 1 month. Effects claimed by his father. Medal and clasp '1879'.

25B/856   Private   PUGH William
            Attested at Brecon on 16/10/76. Effects claimed by next of kin. Medal and clasp '1879'.

25B/513   Private   QUIRK James
            Attested at Clonmel on 7/12/74, aged 23 years. Effects claimed by next of kin. Medal and clasp '1877–8–9'.

1–24/1826   Private   REMINGTON Edward
            Born on 9/7/57 and attested as a Boy. To service companies on 31/1/72. Effects claimed by next of kin. Medal and clasp '1879'.

1–24/1650   Private   RETFORD William H. J.
            Attested as a Boy on 4/1/70. Deserted on 25/1/75, rejoined on 18/5/75. Sentenced to 112 days imprisonment. Effects claimed bv next of kin. Medal and clasp '1877–8–9'.

1–24/840   Private   RICHARDS George
            Born at Birmingham; trade – gun barrel forger. Attested on 25/2/63, aged 20 years. Re-engaged at Malta on 27/10/69. Effects claimed by his mother. Medal and clasp '1879'.

25B/265   Boy   RICHARDS Robert
            His name does not appear in the medal roll, but he is named in the pay list as 'Killed on 22/1/79'. There is no trace of his effects having been claimed. It is presumed that he was entitled to the medal and clasp.

25B/871   Private   RICHARDSON Mitchell
            To service companies on 2/8/77. Effects claimed by his father. Medal and clasp '1879'.

1–24/808   Private   RIGNEY John
            Attested on 18/10/62, aged 18 years. Re-engaged in Malta on 16/9/69. Effects claimed by his brother and sisters. Medal and clasp '1877–8–9'.

1–24/504   Private   RITTMAN John
            Number in medal roll originally given as '804' – later amended to correct number 504. Attested on 4/11/59, aged 18 years. Re-engaged at Malta on 22/9/68. Effects claimed by next of kin. Medal and clasp '1877–8–9'.

25B/355   Private   ROBERTS William
Attested at Manchester on 6/7/74, aged 24 years 1 month. Effects claimed by his brother. Medal and clasp '1877–8–9'.

1–24/1866 Private   RODGERS Henry
To service companies on 15/4/72. Effects claimed by his bother, brothers and sisters. Medal and clasp '1877–8–9'.

1–24/740   Private   ROUBREY Patrick
Attested on 13/5/61, aged 18 years. Re-engaged at Malta on 7/4/69. Effects claimed by next of kin. Medal and clasp '1877–8–9'.

25B/210   Private   ROWMAN Henry
Named in the muster roll as 'H. Rowan'. Effects claimed by next of kin. Medal and clasp '1877–8–9'.

25B/548   Private   RULE Walter
Born on 28/1/61. Attested as a Boy and posted to 2/24th on 15/5/75. Effects claimed by next of kin. Medal and clasp '1879'.

25B/40   Private   RUSSELL Frederick
Attested circa April 1873. Posted to 2/24th (2–24/2451). Given new brigade number and transferred to 1/24th in October 1873. Effects claimed by next of kin. Medal and clasp '1877–8–9'.

1–24/1452 Private   RUTTER Thomas
Attested at Wolverhampton on 15/8/67, aged 19 years. Served in 'H' Company at St. Helena during 1876/77. Effects claimed by next of kin. Medal and clasp '1877–8–9'.

25B/909   Private   RYAN James
Attested at Brecon on 20/11/76. Effects claimed by his father. **Medal and clasp '1879'.**

25B/488   Private   SALTER George
Attested at Newport on 28/11/74, aged 19 years. Effects claimed by his mother and brothers. Medal and clasp ' 1877–8–9'.

25B/529   Private   SARNEY Frederick
Transferred from 2/24th 15/5/75. Effects claimed by his father. Medal and clasp '1877–8–9'.

25B/279   Private   SEARS Henry
Attested at Liverpool on 13/6/74, aged 18 years 2 months. Effects claimed by his father. Medal and clasp '1879'.

1–24/1971 Private   SELLWOOD William
Attested circa January 1873. Effects claimed by mother, brothers and sisters. Medal and clasp '1877–8–9'.

25B/147   Private   SHARP Frederick
Attested at Salisbury on 22/4/74, aged 18 years. Effects claimed by next of kin. Medal and clasp '1877–8–9'. [Medal returned 'found' on 4/8/32. On long loan to Officer Commanding Depot, South Wales Borderers.]

25B/200   Private   SHAW Robert
Attested at Liverpool on 18/5/74, aged 19 years. Effects claimed by his father. Medal and clasp '1877–8–9'.

25B/497   Private   SHEA Daniel
Attested at Tralee on 27/11/74, aged 18 years. Effects claimed by next of kin. Medal and clasp '1877–8–9'.

1–24/1130 Private   SHEATHER Henry
Attested on 27/2/65, aged 19 years. Re-engaged at Malta on 11/12/71. Effects claimed by next of kin. Medal and clasp '1877–8–9'.

1–24/1396 Private   SHRIMPTON John
Attested on 10/1/66, aged 18 years. Re-engaged at Gibraltar on 20/9/73. Effects claimed by his brother. Medal and clasp '1879'.

25B/649   Private   SILCOCK Robert
Attested on 8/10/75. Effects claimed by his father. Medal and clasp '1877–8–9'.

25B/384   Private   SKELTON Walter
Attested at Manchester on 16/7/74, aged 20 years 10 months. Effects claimed by next of kin. Medal and clasp '1877–8–9'.

25B/506   Private   SMITH Charles
Attested at Liverpool on 2/12/74, aged 20 years. Effects claimed by his father. Medal and clasp '1879'.

1–24/1867 Private   SMITH Charles
Attested circa April 1872. Effects claimed by next of kin. Medal and clasp '1877–8–9'.

25B/1047 Private   SMITH Edwin
Attested on 14/1/77. Effects claimed by next of kin. Medal and clasp '1879'.

25B/58   Private   SMITH George
Attested at Newport on 6/2/74, aged 18 years. Effects claimed by next of kin. Medal and clasp '1877–8–9'.

1–24/1903 Private   SMITH James
Attested circa Sept. 1872. Effects claimed by his father. Medal and clasp '1879'.

1–24/396   Private   SPEED Thomas
Attested on 23/6/58, aged 18 years 4 months. Re-engaged at Sheffield on 5/5/68 to complete 21 years service. Effects claimed by his uncles. Medal and clasp '1877–8–9'.

1–24/851   Private   STEVENS Henry
Attested on 6/7/63, aged 19 years. Re-engaged at Malta on 23/4/70. Effects claimed by his widow, mother and sisters. Medal and clasp '1877–8–9'.

25B/20   Private   STEVENS William
Attested circa April 1873. Posted to 2/24th (2–24/2484). Given a new brigade number and transferred to 1/24th in October 1873. Effects claimed by next of kin. Medal and clasp '1877–8–9'.

25B/900　Private　STRANGE Edward
To service companies on 2/8/77. Effects claimed by next of kin. Medal and clasp '1879'.

1-24/1495　Private　SULLIVAN John
Transferred from 1/14th Regiment on 1/1/68. Served in 'H' Company at St. Helena during 1876/77. Effects claimed by his mother, brothers and sisters. Medal and clasp '1877-8-9'.

25B/888　Private　SULLIVAN Patrick
Attested at Brecon on 14/11/76. Effects claimed by his father. Medal and clasp '1877-8-9'.

25B/161　Private　SUTTON Patrick
Attested at Newport on 5/5/74, aged 24 years. Effects claimed by next of kin. Medal and clasp '1877-8-9'.

25B/664　Private　SWOFFER Richard
Attested on 2/10/75. Posted to 2/24th on 6/1/76. Transferred to 1/24th on arrival in South Africa on 2/8/77. Medal and clasp '1879'.

1-24/1779　Private　TATE Reuben
To service companies on 4/2/71. Effects claimed by his father. Medal and clasp '1877-8-9'.

25B/659　Private　TAYLOR Edward
Attested at Monmouth on 26/10/75, aged 22 years. Effects claimed by his father. Medal and clasp '1877-8-9'.

1-24/1760　Private　TERRY James
Number on medal roll given incorrectly as 1670. Posted to service companies on 4/2/71. Effects claimed by next of kin. Medal and clasp '1877-8-9'.

1-24/1753　Private　THEOBALD William
Posted to service companies on 4/2/71. Effects claimed by his mother. Medal and clasp '1879'.

25B/636　Private　THOMAS John
Attested at Brecon on 27/8/75, aged 24 years. Effects claimed by next of kin. Medal and clasp '1879'.

25B/765　Private　THOMAS John B.
Attested at Newport on 17/2/76, aged 22 years 2 months. Effects claimed by his father. Medal and clasp '1877-8-9'.

25B/34　Private　THORNETT Thomas
Attested circa April 1873. Posted to 2/24th (2-24/2463). Given new brigade number and transferred to 1/24th in October 1873. Served in 'H' Company at St. Helena during 1876/77. Effects claimed by next of kin. Medal and clasp '1877-8-9'.

25B/33　Private　THROSSELL Charles
Attested circa April 1873. Posted to 2/24th (2-24/2464). Given new brigade number and transferred to 1/24th in October 1873. Effects claimed by next of kin. Medal and clasp '1877-8-9'.

25B/317　Private　TILLISON Henry
Attested at Burnley on 29/6/74, aged 20 years. Effects claimed by next of kin. Medal and clasp '1877-8-9'.

25B/383　Private　TINNERY Thomas
Attested at Manchester on 15/7/74, aged 24 years 6 months. Effects claimed by his father. Medal and clasp '1877-8-9'.

1-24/1782　Private　TODD George
Posted to service companies on 4/2/71. Effects claimed by his aunt. Medal and clasp '1879'.

25B/209　Private　TOWNSEND Joseph
Attested at Devizes on 23/5/74, aged 18 years 6 months. Effects claimed by his mother and father. Medal and clasp '1877-8-9'.

25B/543　Private　TROWELL Edward
Born on 13/7/60. Attested, as a Boy, circa 24/8/74. Effects claimed by his brother and sister. Medal and clasp '1879'.

25B/14　Private　TULLETT James
Attested circa April 1873. Posted to 2/24th (2-24/2494). Given new brigade number and transferred to 1/24th in October 1873. Served in 'H' Company at St. Helena during 1876/77. Effects claimed by his brother and sisters. Number on medal roll given incorrectly as '16'. Medal and clasp '1877-8-9'.

25B/946　Private　TURNER Edward
Attested on 13/4/64, aged 21 years. Re-engaged on 9/3/71. Served in the Mounted Infantry. Effects claimed by his father. Medal and clasp '1877-8-9'.

25B/85　Private　VINES George
Attested at Trowbridge on 17/3/74, aged 18 years. Effects claimed by his mother. Medal and clasp '1877-8-9'.

1-24/925　Private　WALKER Edward
Attested on 10/5/58, as a Drummer, aged 14 years. Re-engaged at Malta on 27/3/69. Effects claimed by his father. Medal and clasp '1877-8-9'.

25B/444　Private　WALKER Edward
Shown as 'Wallor' in muster roll. Attested at Warley on 24/9/74, aged 15 years 5 months. Effects claimed by next of kin. Medal and clasp '1877-8-9'.

25B/285　Private　WALSH Thomas
Attested at Manchester on 15/6/74, aged 19 years. Effects claimed by his mother and sisters. Medal and clasp '1877-8-9'.

24B/493 Private WALSH Thomas
Attested at Liverpool on 30/11/74, aged 21 years 6 months. Effects claimed by next of kin. Medal and clasp '1877–8–9'.

25B/851 Private WALSH Thomas
Shown as 'Welsh' in muster roll. Attested at Newport on 20/9/76, aged 22 years. Effects claimed by his mother. Medal and clasp '1879'.

25B/596 Private WALTON William
Attested at Cardiff on 5/4/75, aged 21 years. Deserted on 8/4/75 – rejoined on 1/6/75. Released on 2/6/75 as a pardoned deserter. Effects claimed by his mother, brother and sister. Medal and clasp '1877–8–9'.

1–24/531 Private WARNER Joseph
Attested on 1/6/60, aged 18 years. Re-engaged at Malta on 26/7/67. Effects claimed by his brother and sisters. Medal and clasp '1877–8–9'.

25B/380 Private WATKINS William Henry
Attested at Abergavenny on 15/7/74, aged 17 years 8 months. Effects claimed by his father. Medal and clasp '1877–8–9'.

1–24/1152 Private WATLEY John
Attested on 15/4/65, aged 19 years. Re-engaged at Gibraltar on 6/5/73. Effects claimed by his mother, brother and sister. Medal and clasp '1877–8–9'.

1–24/1919 Private WATTS Henry
Posted to Gibraltar in October 1872. Effects claimed by his sister. Medal and clasp '1877–8–9'.

25B/697 Private WEBB Thomas
Attested on 15/12/75. Effects claimed by his father. Medal and clasp '1879'.

1–24/489 Private WETHERHEAD Henry
Attested on 28/7/59, aged 19 years. Re-engaged at Malta on 10/12/67. Effects claimed by next of kin. Medal and clasp '1879'.

25B/642 Private WHELAN John
Attested at Brecon on 24/9/75, aged 23 years. Effects claimed by his aunt. Medal and clasp '1877–8–9'.

1–24/1184 Private WHELAN Thomas
Attested on 15/6/65, aged 19 years. Re-engaged at Gibraltar on 9/4/72. Served in 'H' Company at St. Helena during 1876/77. Effects claimed by next of kin. Medal and clasp '1877–8–9'.

1–24/591 Private WHYBROW Elijah
Attested on 11/12/60, aged 20 years. Re-engaged, as a Corporal, at Malta on 27/3/69. Later reduced to Private. Effects claimed by next of kin. Medal and clasp '1877–8–9'.

25B/297 Private WILKINSON Arthur
Attested at Manchester on 18/6/74, aged 21 years 7 months. Effects claimed by his mother. Medal and clasp '1877–8–9'.

25B/134 Private WILKS Frederick
Attested at Monmouth on 17/4/74, aged 25 years. Effects claimed by next of kin. Medal and clasp 1877–8–9'.

25B/455 Private WILLIAMS Ellis
Attested at Caernarvon on 21/10/74, aged 21 years. Effects claimed by next of kin. Medal and clasp '1879'.

25B/778 Private WILLIAMS Evan
Attested at Brecon on 9/3/76, aged 22 years. Effects claimed by next of kin. Medal and clasp '1879'.

25B/545 Private WILLIAMS James
Attested at Pontypool on 21/1/75, aged 19 years. Effects claimed by next of kin. Medal and clasp '1879'.

25B/582 Private WILLIAMS John
Attested at Cardiff on 20/4/75, aged 20 years. Effects claimed by next of kin. Medal and clasp '1879'.

25B/868 Private WILLIAMS Joseph
Attested at Monmouth on 26/10/76. Effects claimed by next of kin. Named in the Regimental History and also given by Bourne as being killed at Rorke's Drift. It would appear that he may have been confused with 1398 Private Joseph Williams (2/24th) who was killed at Rorke's Drift. Medal and clasp '1877–8–9'.

25B/288 Private WILLIAMS Matthew
Shown in muster roll as 'Mathias'. Attested at Liverpool on 16/6/74, aged 22 years. Effects claimed by his mother. Medal and clasp '1877–8–9'.

25B/534 Private WILLIAMS Thomas
Attested at Wrexham on 5/12/74, aged 18 years 1 month. Effects claimed by his brother and sisters. Medal and clasp '1877–8–9'.

25B/624 Private WILLIAMS Thomas
Attested at Newport on 30/7/75, aged 19 years 6 months. Effects claimed by his uncle. Medal and clasp '1877–8–9'.

25B/698 Private WILLIAMS William E.
Attested on 15/12/75. Effects claimed by next of kin. Medal and clasp '1879'.

1–24/1267 Private WILSON John
Attested on 12/6/66, aged 17 years 10 months. Re-engaged at Cape Town on 9/10/76. Effects claimed by next of kin. Medal and clasp '1877–8–9'.

1–24/533   Private   WILSON Samuel
        The medal roll gives his initial incorrectly
as 'F'. His number is given as '553' in the
effects roll. Attested on 8/10/60, aged 19
years. Re-engaged at Malta on 22/7/67.
Effects claimed by his mother and sisters.
Medal and clasp '1879'.

1–24/227   Private   WISHER William
        Attested in 1857. Effects claimed by next of
kin. Medal and clasp '1877–8–9'.

1–24/888   Private   WOOD James
        Attested on 7/10/63, aged 22 years. Re-
engaged at Malta on 8/6/70. Effects claimed
by next of kin. Medal and clasp '1877–8–9'.

1–24/1266   Private   WOOLLEY John
        Attested on 9/6/66, aged 20 years. Re-
engaged at Gibraltar on 15/2/73. Effects
claimed by next of kin. Medal and clasp
'1877–8–9'.

25B/589   Private   WORTHINGTON Enoch
        Attested at Newcastle-under-Lyme on
23/4/75, aged 20 years 2 months. Effects
claimed by his father. Medal and clasp
'1877–8–9'.

1–24/1768   Private   WRIGHT Robert
        Posted to Malta on 4/2/72. Effects claimed
by his mother. Medal and clasp '1879'.

1–24/1654   Private   YOUNG Thomas
        Attested in 1869. Effects claimed by next of
kin. Medal and clasp '1877–8–9'.

2nd Battalion

24th Regiment of Foot

List of Officers, Non-commissioned Officers and Men killed at the
battle of Isandhlwana, 22nd January, 1879

Henry Julian DYER
(Lieutenant and Adjutant)

Born on 21st October 1854 at Redhill, Surrey, he was the eldest son of Henry Julian Dyer, and Emma, eldest daughter of Francis Glass of Beckenham, Kent. He was educated at the Institute Taplin, Lohnstein-on-Rhine. On 11th October 1876 he was gazetted to a Lieutenancy in the 2nd Battalion, 24th Regiment, which he joined at Dover and later proceeded with his battalion to Chatham. In 1877 he was successful in passing through the School of Musketry at Hythe.

On 2nd February 1878 he embarked with the regiment for South Africa where, after arriving, he served throughout the whole of the operations in connection with the suppression of the Galeka outbreak. In November 1878, Lieutenant Dyer proceeded with the regiment to Natal to join the force being prepared for the forthcoming hostilities with the Zulus, having prior to this held an appointment as principal officer at Durban. He took part in the advance into Zululand and was present at the storming of Sirayo's stronghold in the Bashee Valley, afterwards proceeding to the camp at Isandhlwana.

On the morning of the 22nd January, he left Isandhlwana with the main body of the column, under Lord Chelmsford; but subsequently rode back on special service with Major Smith, Captain Gardner and Sub-Lieutenant Griffith, to convey the General's order to advance the camp. On returning to the camp he became involved in the battle, and it has been testified that his body was found together with a group of some sixty other men who had formed a rallying point during the retreat, and had fought desperately to the end.

Medal for South Africa with clasp '1877–8–9'.

Frederick GODWIN-AUSTEN
(Lieutenant)

Born on 3rd August 1853 at Chilworth Manor, Surrey, he was the fourth surviving son of Robert Alfred Cloyne Godwin-Austen, D.L., J.P., F.R.S., of Shalford House, Surrey, and Maria Elizabeth, only daughter of General Sir Henry Thomas Godwin, K.C.B., who served in the Peninsula and at Waterloo.

He was commissioned on 28th February 1875 and posted to the 2nd West India Regiment, with which he served in both the West Indies and on the Gold Coast. In 1877 he exchanged into the 2nd Battalion, 24th Regiment, which he joined at Chatham, and later proceeded with his battalion to South Africa.

Lieutenant Godwin-Austen served through the Kaffir war of 1878, and later proceeding to Natal, he joined the forces then preparing for the invasion of Zululand. He took part in the subsequent advance into that country and was present at the storming of Sirayo's stronghold in the Bashee Valley, afterwards proceeding to the camp at Isandhlwana. An induna who was present at the battle on 22nd January 1879 subsequently gave a minute description of the deaths of two officers, since ascertained to have been Lieutenants Godwin-Austen and Pope. The Zulu stated that when surrounding the 24th Regiment at the Neck at Isandhlwana, two officers with pieces of glass in their eye came forward, shooting at him with their revolvers. One fell from a gunshot, and the other kept firing his revolver at the induna, grazing the right side of his neck with one bullet, the left side with another, and wounding him in the leg with a third. The induna then flung an assegai which entered the officer's breast. The officer, with a supreme effort, almost succeeded in pulling out the weapon, but the induna fell on him and finished his work with another assegai.

Lieutenant Frederick Godwin-Austen's two elder brothers both served in the 24th Regiment, Lieutenant-Colonel H. H. Godwin-Austen serving from 1852 to 1861, and Captain A. G. Godwin-Austen who served throughout the Kaffir war of 1878, in which he was wounded.

Medal for South Africa with clasp '1877–8–9'.

Charles D'Aguilar POPE
(Lieutenant)

Born on 23rd August 1849, he was the eldest son of the Reverend J. P. Pope, Assistant Chaplain, H.E.I.C.S. He was educated at Bath, and in 1865 he entered Sandhurst, passing out in 1868. On 8th January 1868 he was gazetted to an Ensigncy in the 2nd Battalion, 24th Regiment. He was promoted to Lieutenant on 4th February 1871, and shortly afterwards embarked for Madras, where he served for a period of three years. Returning to England in 1876, he undertook a course of garrison gunnery instruction and obtained an extra first class certificate from the School of Musketry at Hythe.

In February 1878, Lieutenant Pope embarked for South Africa, and arriving at the Cape, served with his battalion through the Kaffir war of that year. In the following November he proceeded with the regiment to Natal to join the force then being prepared for the invasion of Zululand. He took part in the subsequent advance of the column, and was present at the reduction of Sirayo's stronghold in the Bashee Valley, afterwards proceeding to the camp at Isandhlwana.

On 22nd January 1879 Lieutenant Pope, in command of his company, was on picquet duty. Several survivors of the battle testified to the remarkable self-possession with which Lieutenant Pope encouraged his men, and restrained their wasteful fire when the order 'to retire' was given; and the record of the part he played on the fatal day is supplemented by a statement made by an induna who was present at the battle. The Zulu reported that, when surrounding the 24th Regiment at the Neck of Isandhlwana, two officers (subsequently ascertained to have been Lieutenants Pope and Godwin-Austen), with pieces of glass in their eye, came forward shooting at him with their revolvers. One fell from a gunshot, and the other kept firing his revolver at the induna, grazing the right side of his neck with one bullet, the left side with another, and wounding him in the leg with a third. The induna then flung an assegai which entered the officer's breast. The officer, with a supreme effort, almost succeeded in pulling out the weapon, but the induna fell on him and instantaneously finished his work with another assegai.

Lieutenant Pope, beside being an excellent linguist, was also an accomplished draughtsman, and many of his sketches were reproduced in the *Graphic*.

Medal for South Africa with clasp '1877–8–9'
issued on 11th April 1881.

Thomas Llewelyn George GRIFFITH
(Sub-Lieutenant)

Born on 8th October 1857 at Chadlington, Oxon, he was the eldest son of the Reverend Thomas Llewelyn Griffith, M.A. (of Pen-y-Nant, near Ruabon, North Wales, and Rector of Deal, Kent), and Mary Moncreiff, daughter of the late Brevet-Major George St. Vincent Whitmore, Royal Engineers.

He was educated at Marlborough College and at the Priory at Croydon, passing his army entrance examination as well as those at Sandhurst and Edinburgh, where for a period of time he was attached to the 78th Highlanders. On 14th August 1877 he was gazetted to a Sub-Lieutenantcy in the 2nd Battalion, 24th Regiment. His commission was antedated to the 11th November 1876.

He joined the regiment at Chatham in October 1877, and on 1st February 1878 he proceeded to the Cape of Good Hope. He was present during many operations in the Kaffir war, and saw much service with his battalion. In November 1878 he joined the force preparing for the invasion of Zululand, and took part in the subsequent advance into that country, being present at the storming of Sirayo's stronghold in the Bashee Valley, afterwards proceeding to Isandhlwana.

On the morning of 22nd January 1879 he left Isandhlwana with the main body of the column under Lord Chelmsford, but subsequently rode back on special service with Major Smith, Captain Gardner and Lieutenant Dyer, to convey the General's orders to advance the camp. Colonel Black, visiting the battlefield five months afterwards for the purpose of burying the dead, found the bodies of some sixty officers and men lying in a group, giving evidence of their having gathered together and fought desperately to the last. Among them were the remains of Captain Wardell, Lieutenant Dyer and a captain and subaltern of the 2nd Battalion, the latter, it is believed, being the body of young Griffith.

A memorial lectern in the parish church of St. Leonard's, Deal, marks the estimation in which he was held by those round his own home, having been placed there by friends in his father's parish and the neighbourhood.

Medal for South Africa with clasp '1877–8–9'
issued on 30th June 1882.

Edward BLOOMFIELD
(Quartermaster)

Born on 7th November 1835, he enlisted in the Scots Fusilier Guards at the age of eleven years. He was transferred to the 2nd Battalion of the 24th Regiment on its formation, and subsequently served in Mauritius, Burma and India. In 1868, after twenty-two years service, he was promoted from Colour-Sergeant to Sergeant-Major. He

returned from India to England in 1873, when he was awarded the good conduct medal, and in September of the same year was promoted to Quartermaster.

In February 1878 he proceeded to the Cape of Good Hope, and subsequently served through the whole of the operations in connection with the suppression of the Galeka outbreak. In November of the same year he proceeded with his regiment to Natal to join the force being prepared to act against the Zulus. Taking part in the subsequent advance of the column, he was present at the storming of Sirayo's stronghold in the Bashee Valley, afterwards proceeding to Isandhlwana.

In the engagement on the 22nd January 1879 he shared the fate of the officers and men of the regiment who fell. He was killed in the act of serving out to the men, in the thick of the engagement, the cartridges which enabled them to make their last desperate stand.

Quartermaster Bloomfield was married and had one child.

Medal for South Africa with clasp '1877–8–9'.

Staff

—————　Bandmaster BULLARD　Harry T.
Effects claimed by his mother-in-law. Medal and clasp '1877–8–9'.

2-24/1689　Q.M.S.　DAVIS George H.
Attested at Birmingham on 9/2/65, aged 18 years. Promoted Corporal 5/5/72, Sergeant 21/5/73. Appointed Colour-Sergeant 4/1/76, Sergeant Instructor of Musketry 21/5/78, Q.M.S. 27/4/78. Served in 'D' Company. Medal and clasp '1877–8–9' issued on 7/5/81.

Sergeants

25B/927　Sergeant　CARSE　Henry
Attested on 30/11/76. Appointed Lance-Corporal on 20/7/77, promoted Corporal 1/5/78, Sergeant 26/8/78. Served in 'G' Company. Medal and clasp '1877–8–9'.

2-24/1416　Sergeant
(Cook)　CHEW　Charles
Promoted Corporal 21/7/63, Sergeant 1/10/68. Served in 'E' Company. Medal and clasp '1877–8–9'.

2-24/2227　Sergeant LINES　John
Transferred from 1/24th (1-24/897) on 15/3/70. Promoted Corporal 31/1/72, Sergeant circa 1874. Served in 'A' Company. Medal and clasp '1877–8–9' issued on 25/8/82.

2-24/1078　Sergeant　REEVES William J. G.
Detached to School of Engineering and served as Pioneer Sergeant in 1877. To Sergeant 20/4/78. Served in 'G' Company. Medal and clasp '1877–8–9' issued on 25/8/82.

25B/50 Sergeant ROSS John
Attested at Brecon on 24/12/73, aged 18 years 9 months. Confined on 27/11/78, tried on 30/11/78 – remustered to prevent sentence. Served in 'F' Company. Medal and clasp '1877–8–9'.

2–24/2336 Sergeant SHAW William
Number given as '2236' in some muster rolls. Posted to India on 28/12/70. Promoted Corporal 22/1/73, Sergeant 8/4/77. Served in 'H' Company. Medal and clasp '1877–8–9'.

25B/899 Sergeant WILKINS George
Number in medal roll given incorrectly as '889'. Originally attested in 1865 (2–24/1742), aged 18, height 5' 6¾", and discharged on completion of service. Re-attested on 20/11/76. Promoted Corporal 1/2/78, Sergeant 3/12/78. Served in 'E' Company. Medal and clasp '1877–8–9'.

Lance-Sergeants

25B/1217 Lance-Sergeant HAIGH Joseph
Attested on 20/2/77. Promoted Corporal 1/2/78. Served in 'G' Company. Effects claimed by his mother. Medal and clasp '1877–8–9'.

2–24/1755 Lance-Sergeant McCAFFERY James
Attested on 9/9/65, aged 21 years. Re-engaged at Aldershot on 31/5/75. Appointed Lance-Corporal 2/11/76, promoted Corporal 1/2/77, appointed Lance-Sergeant 1/11/77. Made remittances to his wife, then living in Limekiln St., Dover. See letter written by Sgt. E. Daly (page 103, *The Red Soldier*). Served in 'A' Company. Medal and clasp '1877–8–9'.

Corporals

2–24/1268 Corporal GREENHILL William
Promoted Corporal 5/9/64. Served in 'G' Company. Effects claimed by his wife and two children. Medal and clasp '1877–8–9'.

25B/1248 Corporal HENSHAW James
Attested on 24/2/77. Appointed Lance-Corporal 1/2/78, promoted Corporal 2/11/78. Served in 'A' Company. Effects claimed by his mother. Medal and clasp '1877–8–9'.

25B/657 Corporal LOW John M.
Attested at Newport on 20/10/75, aged 24 years 10 months. Promoted Corporal 3/10/78. Medal and clasp '1879'.

25B/725 Corporal MORTLOCK Henry
Attested on 28/1/76. Promoted Corporal 16/9/78. Served in 'G' Company. Effects claimed by his sister. Medal and clasp '1877–8–9'.

25B/673 Corporal SIMS George
Attested on 14/11/75. Appointed Lance-Corporal 1/5/78, promoted Corporal 14/7/78. Served in 'F' Company. Effects claimed by his father. Medal and clasp '1877–8–9'.

25B/1103 Corporal THOMPSON George
Attested on 26/1/77. Promoted Corporal 22/7/78. Served in 'G' Company. Medal and clasp '1877–8–9'.

Lance-Corporal

25B/929 Lance-Corporal ELVEY John
Attested on 1/12/76. Appointed Lance-Corporal 14/8/78. Served in 'D' Company. Medal and clasp '1877–8–9'.

Drummers

2–24/2161 Drummer ANDERSON John
Attested at Preston on 21/8/69, aged 14 years. Trained at the Royal School of Military Music, Kneller Hall. Joined the 2nd/24th, as a Drummer, on 6/2/73. Awarded a good shooting prize in 1878. Served in 'G' Company. Effects claimed by next of kin. Medal and clasp '1877–8–9' issued on 19/3/81.

2–24/2153 Drummer HOLMES JOHN
Transferred from 90th Regiment (90/1343) 19/5/69. Posted to India on 11/2/70. Served in 'G' Company. Effects claimed by his wife and child. Medal and clasp '1877–8–9' issued on 29/7/81.

Privates

25B/1266 Private ALLEN Joseph
Attested on 28/2/77. Served in 'G' Company. Effects claimed by his father. Medal and clasp '1877–8–9' issued on 3/8/81.

25B/1142 Private BARTON J. William
Attested at Brecon on 2/2/77. Served in 'G' Company. Medal and clasp '1877–8–9'.

25B/1471 Private BEAVAN Samuel
Attested at Pontypool on 23/11/77. Served in 'G' Company. Effects claimed by his father. Medal and clasp '1877–8–9'.

25B/1413 Private BENNETT Thomas
Attested into the 36th Brigade on 2/9/77 from the Monmouth Militia. Transferred to 2/24th on 2/8/77. Served in 'G' Company. Effects claimed by his mother, brother and sisters. Medal and clasp '1877–8–9' issued on 18/10/82.

25B/1550 Private BISHOP Henry
Medal and clasp '1879'.

25B/854   Private   BRAY Arthur
Attested at Brecon on 13/10/76. Served in 'G' Company. Effects claimed by his mother. Medal and clasp '1877–8–9'.

25B/1141   Private   BRIDGEWATER Francis
Attested at Tredegar on 1/2/77. Served in 'G' Company. Effects claimed by his mother, brother and sisters. Medal and clasp '1877–8–9' issued on 25/8/81.

2–24/2053 Private   BRIERLY George P.
Attested at Manchester on 27/7/68, aged 18 years. Served in 'C' Company. Effects claimed by his father. Medal and clasp '1877–8–9' issued on 25/8/81.

25B/960   Private   BRODERICK Michael
Attested on 10/12/76. Served in 'A' Company. Medal and clasp '1877–8–9'.

25B/1177   Private   BRYANT William
Initial given incorrectly as 'J' in medal roll. Attested on 11/2/77. Served in 'B' Company. Medal and clasp '1877–8–9'.

25B/517   Private   BUCKLEY Robert
Attested at Cork on 30/11/74, aged 24 years. Served in 'G' Company. Effects claimed by next of kin. Medal and clasp '1877–8–9'.

25B/1262   Private   BULL Thomas
Attested on 28/2/77. Served in 'E' Company. Medal and clasp '1877–8–9'.

2–24/1500 Private   BYARD Edward A.
Attested at Birmingham on 23/6/64, aged 18 years. No trace of effects having been claimed. Medal and clasp '1877–8–9'.

25B/721   Private   BYRNE John
Attested on 22/1/76. Served in 'A' Company. Effects claimed by his mother. Medal and clasp '1877–8–9' issued on 29/1/81.

2–24/1671 Private   BYRNE John
Attested at Leeds on 6/3/65, aged 18 years 6 months. Served in 'A' Company. Medal and clasp '1877–8–9'.

25B/1336   Private   CARROLL Thomas
Attested on 6/3/77. Served in 'D' Company. Effects claimed by his father. Medal and clasp '1877–8–9'.

25B/1510   Private   CHARLES William
Attested at Monmouth on 24/1/78. Served in 'G' Company. Effects claimed by his father. Medal and clasp '1879'.

2–24/1598 Private   CHERRY Fred
Attested at Reading on 19/1/65, aged 18 years 6 months. Served in 'G' Company. Effects claimed by his widow and child. Medal and clasp '1877–8–9' issued on 25/8/82.

25B/723   Private   CLEARY Maurice
Attested at Brecon on 22/1/76, aged 22 years 6 months. Served in 'G' Company. No trace of effects having been claimed. Medal and clasp '1877–8–9'.

25B/819   Private   CORNISH Thomas
Attested at Monmouth on 24/4/76, aged 20 years. Served in 'D' Company. Effects claimed by his mother. Medal and clasp '1877–8–9' issued on 29/3/82.

25B/1031   Private   DAVIES George
Attested on 4/1/77. Served in 'G' Company. Effects claimed by his father. Medal and clasp '1877–8–9'.

25B/743   Private   DAVIES John James
Attested at Brecon on 2/2/76, aged 24 years. Served in 'D' Company. Effects claimed by his brother. Medal and clasp '1877–8–9'.

25B/1414   Private   DAVIS David
Attested at Brecon on 7/6/77. Served in 'G' Company. Effects claimed by his father. Medal and clasp '1877–8–9' issued on 22/9/81.

25B/894   Private   DAVIS James
Attested at Monmouth on 13/11/76. Served in 'A' Company. Effects claimed by his brother and sister. Medal and clasp '1877–8–9'.

25B/121   Private   DAVIS John
Attested at Cardiff on 2/4/74, aged 19 years. Served in 'E' Company. Medal and clasp '1877–8–9'.

25B/1026   Private   DONEGAN Michael
Attested on 7/1/77. Served in 'G' Company. Effects claimed by his wife. Medal and clasp '1877–8–9' issued on 26/1/81.

25B/872   Private   DOWLE John
In Millbank Prison early in 1877. To service companies on 24/5/77. Served in 'G' Company. Effects claimed by mother and brother. Medal and clasp '1877–8–9' issued on 17/5/81.

2–24/2081 Private   EARISH John
The effects roll gives his number incorrectly as '281'. To service companies on 5/4/69. Served in 'G' Company. Effects claimed by his wife and father. Medal and clasp '1877–8–9'.

25B/1166   Private   EDWARDS Edmund
Attested at Brynmawr on 1/2/77. Served in 'A' Company. Effects claimed by next of kin. Medal and clasp '1877–8–9'.

25B/786   Private   EDWARDS John
Attested at Brecon on 14/3/76, aged 20 years. Served in 'G' Company. Effects claimed by his mother. Medal and clasp '1877–8–9'.

25B/1378 Private EMERSON Robert
Attested on 27/3/77. Served in 'A' Company. Effects claimed by his aunt and uncle. Medal and clasp '1877–8–9' issued on 29/8/81.

25B/1389 Private EVANS John
Attested at Brecon on 27/4/77. Served in 'A' Company. Medal and clasp '1877–8–9'.

25B/1041 Private FARR Alfred
Attested at Brecon on 4/1/77. Effects claimed by his mother, brothers and sisters. Medal and clasp '1877–8–9' issued on 1/10/81.

2–24/1963 Private FINN Thomas
Attested circa 1868. Promoted Corporal 11/5/74. Detached to 105th Regiment in March 1876, returned to 2/24th Regiment shortly afterwards. Appointed Lance-Sergeant 1/2/78, promoted Sergeant 12/3/78. Reduced to Private 2/12/78. Served in 'G' Company. Medal and clasp '1877–8–9'.

2–24/2307 Private FITTON George
Born at St. Andrew's; trade - labourer. Attested on 8/7/70. Deserted on 31/3/73, rejoined on 1/9/73. Served in 'G' Company. Medal and clasp '1877–8–9'.

25B/1519 Private FITZPATRICK Michael
Transferred from 2/25th Regiment (No. 2374) to 2/24th on 1/2/78. To 88th Regiment on 1/7/78, returning on 1/8/78. Medal and clasp '1877–8–9'.

25B/1030 Private FLYN David
Attested on 10/1/77. Sentenced to 42 days hard labour at Fort Clarence in June 1877. Served in 'G' Company. Medal and clasp '1877–8–9'.

2–24/2222 Private FLYN Joseph
Attested in 1/24th (1–24/1557) in 1869. Transferred to 2/24th and posted to service companies on 28/12/70. Served in 'A' Company. Effects claimed by his widow. Medal and clasp '1877–8–9' issued on 5/4/81.

25B/738 Private FORTUNE Michael
Attested at Tredegar on 29/1/76, aged 20 years. Served in 'E' Company. Effects claimed by his father. Medal and clasp '1877–8–9' issued on 20/5/81.

25B/1162 Private FOX Thomas
Attested on 10/2/77. Served in 'G' Company. Effects claimed by his mother. Medal and clasp '1877–8–9' issued on 20/5/81.

2–24/2335 Private FRY James
Reached service companies 28/12/70. Served in 'G' Company. Good shooting prize 1878. Medal and clasp '1877–8–9'.

2–24/1771 Private GEE William
Born on 4/7/52. Attested at London on 6/12/65. Sent to Kneller Hall, returning to service companies as a Bandsman on 4/11/67. Served in 'G' Company. Effects claimed by his widow and child. Medal and clasp '1877–8–9' issued on 7/5/81.

25B/619 Private GHOST George
Attested at Aldershot on 16/7/75, aged 14 years. Served in 'G' Company. Effects claimed by his mother. Medal and clasp '1877–8–9' issued on 24/9/81.

25B/1491 Boy GORDON Daniel
Attested at Chatham on 6/12/77, aged 13 years. Served in 'B' Company. Medal and clasp '1877–8–9' issued on 16/12/82.

2–24/1056 Private GRIFFITHS William V.C.
Born at Roscommon; trade – collier. He was awarded the Victoria Cross, together with Assistant-Surgeon C. M. Douglas and Privates D. Bell, J. Cooper and T. Murphy: 'For the very gallant and daring manner in which, on 7th May 1867, they risked their lives in manning a boat and proceeding through dangerous surf to the rescue of some of their comrades who formed part of an expedition that had been sent to the Island of Little Andaman –'. Served in 'G' Company. Effects claimed by his mother. Medal and clasp '1877–8–9' issued on 2/9/81.

25B/1494 Private GURNEY James
Attested at Chatham on 20/12/77, aged 15 years. Served in 'D' Company. Effects claimed by next of kin. Medal and clasp '1877–8–9' issued on 16/12/82.

25B/1272 Private HACKER Samuel
Attested at Newport on 27/2/77. Served in 'D' Company. Effects claimed by his father. Medal and clasp '1877–8–9' claimed and issued in 1973.

25B/1527 Private HALL Benjamin
Attested at Brecon on 4/2/78. Served in 'G' Company. Medal and clasp '1879' issued on 12/1/82.

2–24/1636 Private HALL Charles
Attested circa December 1864. Served in 'D' Company. Medal and clasp '1877–8–9'.

25B/1260 Private HALL John
Attested on 28/1/77. Served in 'E' Company. Effects claimed by his father. Medal and clasp '1877–8–9' issued on 15/12/81.

25B/1297 Private HALL William
Attested on 3/3/77. Served in 'G' Company. Effects claimed by his brother. Medal and clasp '1877–8–9'.

25B/618 Private HANKIN Leonard
Attested at Aldershot on 16/7/75, aged 14 years. Served in 'G' Company. Effects claimed by his mother. Medal and clasp '1877–8–9'.

2–24/2323 Private   HAWKINS William
Posted to service companies on 28/12/71. Served in 'A' Company. Effects claimed by next of kin. Medal and clasp '1877–8–9'.

25B/1219 Private   HEALEY John
Attested on 20/2/77. Served in 'G' Company. Effects claimed by next of kin. Medal and clasp '1877–8–9'.

25B/1313 Private   HILL James Edward
Also shown as 'John' in musters. Attested on 6/3/77. Effects claimed by his mother. Medal and clasp '1877–8–9'.

25B/887 Private   HOPKINS Robert Harry
Attested at Brecon on 14/11/76. Served in 'D' Company. Effects claimed by his father, brothers and sisters. Medal and clasp '1877–8–9' issued on 25/8/81.

25B/886 Private   HORROCKS George
Attested at Brecon on 26/10/76. Served in 'A' Company. Medal and clasp '1877–8–9'.

25B/791 Private   HOWELLS Robert
Attested at Brecon on 22/3/76, aged 18 years. Served in 'A' Company. Effects claimed by his father. Medal and clasp '1877–8–9'.

2–24/1678 Private   HUDSON George
Born at Bakewell; trade – striker. Attested at Manchester on 19/5/69, aged 21 years 10 months. Previously served in 6th Lancashire Militia. Served in 'D' Company. Effects claimed by his father. Medal and clasp '1877–8–9'.

25B/1024 Private   HUGHES Francis
Attested at Brecon on 7/1/77. Served in 'G' Company. Medal and clasp '1877–8–9'.

2–24/1593 Private   HUNT John
Attested at Westminster on 25/1/65, aged 19 years. Served in 'G' Company. Effects claimed by his mother and brothers. Medal and clasp '1877–8–9'.

25B/1135 Private   JENKINS William
Attested on 2/2/77. Served in 'G' Company. Medal and clasp '1877–8–9'.

25B/1025 Private   JOHNSTONE William
Attested on 7/1/77. Served in 'G' Company. Effects claimed by his father. Medal and clasp '1877–8–9'.

25B/1097 Private   JONES Abraham
Attested at Pontypool on 20/1/77. Served in 'G' Company. Effects claimed by his mother, brothers and sisters. Medal and clasp '1877–8–9'.

25B/983 Private   JONES Edward
Attested on 19/12/76. Served in 'G' Company. Medal and clasp '1879'.

25B/948 Private   JONES James
Attested on 4/12/76. Served in 'G' Company. Medal and clasp '1877–8–9'.

25B/976 Private   JONES Thomas
Attested at Brecon on 13/12/76. Served in 'C' Company. Effects claimed by his father. Medal and clasp '1877–8–9' issued on 29/8/81.

25B/1382 Private   JONES Thomas
Attested at Newport on 19/4/77. Served in 'A' Company. Effects claimed by his mother. Medal and clasp '1877–8–9'.

25B/1511 Private   JONES Thomas
Served in 'A' Company. Medal and clasp '1879'.

25B/804 Private   JONES William
Attested at Brecon on 30/3/76, aged 19 years 6 months. Served in 'C' Company. Effects claimed by his mother. Medal and clasp '1877–8–9' issued on 20/6/81.

2–24/2400 Private   KELLY John
Born at Drung, Co. Cavan; trade – labourer. Attested circa January 1873. Served in 'A' Company. Medal and clasp '1877–8–9'.

2–24/1707 Private   KENNEDY Thomas
Attested at Clonmel on 27/2/65, aged 19 years. Served in 'A' Company. Medal and clasp '1877–8–9'.

2–24/1707 Private   KING Joseph
Promoted Corporal 3/5/66, but later reduced to Private. Attended musketry course in 1873. Effects claimed by his father. Medal and clasp '1877–8–9'.

25B/654 Private   LATHAM Benjamin
Attested at Newport on 18/10/75, aged 18 years. Served in 'C' Company. Medal and clasp '1877–8–9'.

25B/1532 Private   LEWIS Edward
Attested at Newport on 16/1/78. Served in 'E' Company. Effects claimed by his father. Medal and clasp '1879'.

2–24/1957 Private   LEWIS James
Incorrectly given in the medal roll as serving in 1881. Reduced from Corporal to Private on 17/4/69. Served in 'G' Company. Medal and clasp '1877–8–9'.

25B/70 Private   LLEWELLYN James
Attested at Manchester on 5/3/74, aged 22 years. Served in 'G' Company. Effects claimed by his widow. Medal and clasp '1877–8–9' issued on 5/4/81.

25B/762 Private   LONG Charles
Attested at Brecon on 16/2/76, aged 19 years 10 months. Appointed Lance-Corporal. Deprived of appointment on 10/10/78. Served in 'A' Company. Effects claimed by his mother, brothers and sister. Medal and clasp '1877–8–9' issued on 29/8/81.

25B/1273 Private LYNCH Thomas
Attested on 2/3/77. Previously served in Glamorgan Militia. Served in 'A' Company. Effects claimed by his father. Medal and clasp '1879' issued on 29/4/81.

25B/671 Private MACHIN Joseph
Attested on 13/11/75. Medal and clasp '1877-8-9'.

25B/1225 Private McCAFFREY Patrick
Attested on 21/2/77. Served in 'F' Company. Medal and clasp '1877-8-9'.

2-24/2276 Private McCORMACK James
Served in 'D' Company. Medal and clasp '1877-8-9'.

2-24/1458 Private McCRACKEN Samuel
Attested circa 1861. Medal and clasp '1877-8-9' issued on 21/7/81.

25B/1221 Private McDOON George
Attested on 20/2/77. Served in 'G' Company. Medal and clasp '1877-8-9'.

25B/1387 Boy McEWAN Joseph S.
Attested at Dover on 20/4/77, aged 14 years. Served in 'E' Company. Effects claimed by his mother, brother and sister. Medal and clasp '1877-8-9'.

25B/1388 Private McGUIRE James
Attested on 21/4/77. Served in 'A' Company. Medal and clasp '1877-8-9'.

25B/1197 Private MACK James
Attested on 17/2/77. Served in 'C' Company. Effects claimed by his father. Medal and clasp '1877-8-9' issued on 5/4/81.

25B/1050 Private MALLEY Edward
Attested on 16/1/77. Served in 'A' Company. Effects claimed by his brother and sisters. Medal and clasp '1877-8-9' issued on 25/8/81.

25B/1349 Private MARSH John
Attested on 9/3/77. Served in 'G' Company. Effects claimed by next of kin. Medal and clasp '1879' issued on 26/5/81.

2-24/2434 Private MARTINGALE Ernest
Transferred from 1/24th (1-24/1935) on 1/4/73. Served in 'G' Company. Medal and clasp '1877-8-9' issued on 14/6/82.

25B/1168 Private MOCKLER Michael
Attested on 7/2/77. Served in 'A' Company. Effects claimed by his father. Medal and clasp '1877-8-9'.

25B/1128 Private MONTGOMERY Thomas
Attested on 31/1/77. Served in 'F' Company. Effects claimed by his widow. Medal and clasp '1877-8-9' issued and returned to Mint on 17/9/85.

25B/726 Private MOORE Frederick
Attested on 28/1/76. Served in 'G' Company. Medal and clasp '1877-8-9'.

25B/1506 Private MORGAN James
Attested at Tredegar on 21/1/78. Served in 'G' Company. Effects claimed by next of kin. Medal and clasp '1877-8-9' issued on 9/2/81.

25B/788 Private MORRIS Alfred
Attested at Tredegar on 14/3/76, aged 20 years 7 months. Served in 'G' Company. Effects claimed by his brother and sisters. Medal and clasp '1877-8-9' issued on 20/5/81.

25B/1412 Private MORRISEY James
Attested at Brecon on 6/6/77. Previously in South Wales Borderers Militia. Served in 'G' Company. Effects claimed by his mother. Medal and clasp '1877-8-9' issued on 9/6/82.

2-24/1994 Private MULROY Patrick
Attested at Sheffield on 24/6/68, aged 22 years. To India on 5/4/69. Served in 'G' Company. Medal and clasp '1879'.

25B/1469 Private MURPHY John
Attested at Brecon on 15/11/77. Served in 'G' Company. Medal and clasp '1877-8-9' issued on 17/6/81.

25B/1036 Private NEAGLE Timothy
Attested at Newport on 21/1/77. Effects claimed by his mother, brother and half-sisters. Medal and clasp '1877-8-9'.

2-24/1901 Private NOBES Robert
Attested at Sheffield on 29/4/67. Medal and clasp '1877-8-9'.

2-24/1549 Private O'KEEFE Terence
Attested at Westminster on 19/12/64, aged 18 years. Served in 'G' Company. Medal and clasp '1877-8-9'.

25B/1134 Private PERKINS Hugh
Attested on 2/2/77. Served in 'F' Company. Effects claimed by his mother, brothers and sisters. Medal and clasp '1877-8-9'.

25B/1383 Private PHILLIPS David
Attested at Brecon on 23/4/77. Served in 'A' Company. Effects claimed by his mother, brothers and sisters. Medal and clasp '1877-8-9' issued on 14/11/81.

25B/586 Private POOLE Samuel
Attested at Hanley on 27/4/75, aged 21 years. Served in 'G' Company. Effects claimed by his brothers. Medal and clasp '1877-8-9' issued on 7/5/81.

2–24/1709 Private   POPPLE Samuel
The effects roll gives his number incorrectly as '1079'. Attested at Southwick on 21/2/65, aged 23 years 10 months. Served in 'G' Company. Effects claimed by his widow. Medal and clasp '1877–8–9' issued on 7/4/81.

25B/945 Private   PRICE Henry
Attested on 7/12/76. Served in 'G' Company. Medal and clasp '1877–8–9' issued on 25/1/81.

25B/1098 Private   PRICE John
Attested at Pontypool on 20/1/77. Served in 'G' Company. Medal and clasp '1877–8–9'.

2–24/1576 Private   PRITCHARD David
Attested at Hanley on 11/1/65, aged 20 years. Served in 'B' Company. Effects claimed by his sister. Medal and clasp '1877–8–9'.

25B/949 Private   QUILFORD Thomas
Attested at Brecon on 5/12/76. Effects claimed by his sister. Medal and clasp '1877–8–9'.

2–24/1868 Private   QUINN John
Born at Wigan, Lancashire; trade – labourer. Attested on 17/4/64. Deserted on 31/3/73, rejoined on 1/6/73. Confined by Civil Power from 1/10/78 to 31/10/78. Served in 'A' Company. Medal and clasp '1877–8–9'.

25B/1411 Private   REES William
Attested at Monmouth on 5/6/77. Previously served in Monmouth Militia. Served in 'G' Company. Effects claimed by his father. Medal and clasp '1877–8–9' issued on 5/9/81.

25B/692 Private   RICE Walter
Attested at Newport on 1/12/75, aged 18 years. Served in 'G' Company. Effects claimed by his father. Medal and clasp '1877–8–9' issued on 7/5/81.

25B/781 Private   ROCHE John
Named as 'Roach' in muster roll. Attested at Brecon on 4/3/76, aged 19 years 8 months. Served in 'G' Company. Effects claimed by his father. Medal and clasp '1877–8–9' issued on 28/9/81.

25B/1505 Private   ROCHE Michael
Named as 'Roach' in muster roll. Attested at Tredegar on 21/1/78. Confined in cells from 11/10/78 to 17/10/78. Served in 'G' Company. He is included in the medal roll of the 1/24th named as '1505 M. Roche'. His name also appears in the medal roll of the 2/24th as '1505 M. Roach'. Medal and clasp '1877–8–9'.

25B/850 Private   SAUNDERS Thomas
Attested at Newport on 19/9/76, aged 22 years. Served in 'G' Company. Medal and clasp '1877–8–9'.

2–24/813 Private   SCOTT James
Attested circa 1860. Served in 'G' Company. Medal and clasp '1877–8–9' issued on 7/4/81.

25B/779 Private   SHEAN John
Attested at Tredegar on 10/3/76, aged 18 years. Served in 'G' Company. Effects claimed by next of kin. Medal and clasp '1877–8–9' issued on 2/9/81.

25B/1169 Private   SHERWOOD Samuel
Attested on 11/2/77. Served in 'A' Company. Effects claimed by his father. Medal and clasp '1877–8–9'.

25B/79 Private   SHUTTLEWORTH William
Attested at Liverpool on 12/3/74, aged 18 years 11 months. Served in 'G' Company. Effects claimed by his sister. Medal and clasp '1877–8–9' issued on 29/8/81.

25B/895 Private   SLADE Henry
Attested on 19/11/76. Served in 'D' Company. Medal and clasp '1877–8–9' issued on 29/8/82.

2–24/1487 Private   SMITH Charles M.
Attested on 18/5/64 from the Militia. Served in 'G' Company. Effects claimed by his sister. Medal and clasp '1877–8–9'.

25B/1096 Private   SMITH Daniel
Attested on 25/1/77. Served in 'G' Company. Effects claimed by next of kin. Medal and clasp '1877–8–9'.

25B/1143 Private   SMITH Frank
Attested on 14/2/77. Absent without leave from 5th–6th October 1878. Sentenced on 9/10/78 to 42 days hard labour. Served in 'G' Company. Effects claimed by his mother, brothers and sisters. Medal and clasp '1877–8–9' issued on 17/5/81.

25B/907 Private   SMITH Henry
Attested at Brecon on 20/11/76. Served in 'G' Company. Effects claimed by his father. Medal and clasp '1877–8–9'.

25B/1056 Private   SMITH John
Attested at Newport on 4/1/77. Served in 'A' Company. Medal and clasp '1877–8–9' issued on 17/3/82.

25B/912 Private   SMITH Patrick
Attested on 24/11/76. Served in 'A' Company. Effects claimed by his brother. Medal and clasp '1877–8–9' issued on 19/3/81.

25B/1495 Private   SMITH Robert
Attested at Chatham on 20/12/77, aged 24 years. Served in 'B' Company. Effects claimed by his uncle. Medal and clasp '1877–8–9'.

25B/1484 Private STEPHENS Robert
Shown as 'Stevens' in the medal roll. Attested at Newport on 4/12/77. Served in 'C' Company'. Medal and clasp '1877–8–9'.

25B/782 Private TERRETT William
Attested at Brecon on 13/3/76, aged 21 years. Served in 'G' Company. Medal and clasp '1877–8–9' issued on 29/7/81.

25B/1218 Private THOMAS David
Attested on 20/2/77. Served in 'G' Company. Effects claimed by his father. Medal and clasp '1877–8–9'.

2–24/1107 Private THOMPSON George
Rejoined from desertion on 7/1/64 – obtained from Marine Light Infantry. Served in 'D' Company. Medal and clasp '1877–8–9'.

25B/951 Private TREVERTON Richard
Attested at Monmouth on 2/12/76. Served in 'G' Company. Effects claimed by his mother, brother and sisters. Medal and clasp '1877–8–9' issued on 23/5/81.

2–24/2358 Private TURNER Edmund
Posted to service companies in India on 5/4/69. Medal and clasp '1877–8–9'.

25B/653 Private VEDLER Thomas
Attested on 15/10/75. Served in 'C' Company. Medal and clasp '1877–8–9' issued on 5/4/81.

2–24/2038 Private WALKER Samuel
Attested at Sheffield on 23/7/68, aged 19 years. Served in 'G' Company. Effects claimed by his father. Medal and clasp '1877–8–9' issued on 28/3/82.

25B/1543 Private WATERS Edmund
Attested at Brecon on 12/3/78. Served in 'G' Company. Medal and clasp '1879'.

2–24/513 Private WATERHOUSE William
Attested circa 1856 with 25 Brigade for 2½ years before returning to 2/24th 26/1/78. Served in 'F' Company. Effects claimed by his uncle and step-father. Medal and clasp '1877–8–9'.

25B/1191 Private WATKINS John
Attested on 14/2/77. Served in 'C' Company. Medal and clasp '1877–8–9'.

25B/1518 Private WATSON George
Transferred from 31st Regiment (No. 2124) to 2/24th on 1/2/78. Medal and clasp '1877–8–9'.

25B/1132 Private WHITE James
Attested on 3/2/77. Served in 'C' Company. Medal and clasp '1877–8–9'.

25B/794 Private WHITE Thomas
Attested at Monmouth on 22/3/76, aged 19 years 5 months. Served in 'A' Company. Medal and clasp '1877–8–9'.

25B/1095 Private WIGHTMAN Adam
Attested on 25/1/77. Served in 'G' Company. Effects claims by his sisters. Medal and clasp '1877–8–9' issued on 5/9/81.

25B/463 Private WILLIAMS Edward
Attested at Pontypool on 29/10/74, aged 22 years. Served in 'G' Company. Effects claimed by his father. Medal and clasp '1877–8–9'.

25B/1470 Private WILLIAMS Edward
Attested at Monmouth on 21/11/77. Served in 'G' Company. Effects claimed by his mother. Medal and clasp '1877–8–9'.

25B/1023 Private WILLIAMS Evan
Attested on 7/1/77. Served in 'G' Company. Effects claimed by his brother. Medal and clasp '1877–8–9' issued on 12/12/81.

25B/987 Private WILLIAMS George
Served in 'E' Company. Effects claimed by his mother and brother. Medal and clasp '1877–8–9'.

25B/1140 Private WILLIAMS Theophilus
Attested at Tredegar on 1/2/77. Served in 'G' Company. Medal and clasp '1877–8–9'.

2–24/2047 Private WILLIAMSON James
Attested at Sheffield on 28/7/68, aged 19 years. Shown as a 'Mess waiter' in 1873. Served in 'G' Company. Effects claimed by his father. Medal and clasp '1877–8–9' issued on 29/9/81.

25B/689 Private WOOD George
Attested on 3/12/75. Served in 'C' Company. Medal and clasp '1877–8–9'.

25B/1138 Private WRIGHT John
Attested on 3/2/77. Served in 'G' Company. Effects claimed by his mother. Medal and clasp '1877–8–9'.

25B/1093 Private YOUNG Edward
Attested on 24/1/77. Served in 'G' Company. Effects claimed by his daughter. Medal and clasp '1877–8–9'.

Statements of the six private soldiers of the 1st Battalion, 24th Regiment who escaped from the battlefield of Isandhlwana, 22nd January, 1879

1173 Private J. Bickley, 1/24th Regiment

At about 7.45 a.m. on 22nd January 1879 one of the Volunteers who had been away from Camp on Picquet duty came in and made a report to the Commanding Officer; immediately after this I heard Mr. Melvill give the order to the Bugler to sound the 'Fall in' and add 'Sound the Column call.' Each corps fell in in front of its own Camp and the Picquets were then brought in, consisting of a Company of each Battalion of the 24th Regiment. The Infantry formed up in front of an open space between the Camps of the 2/24th Regiment and the R.A. At this time I was posted as a picquet sentry on the Officers mess, all the Servants having fallen in with their Companies. About half an hour after the Column had fallen in Colonel Durnford's Column marched in, some twenty minutes to half an hour later a part of Colonel Durnford's Mounted Basutos was sent up a hill to our left, at this time we could see, with field glasses, Kaffirs on the hills to the left quite distinctly. Cetywayo's half-brother in charge of some of the Native Contingent came in soon after, and in my hearing reported himself to Colonel Pulleine as having come off Piquet, and obtained permission to bring in some of his men from the rear of (the) hill behind the Camp. About this time a second mounted messenger was sent out to bring in a party working on the road under Lieutenant Anstey which came in some three-quarters of an hour later. After remaining under arms for some hour and a half to two hours the men were dismissed with orders not to take off their accoutrements. Very shortly after we had been dismissed we heard very rapid firing from the hill on the left where the Basutos had been sent, and the 'Fall in' was immediately sounded the second time, and number 5 Company, 1/24th, sent soon afterwards on to the hill to support the Basutos. By the time the Column was formed up the Basutos were coming down the ridge pursued by the Zulus, and the Company 1/24th had opened fire. The Native Contingent and rocket party under Colonel Durnford was also engaged at this time about a mile to our left front. The guns opened fire about this time, one on to the Zulus coming down the ridge on our left flank and the other on to those advancing on Colonel Durnford's party to our left front. The Mounted Police and our Company 1/24th was sent out after this in support of Colonel Durnford's party. The gun firing at the enemy in this direction appear to have great effect, and soon after it began firing they made a retreat, but afterwards they reappeared in extended order coming over a rise to the left front and near a conical hill. At the same time the line of the Zulus appeared right across the plain in front of the Camp, completely outflanking that of our skirmishers. There were Kraals on both flanks of the Camp which were occupied by the Zulus, and our men began to retire on to the Camp, making a stand in a ravine which crossed the front of the Camp.

The Companies out skirmishing were now apparently getting short of ammunition, and it was carried out to them by the Bandsmen and wagon drivers and other unarmed people about the Camp; and the Native Contingent had been driven into the Camp and together with most of the transport and other employed natives were rushing out of Camp towards the road for Rorke's Drift. The Quarter-Master then came up and asked me if I could saddle his horse for him. I took it behind a wagon near the Officers Mess to do so, but could find no bridle. I left the horse tied up to the wagon by the headstall, but saw no more of the Quarter-Master who had gone away in the direction of the Officers latrine. By this time all the idlers were clearing out of Camp, and the skirmishers driven in, I made for the neck of land over which the road ran, and on gaining it, saw that retreat by the road to Rorke's Drift was cut off, and struck off to the left, about a quarter of a mile on I found a pony standing in the path which I mounted and shortly after caught up Lieutenant Melvill who was carrying the Queen's Colour. Mr. Coghill afterwards joined us and reported to the Adjutant that Colonel Pulleine had been shot.

Corporal Richardson, the Pioneer Corporal, came up soon after and said he was wounded in the arm and soon after I saw him fall off his horse and lie on the ground unable to remount. When I got down to the drift I could see nothing of the Officers who had passed me. From the drift I found my way with Captain Essex whom I met at the top of the hill to Helpmakaar.

Statement of
665 Private H. Grant, 1/24th Regiment.

I was one of the Rocket Battery under command of the late Captain Russell, R.A., attached to Colonel Durnford's Column. On the 22nd January 1879 we left Rorke's Drift early in the morning to reinforce the main column at Isandhlwana Camp where we arrived about 11 a.m. and remained near the Camp about $\frac{1}{4}$ of an hour. Captain Russell received orders from Colonel Durnford to advance from the Camp towards the right front, saying that the Zulus were retiring and he must make haste and outflank them. We started at once and went from 3 to 4 miles as far as I can judge. We then came to the foot of a hill on which the enemy were posted in force. We received orders from Captain Russell to come into action as quickly as possible : we fired one rocket when we were overpowered by the enemy owing to the bad position we were in at the foot of the hill. When the enemy fired their first volley the Native Contingent ran away and the mules with the rockets also broke away. I had been told off to hold the horses belonging to the Rocket Battery and was holding them close to the troughs. Captain Russell and five of the men of the Rocket Battery were killed by the first volley, leaving only three of us. Not knowing what to do and having no leader, we tried to reach the nearest party of our own troops. I got back to Camp with three of the Battery horses and on arriving there found that the Companies on the left were completely surrounded by the enemy, and everyone making the best of their way out of the Camp, as the Zulus were entering it from the left and rear. Privates Johnson and Trainer of the Rocket Battery came in soon after with some Basutos and I gave them each a horse, we then made our way to the Buffalo, after crossing which Private Johnson and I went to Rorke's Drift and reported the advance of the enemy, and further on on the Helpmakaar road met Major Spalding to whom we reported what had occurred; he ordered us to go back with him to see what was going on at the drift. We got within about two miles of the Camp, when we saw smoke from one of the buildings on fire. We then retired and met 2 Companies 1/24th under Major Upcher and returned with them to Helpmakaar.

Statement of
299 Private D. Johnson, 1/24th Regiment

I was one of the Rocket Battery under command of the late Captain Russell, R.A., which was attached to Colonel Durnford's Column. We got to Isandhlwana Camp about 11 a.m. on the 22nd January 1879. We halted there about 10 minutes when Colonel Durnford came down from the Camp of the 1/24th Regiment and gave orders that, as the Zulus were retiring fast, the mounted men should advance up a hill about 2½ miles from Camp, and that the Rocket Battery supported by the Infantry of the Native Contingent should follow in rear of the Mounted Basutos. About 2 miles out we met a 'vidette' of the Natal Carbineers who reported that the Mounted Basutos were heavily engaged on the opposite side of a hill on our left, at the same time offering to show us a short cut to the place where the engagement was going on. The Captain galloped up the hill and before he returned to us shouted 'Action front'.

While we were getting into action the Zulus kept coming out of a kloof on our left, which the big guns had been shelling from the Camp. We had time to fire our rocket when they came over the hill in masses, and commenced to fire on us. As soon as they opened fire the mules carrying the rockets broke away. The Native Contingent, who were in the rear of us, after firing a few shots ran away. I observed that a great number of them were unable to extract the empty cartridge cases after firing, and offered to do so for some of them but they would not give me their rifles. Before this the horses had broken away and I tried to help Captain Russell off the field, but he was shot before we had gone many paces. I made my escape to a donga held by some of the Police, Mounted Infantry and Carbineers. On my way to this place I met Colonel Durnford and he asked me where my Battery was; I told him that the Battery was cut up and the Captain shot, when he said you had better go back and fetch him. I then pointed out to him that the enemy had already nearly surrounded us. At this time he was mounted as well as his orderly who had a spare horse, and he retired with a few Basutos towards the left of the Camp. Just below the Camp I met Privates Trainer and Grant with Bombardier Gough, they gave me a horse. We then went up to the Camp and found the Police extended in front of it and they were shortly afterwards driven in. The Camp was now almost completely surrounded and I made for the Buffalo following some of the Police and other mounted men, and crossed it below Rorke's Drift. I afterwards met Major Spalding on the road to Helpmakaar, and turned back and joined the Companies 1/24th under Major Upcher. We met a lot of natives on the left of the road to the Drift but could not make out what they were for certain.

Statement of
196 Private J. Trainer, 1/24th Regiment.

I was one of the Rocket Battery under Captain Russell, R.A., attached to Colonel Durnford's Column: on the 22nd January 1879 at about 10.30 a.m. we arrived in Isandhlwana Camp and went to the Native Contingent huts. Colonel Durnford gave us orders not to off saddle, and went away himself to the tents of the 1/24th Regiment. He returned about 10 minutes to 11 and ordered the contingent Officers to fall in. I heard him tell them that

the enemy was retreating and he was going to take out two troops of Basutos to the front and gave Captain Russell orders to accompany him with the Rocket Battery, and two Companies of Native Infantry as a support to the Battery. When we had got from 2 to 3 miles to the front we met one of the Natal Carbineers, who offered to show us a short cut to where the Mounted Basutos in front of us were engaged; we were going up a hill to reach them when we saw some of the Enemy at the top of it, and shortly after got the order to come into action; when the first rocket was fired they appeared in force over the top of the hill and fired a volley at us by which Captain Russell was killed, and the horses and mules got so frightened by this and the Native Infantry running away through them that they broke away. The Native Infantry made no stand at all, but ran away immediately the first volley was fired.

On seeing that they had all gone, I tried to make my way back to Camp. On the way I saw some of the Basutos, 2 of whom came along with me. I stayed with the Basutos, who, for some time held a portion of the donga that crossed the front of the Camp. Some of the Police, Mounted Infantry and Natal Carbineers were also for a considerable time in this donga, and after some time we retired into Camp, where I found Private Grant of the Rocket Battery with some of the horses that had broken loose and got one of them from him. As soon as the Camp was surrounded, which was very soon after I got into it, I made the best of my way out for the Buffalo after crossing which I made for Helpmakaar and fell in with 2 Companies 1/24th under Major Upcher with whom I remained.

Statement of
139 Private John Williams, 1/24th Regiment
(Colonel Glyn's Groom).

On the 22nd January 1879 I was calling up at 2 a.m. to get Colonel Glyn's horse ready, he started about 4 a.m. with the patrol under the General. I remained in Camp to look after the Colonel's other two horses; about 9 a.m. a mounted orderly came in to report Zulus on the hills to the left of the Camp, he made his report to Lieutenant Coghill at the Column Office; that officer went to Colonel Pulleine to inform him. The 'Column Alarm' was then sounded. The five Companies 1/24th fell in, and the Company of the 2/24th and the Artillery harnessed their horses. The Column was marched below the Native Contingent Camp where they waited for orders about half an hour; they were then sent back to their own Camp where they stood under arms about three quarters of an hour. After which Colonel Pulleine gave them permission to fall out without taking their accoutrements off.

During this time Zulus were visible on the hill to the left front, sometimes in small numbers at others in large bodies. The 'fall in' was sounded a second time about 11 a.m. and the Column was formed up in the same spot as before, below the space between the 2/24th and Native Contingent Camps. The Kaffirs were now advancing on the Camp along the top of the hills to the left, Colonel Durnford's Column had come in by this time, and his party went out of Camp towards our left front some three quarters of a mile off and went round a small conical hill, No. 5 Company, 1/24th was sent out to the left in skirmishing order to support some of the Native Contingent who were already there. A soon as Colonel Durnford's mounted party got out of sight we heard firing from their direction but could not tell whether it was them or the enemy, and five minutes afterwards the party on the left were engaged, and we could see masses of Zulus coming over the hills in that direction. Number 1 Company 1/24th was now sent out in support of Colonel Durnford and the guns of the Artillery commenced firing on the Zulus as they came down the hills to our left and left front with great effect; and the Zulus began to retreat behind the hill Colonel Durnford had gone round, his party having commenced to retire on its supports. The enemy occupied some Kraals which were to the right of the hill but were driven out by the Artillery fire, when they extended in skirmishing order, to the right I should say from 2 to 300 yards deep. They then advanced round towards the right of the Camp out-flanking the mounted men who were extended on that side. Meanwhile there was very heavy firing on the left and left centre. I myself and Private Hough, the Colonel's Cook, went to the left beyond the General's tents where we were joined by three of the General's servants, and began to fire from the left of No. 5 Company, 1/24th Regiment. We fired 40 to 50 rounds each when the Native Contingent fell back on the Camp and one of their officers pointed out to me that the enemy were entering the right of the Camp. We then went to the right, No. 5 Company still holding their position, and fired away the remainder of our ammunition, the Kaffirs turned the left of No. 5 Company by coming over a high rock. The firing at this point still continuing very heavy.

Meanwhile No. 1 Company and the remainder of the 1/24th together with 2/24th Company were firing volleys into the Zulus who were only 100 to 150 yards distant from them; they kept this up till they got short of ammunition. The right of the Camp was open and undefended except by the few mounted troops left in Camp who had taken cover in a small ravine. The Zulus kept outside Camp some 2 or 300 yards and made round to the right of the Camp apparently intending to take us in rear, and another party had made round to the left completely surrounding the Camp except a small space to the left of the road to Rorke's Drift. The men in Camp, Bandsmen and men on Guard etc., were trying to take ammunition to the Companies but the greater part never got there, as I saw horses and mules with ammunition on their backs galloping about the Camp a short time afterwards.

Lieutenant Coghill galloped up now to Colonel Glyn's tents and gave orders for them to be struck and placed in the wagon which was done, when he came up again and ordered the grooms to take the horses to the rear part of the Camp.

I kept one of the Colonel's horses tied to the wagon and went and got 40 rounds more ammunition of which I then used 29. I then saw Lieutenant Melvill leaving Camp with the Queen's colours and Lieutenant Coghill close behind him; the latter told me to come on or I should get killed; just then the two guns of the R.A. retreated out of Camp past me, and I could see the men on foot who had attempted to escape turned back and coming into Camp. When I got on to the hill overlooking the Rorke's Drift road the Zulus were entering the Camp from that direction and I saw Lieutenant Coghill's horse assegaied in the thigh. About 300 yards out of the Camp the ground became so bad that the guns of the R.A. were upset, and I saw several of the drivers assegaied. I passed them here and saw no more of the guns.

On my way to the drift I passed Band Sergeant Gamble 1/24th Regiment on foot but could give him no assistance. When I got down to the drift I saw Lieutenants Melvill and Coghill coming down the rocks to it, and after I entered the river to cross saw no more of either of these officers. I made my way up to Helpmakaar after crossing the river.

Statement of
13 Private E. Wilson, 1/24th Regiment.

I was one of the band of the 1/24th Regiment, on the 22nd January 1879 I was in the Camp at Isandhlwana. The Regiment fell in at about 8 a.m. the 'Fall in' going while we were at breakfast, and marched to the Camp of the 2/24th Regiment. The bandsmen were told off as Stretcher-bearers, ammunition carriers, and cooks. I was one of the stretcher party which fell in with the Regiment, the remainder remaining in Camp. The Regiment remained under arms up to 10.30 or 11 a.m. when Colonel Durnford's party came in. Soon after which 'E' Company, 1/24th, Lieutenant Cavaye in charge moved out to the left the remainder were marched back to our own private parade grounds, and were dismissed with orders not to take off our accoutrements. We were told to get our dinners as quick as possible, and be in readiness to fall in at any moment. The 'fall in' sounded about ¼ of an hour later, and the Regiment marched off to the left front of the Camp. I myself went to the hospital tent to get a stretcher; while I was on my way to rejoin my Company, I first heard firing on the hills to the left of the Camp. I could not at this time see anything of 'E' Company, 1/24th which was out of sight. The R.A. guns were in action, one firing to the left and one to the left front, a company was lying in support in rear of them. I was going to join this Company but was ordered by the doctor to join the 4 Companies remaining on the parade ground. About 10 minutes after these companies were sent out to the front of the Camp in skirmishing order. The Stretcher-bearers were out with their Companies for some ten minutes when we were ordered by Dr. Sheppard to go to the Hospital tents, as he said there would be too many wounded for us to attend to.

As we were going the ammunition was beginning to be brought down to the Companies.

While in the Hospital tent I saw the hills to the left and in front covered with Zulus advancing on the Camp. To the right front some of the Police, Carbineer and Native Levies were engaged very hotly and retiring on the Camp. They made a stand for some time in a sluit which crossed the front of the Camp, but were driven out of it after a ¼ of an hour or 20 minutes. When the idlers and men among the tents were now making the best of their way out of Camp, the doctor told us we were no longer likely to be of any use, and the Band Sergeant told us we had better get away as best we could. I with another man began to retire on the hill in rear of the Camp taking a stretcher, but were told by a Carbineer that we had better clear out altogether, we then dropped the stretcher and followed the men who had gone before towards the Buffalo. About ½ mile from Camp I caught a horse and rode him down to the river where I lost him in crossing.

Some 50 or 100 yards on the Natal side I met Private Bickley, 1/24th Regiment some way on I got a spare horse from a Volunteer and rode up to Helpmakaar where I arrived about 7.30 p.m. in company with Sergeant Norton of the Mounted Infantry.

Lt. Col. Henry Burmester Pulleine

Capt. William Degacher

Capt. William Eccles Mostyn

Capt. Reginald Younghusband

Capt. George V. Wardell

Lt. Edgar O. Anstey

Lt. Charles John Atkinson

Lt. Charles Walter Cavaye

Lt. Nevill J. A. Coghill, V.C.

Lt. James Patrick Daly

Lt. George Frederick John Hodson

Lt. Teignmouth Melvill, V.C.

Lt. Francis Pender Porteous

Lt. Edwards Hopton Dyson

Py. Mr. Francis Freeman White

Qr. Mr. James Pullen

Lt. Henry Julian Dyer

Lt. Edgar Godwin-Austen

Lt. Charles D'Aguilar Pope

Sub Lt. Thomas Ll. G. Griffith

Qr. Mr. Edward Bloomfield

The Monument at Rorke's Drift

Photo: F. Emery

Lt. Gonville Bromhead, V.C.

Col. Sgt. Frank Bourne, D.C.M.
in 1905, when a Major

Photo: Mary K. Whitby

Cpl. William Allen, V.C.

Pte. Frederick Hitch, V.C.

Pte. Alfred Henry Hook, V.C.

Pte. Robert Jones, V.C.

Pte. William Jones, V.C.

Pte. John Williams, V.C.

RORKE'S DRIFT

The Defence of Rorke's Drift, 22nd-23rd January, 1879

An account of the defence of Rorke's Drift, written by Major J. R. M. Chard, V.C., R.E., at the personal request of Queen Victoria, and submitted to Her Majesty at Windsor Castle on 21st February 1880

Early in January 1879, shortly after the arrival of the 5th Company, Royal Engineers, at Durban, an order came from Lord Chelmsford directing that an officer and a few good men of the R.E., with mining implements, etc., should join the 3rd Column as soon as possible. I was consequently sent on in advance of the company, with a light mule wagon containing the necessary tools, etc., and in which the men could also ride on level ground; with a *Corporal, three Sappers and †one Driver, my batman, who rode one, and looked after my horses. The wagon was driven by a Cape black man, with a Natal Kaffir lad as vorlooper. The roads were so bad that in spite of all our exertions, our progress was slow, and although we got a fresh team at Pietermaritzburg, we did not reach Rorke's Drift until the morning of the 19th January 1879. The 3rd Column was encamped on the other side (left bank) of the river Buffalo, and the wagons were still crossing in the ponts. I pitched my two tents on the right (Natal) bank of the river, near the ponts, and close to the store accommodation there for keeping them in repair. On the 20th January, the 3rd Column broke up its camp on the Buffalo River and marched to Isandhlwana, where it encamped, and the same evening, or following morning, Colonel Durnford's force arrived and took up its camp near where the 3rd Column had been.

There were two large ponts at the river, one of which only was in working order, and my sappers were during this time working at the other, which was nearly finished, to get it also in working order. Late in the evening of the 21st January I received an order from the 3rd Column to say that the *men* of the R.E., who had lately arrived, were to proceed to the camp at Isandhlwana at once – I had received no orders concerning myself. I reported this to Major Spalding, who was now in command at Rorke's Drift, and also pointed out to him that the sappers leaving there were no means at my disposal for putting the ponts in working order, or keeping them so. Major Spalding had also received no orders respecting me, except that I was to select a suitable position protecting the ponts, for Captain Rainforth's Company 1/24th to entrench itself. I consequently asked, and obtained permission from Major Spalding, to go to the camp at Isandhlwana and see the orders.

On the morning of the 22nd January, I put the corporal and three sappers in the empty wagon, with their field kits, etc., to take them to the camp of the 3rd Column; and also rode out myself. The road was very heavy in some places, and the wagon went slowly; so I rode on in advance, arrived at the Isandhlwana Camp, went to the Head-Quarters Tent, and got a copy of the orders as affecting me, and found that I was to keep the ponts in working order, and also the road between Helpmakaar and Rorke's Drift and the orders also particularly stated that my duties lay on the *right* bank of the River Buffalo.

A N.C.O. of the 24th Regiment lent me a field glass,

which was a very good one, and I also looked with my own, and could see the enemy moving on the distant hills, and apparently in great force. Large numbers of them moving to my left, until the lion hill of Isandhlwana, on my left as I looked at them, hid them from my view. The idea struck me that they might be moving in the direction between the camp and Rorke's Drift and prevent my getting back, and also that they might be going to make a dash at the ponts.

Seeing what my duties were, I left the camp, and a quarter of a mile, or less, out of it met with Colonel Durnford, R.E., riding at the head of his mounted men – I told him what I had seen, and took some orders, and a message all along his line, at his request. At the foot of the hill I met my men in the wagon and made them get out and walk up the hill with Durnford's men. I brought the wagon back with me to Rorke's Drift, where on arrival I found the following order had been issued. The copy below was given me, and preserved from the fact of its being in my pocket during the fight :

Camp Rorke's Drift.
Camp Morning Orders.   22nd January 1879.

1. The force under Lt. Col. Durnford, R.E., having departed, a Guard of 6 Privates and 1 N.C.O. will be furnished by the detachment 2/24th Regiment on the ponts.
A Guard of 50 armed natives will likewise be furnished by Capt. Stevenson's detachment at the same spot – The ponts will be invariably drawn over to the Natal side at night. This duty will cease on the arrival of Capt. Rainforth's Company, 1/24th Regiment.

2. In accordance with para. 19 Regulations for Field Forces in South Africa, Capt. Rainforth's Company, 1/24th Regiment, will entrench itself on the spot assigned to it by Column Orders para. – dated –.

H. SPALDING, Major,
Commanding.

The Guard as detailed was over the ponts – Captain Rainforth's Company had not arrived. I went at once to Major Spalding on arrival, told him what I had seen, and pointed out to him that in the event of an attack on the ponts it would be impossible with 7 men (not counting the natives) to make an effective defence. (According to the orders, Capt. Rainforth's Company should have been already at Rorke's Drift.)

Major Spalding told me he was going over to Helpmakaar, and would see about getting it down at once. Just as I was about to ride away he said to me 'Which of you is senior, you or Bromhead?' I said 'I don't know' – he went back into his tent, looked at an Army List, and coming back, said – 'I see you are senior, so you will be in charge, although, of course, nothing will happen, and I shall be back again this evening early.'

I then went down to my tent by the river, had some lunch comfortably, and was writing a letter home when my attention was called to two horsemen galloping towards us

* 862 Corporal Gamble and Sappers Cuthbert, MacLaren and and Wheatley — killed at Isandhlwana.

† Sapper Robson — present at the defence of Rorke's Drift.

from the direction of Isandhlwana. From their gesticulation and their shouts, when they were near enough to be heard, we saw that something was the matter, and on taking them over the river, one of them, Lieut. Adendorff of Lonsdale's Regiment, Natal Native Contingent, asking if I was an officer, jumped off his horse, took me on one side, and told me that the camp was in the hands of the Zulus and the army destroyed; that scarcely a man had got away to tell the tale, and that probably Lord Chelmsford and the rest of the column had shared the same fate. His companion, a Carbineer, confirmed his story – He was naturally very excited and I am afraid I did not, at first, quite believe him, and intimated that he probably had not remained to see what *did* occur. I had the saddle put on my horse, and while I was talking to Lieut. Adendorff, a messenger arrived from Lieut. Bromhead, who was with his Company at his little camp near the Commissariat Stores, to ask me to come up at once.

I gave the order to inspan the wagon and put all the stores, tents, etc., they could into it. I posted the sergeant and six men on the high ground over the pont, behind a natural wall of rocks, forming a strong position from which there was a good view over the river and ground in front, with orders to wait until I came or sent for them. The guard of natives had left some time before and had not been relieved. I galloped up at once to the Commissariat Stores and found that a pencil note had been sent from the 3rd Column by Capt. Allan Gardner to state that the enemy were advancing in force against our post – Lieut. Bromhead had, with the assistance of Mr. Dalton, Dr. Reynolds and the other officers present, commenced barricading and loopholing the store building and the Missionary's house, which was used as a Hospital, and connecting the defence of the two buildings by walls of mealie bags, and two wagons that were on the ground. The Native Contingent, under their officer, Capt. Stephenson, were working hard at this with our own men, and the walls were rapidly progressing. A letter describing what had happened had been sent by Bromhead by two men of the Mounted Infantry, who had arrived fugitives from Isandhlwana, to the Officer Commanding at Helpmakaar. These two men crossed the river at Fugitives Drift, with some others, and as they have since reported to me, came to give notice of what had happened, to us at Rorke's Drift, of their own accord and without orders from anyone.

I held a consultation with Lieut. Bromhead, and with Mr. Dalton, whose energy, intelligence and gallantry were of the greatest service to us, and whom, as I said in my report at the time, and I am sure Bromhead would unite with me in saying again now, I cannot sufficiently thank for his services. I went round the position with them and then rode down to the ponts where I found everything ready for a start, ponts in midstream, hawsers and cables sunk, etc. It was at this time that the Pontman Daniells, and Sergt. Milne, 3rd Buffs, who had been employed for some time in getting the ponts in order, and working them under Lieut. MacDowell, R.E. (killed at Isandhlwana), offered to defend the ponts, moored in the middle of the river, from their decks with a few men. Sergt. Williams 24th and his little guard were quite ready to join them.

We arrived at the Commissariat Store about 3.30 p.m. Shortly afterwards an officer of Durnford's Horse reported his arrival from Isandhlwana, and I requested him to observe the movements, and check the advance, of the enemy as much as possible until forced to fall back. I saw each man at his post, and then the work went on again.

Several fugitives from the Camp arrived, and tried to impress upon us the madness of an attempt to defend the place. Who they were I do not know, but it is scarcely necessary for me to say that there were no officers of H.M. Army among them. They stopped the work very much – it being impossible to prevent the men getting around them in little groups to hear their story. They proved the truth of their belief in what they said by leaving us to our fate, and in the state of mind they were in, I think our little garrison was as well without them. As far as I know, but one of the fugitives remained with us – Lieut. Adendorff, whom I have before mentioned. He remained to assist in the defence, and from a loophole in the store building, flanking the wall and Hospital, his rifle did good service.

There were several casks of rum in the Store building, and I gave strict orders to Sergt. Windridge, 24th Regiment, who was in charge (acting as issuer of Commissariat stores to the troops), that the spirit was not to be touched, the man posted nearest it was to be considered on guard over it, and after giving fair warning, was to shoot without altercation anyone who attempted to force his post, and Sergt. Windridge being there was to see this carried out. Sergt. Windridge showed great intelligence and energy in arranging the stores for the defence of the Commissariat store, forming loopholes, etc.

The Reverend George Smith, Vicar of Estcourt, Natal, and acting Army Chaplain, went for a walk (before the news of the disaster reached us) to the top of the Oscarberg, the hill behind Rorke's Drift. Mr. Witt, the missionary, went with him, or met him there. They went to see what could be seen in the direction of the Isandhlwana camp. He saw the force of the enemy which attacked us at Rorke's Drift, cross the river in three bodies – and after snuff-taking, and other ceremonies, advance in our direction. He had been watching them for a long time with interest, and thought they were our own Native Contingent. There were two mounted men leading them, and he did not realize that they were the enemy until they were near enough for him to see that these two men also had black faces. He came running down the hill and was agreeably surprised to find that we were getting ready for the enemy. Mr. Witt, whose wife and family were in a lonely house not very far off, rode off, taking with him a sick officer, who was very ill in hospital and only just able to ride. Mr. Smith, however, although he might well have left, elected to remain with us, and during the attack did good service in supplying the men with ammunition.

About 4.20 p.m. the sound of firing was heard behind the Oscarberg. The officer of Durnford's returned, reporting the enemy close upon us, and that his men would not obey his orders but were going off to Helpmakaar, and I saw them, about 100 in number, going off in that direction. I have seen these same men behave so well since that I have spoken with several of their conduct – and they all said, as their excuse, that Durnford was killed, and it was no use. About the same time Capt. Stephenson's detachment of Natal Native Contingent left us – probably most fortunately for us. I am sorry to say that their officer, who had been doing good service in getting his men to work, also deserted us. We seemed very few, now all these people had gone, and I saw that our line of defence was too extended, and at once commenced a retrenchment of biscuit boxes, so as to get a place we could fall back upon if we could not hold the whole.

Private Hitch, 24th, was on the top of the thatch roof of the Commissariat Store keeping a look-out. He was severely wounded early in the evening, but notwithstanding, with Corpl. Allen, 24th, who was also wounded, continued to do good service, and they both when incapacitated by their wounds from using their rifles, still continued under fire serving their comrades with ammunition.

We had not completed a wall two boxes high when, about 4.30 p.m., Hitch cried out that the enemy was in sight, and he saw them, apparently 500 or 600 in number, come around the hill to our south (the Oscarberg) and advance at a run against our south wall.

We opened fire on them, between five and six hundred yards, at first a little wild, but only for a short time, a chief on horseback was dropped by Private Dunbar, 24th. The men were quite steady, and the Zulus began to fall very thick. However, it did not seem to stop them at all, although they took advantage of the cover and ran stooping with their faces near the ground. It seemed as if nothing would stop them, and they rushed on in spite of their heavy loss to within 50 yards of the wall, when they were taken in flank by the fire from the end wall of the store building, and met with such a heavy direct fire from the mealie wall, and the Hospital at the same time, that they were checked as if by magic.

They occupied the Cook-house ovens, banks and other cover, but the greater number, without stopping, moved to their left around the Hospital, and made a rush at the end of the Hospital, and at our north-west line of mealie bags. There was a short but desperate struggle during which Mr. Dalton shot a Zulu who was in the act of assegaing a corporal of the Army Hospital Corps, the muzzle of whose rifle he had seized, and with Lieut. Bromhead and many of the men behaved with great gallantry. The Zulus forced us back from that part of the wall immediately in front of the Hospital, but after suffering very severely in the struggle were driven back into the bush around our position.

The main body of the enemy were close behind the first force which appeared, and had lined the ledge of rocks and caves in the Oscarberg overlooking us, and about three or four hundred yards to our south, from where they kept up a constant fire. Advancing somewhat more to their left than the first attack, they occupied the garden, hollow road, and bush in great force. The bush grew close to our wall and we had not had time to cut it down – The enemy were thus able to advance under cover close to our wall, and in this part soon held one side of the wall, while we held the other.

A series of desperate assaults was made, on the Hospital, and extending from the Hospital, as far as the bush reached; but each was most splendidly met and repulsed by our men, with the bayonet. Each time as the attack was repulsed by us, the Zulus close to us seemed to vanish in the bush, those some little distance off keeping up a fire all the time. Then, as if moved by a single impulse, they rose up in the bush as thick as possible, rushing madly up to the wall (some of them being already close to it), seizing, where they could, the muzzles of our men's rifles, or their bayonets, and attempting to use their assegais and to get over the wall. A rapid rattle of fire from our rifles, stabs with the bayonet, and in a few moments the Zulus were driven back, disappearing in the bush as before, and keeping up their fire. A brief interval, and the attack would be again made, and repulsed in the same manner. Over and over again this happened, our men behaving with the greatest coolness and gallantry.

It is impossible for one individual to see all, but I particularly myself noticed the behaviour of Col. Sgt. Bourne 24th, Sergt. Williams 24th, Corpl. Scheis N.N.C., Corpl. Lyons 24th, Private McMahon A.H.C., Privates Roy, Deacon, Bush, Cole, Jenkins 24th, and many others.

Our fire at the time of these rushes of the Zulus was very rapid – Mr. Dalton dropping a man each time he fired his rifle, while Bromhead and myself used our revolvers. The fire from the rocks and caves on the hill behind us was kept up all this time and took us completely in reverse, and although very badly directed, many shots came among us and caused us some loss – and at about 6.00 p.m. the enemy extending their attack further to their left, I feared seriously would get in over our wall behind the biscuit boxes. I ran back with 2 or 3 men to this part of the wall and was immediately joined by Bromhead with 2 or 3 more. The enemy stuck to this assault most tenaciously, and on their repulse, and retiring into the bush, I called all the men inside our retrenchment – and the enemy immediately occupied the wall we had abandoned and used it as a breastwork to fire over.

Mr. Byrne, acting Commissariat Officer, and who had behaved with great coolness and gallantry, was killed instantaneously shortly before this by a bullet through the head, just after he had given a drink of water to a wounded man of the N.N.C.

All this time the enemy had been attempting to fire the Hospital and had at length set fire to its roof and got in at the far end. I had tried to impress upon the men in the Hospital the necessity for making a communication right through the building – unfortunately this was not done. Probably at the time the men could not see the necessity, and doubtless also there was no time to do it. Without in the least detracting from the gallant fellows who defended the Hospital, and I hope I shall not be misunderstood in saying so, I have always regretted, as I did then, the absence of my four poor sappers, who had only left that morning for Isandhlwana and arrived there just to be killed.

The garrison of the Hospital defended it with the greatest gallantry, room by room, bringing out all the sick that could be moved, and breaking through some of the partitions while the Zulus were in the building with them. Privates Williams, Hook, R. Jones and W. Jones being the last to leave and holding the doorway with the bayonet, their ammunition being expended. Private Williams's bayonet was wrenched off his rifle by a Zulu, but with the other men he still managed with the muzzle of his rifle to keep the enemy at bay. Surgeon Reynolds carried his arms full of ammunition to the Hospital, a bullet striking his helmet as he did so. But we were too busily engaged outside to be able to do much, and with the Hospital on fire, and no free communication, nothing could have saved it. Sergeant Maxfield 24th might have been saved, but he was delirious with fever, refused to move and resisted the attempts to move him. He was assegaied before our men's eyes.

Seeing the Hospital burning, and the attempts of the enemy to fire the roof of the Store (one man was shot, I believe by Lt. Adendorff, who had a light almost touching the thatch), we converted two large heaps of mealie bags into a sort of redoubt which gave a second line of fire all around, in case the store building had to be abandoned, or the enemy broke through elsewhere. Assistant Commissary Dunne worked hard at this, and from his height, being a tall man, he was much exposed, in addition to the fact that the heaps were high above our walls, and that most of the Zulu bullets went high.

Trooper Hunter, Natal Mounted Police, escaping from the Hospital, stood still for a moment, hesitating which way to go, dazed by the glare of the burning Hospital, and the firing that was going on all around. He was assegaied before our eyes, the Zulu who killed him immediately afterwards falling. While firing from behind the biscuit boxes, Dalton, who had been using his rifle with deadly effect, and by his quickness and coolness had been the means of saving many men's lives, was shot through the body. I was standing near him at the time, and he handed me his rifle so coolly that I had no idea until afterwards of how severely he was wounded. He waited quite quietly for me to take the cartridges he had left out of his pockets. We put him inside our mealie sack redoubt, building it up around him. About this time I noticed Private Dunbar 24th make some splendid shooting, seven or eight Zulus falling on the ledge of rocks in the Oscarberg to as many consecutive shots by him. I saw Corporal Lyons hit by a bullet which lodged in his spine, and fall between an opening we had left in the wall of biscuit boxes. I thought he was killed, but looking up he said, ' Oh, Sir ! you are not going to leave me here like a dog ? ' We pulled him in and laid him down behind the boxes where he was immediately looked to by Reynolds.

Corporal Scammle (Scammell) of the Natal Native Contingent, who was badly wounded through the shoulder, staggered out under fire again, from the Store building where he had been put, and gave me all his cartridges, which in his wounded state he could not use. While I was intently watching to get a fair shot at a Zulu who appeared to be firing rather well, Private Jenkins 24th, saying ' Look out, Sir,' gave my head a duck down just as a bullet whizzed over it. He had noticed a Zulu who was quite near in another direction taking a deliberate aim at me. For all the man could have known, the shot might have been directed at himself. I mention these facts to show how well the men behaved and how loyally worked together.

Corporal Scheiss, Natal Native Contingent, who was a patient in the Hospital with a wound in the foot, which caused him great pain, behaved with the greatest coolness and gallantry throughout the attack, and at this time creeping out a short distance along the wall we had abandoned, and slowly raising himself, to get a shot at some of the enemy who had been particularly annoying, his hat was blown off by a shot from a Zulu the other side of the wall. He immediately jumped up, bayonetted the Zulu and shot a second, and bayonetted a third who came to their assistance, and then returned to his place.

As darkness came on we were completely surrounded. The Zulus wrecking the camp of the Company 24th and my wagon which had been left outside, in spite of the efforts of my batman, Driver Robson (the only man of the Royal Engineers with us), who had directed his particular attention to keeping the Zulus off this wagon in which were, as he described it, ' Our things.'

They also attacked the east end of our position, and after being several times repulsed, eventually got into the Kraal, which was strongly built with high walls, and drove us to the middle, and then to the inner wall of the Kraal – the enemy occupying the middle wall as we abandoned it. This wall was too high for them to use it effectively to fire over, and a Zulu no sooner showed his head over it than he was dropped, being so close that it was almost impossible to miss him. Shortly before this, some of the men said they saw the red-coats coming on the Helpmakaar road. The rumour passed quickly round – I could see nothing of the sort myself, but some men said they could. A cheer was raised, and the enemy seemed to pause, to know what it meant, but there was no answer to it, and darkness came. It is very strange that this report should have arisen amongst us, for the two companies 24th from Helpmakaar did come down to the foot of the hill, but not, I believe, in sight of us. They marched back to Helpmakaar on the report of Rorke's Drift having fallen.

After the first onslaught, the most formidable of the enemy's attacks was just before we retired behind our line of biscuit boxes, and for a short time after it, when they had gained great confidence by their success on the Hospital. Although they kept their positions behind the walls we had abandoned, and kept up a heavy fire from all sides until about 12 o'clock, they did not actually charge up in a body to get over our wall after about 9 or 10 o'clock. After this time it became very dark, although the Hospital roof was still burning – it was impossible from below to see what was going on, and Bromhead and myself getting up on the mealy sack redoubt, kept an anxious watch on all sides.

The enemy were now in strong force all around us, and every now and then a confused shout of 'Usutu' from many voices seemed to show that they were going to attack from one side and immediately the same thing would happen on the other, leaving us in doubt as to where they meant to attack. About midnight or a little after the fire slackened, and after that, although they kept us constantly on the alert, by feigning, as before, to come on at different points, the fire was of a desultory character. Our men were careful, and only fired when they could see a fair chance. The flame of the burning Hospital was now getting low, and as pieces of the roof fell, or hitherto unburnt parts of the thatch ignited, the flames would blaze up illuminating our helmets and faces. A few shots from the Zulus, replied to by our men – again silence, broken only by the same thing repeatedly happening. This sort of thing went on until about 4 a.m. and we were anxiously waiting for daybreak and the renewal of the attack, which their comparative, and at length complete silence, led us to expect. But at daybreak the enemy were out of sight, over the hill to our south-west. One Zulu had remained in the Kraal and fired a shot among us (without doing any damage) as we stood on the walls, and ran off in the direction of the river – although many shots were fired at him as he ran. I am glad to say the plucky fellow got off.

Taking care not to be surprised by any ruse of the enemy, we patrolled the ground around the place, collecting the arms, and ammunition, of the dead Zulus.

Some of the bullet wounds were very curious. One man's head was split open, exactly as if done with an axe. Another had been hit just between the eyes, the bullet carrying away the whole of the back of his head, leaving his face perfect, as though it were a mask, only disfigured by the small hole made by the bullet passing through. One of the wretches we found, one hand grasping a bench that had been dragged from the Hospital, and sustained thus in the position we found him in, while in the other hand he still clutched the knife with which he had mutilated one of our poor fellows, over whom he was still leaning.

We increased the strength of our defences as much as possible, strengthening and raising our walls, putting sacks on the biscuit boxes, etc., and were removing the thatch from the roof of the Commissariat Store, to avoid being burnt out in case of another attack, when at about 7 a.m. a large body of the enemy (I believe the same who had attacked us) appeared on the hills to the south-west. I thought at the time that they were going to attack us, but from what I now know from Zulus, and also of the number we put hors de combat, I do not think so. I think that they came up on the high ground to observe Lord Chelmsford's advance; from there they could see the Column long before it came in sight of us.

A frightened and fugitive Kaffir came in shortly before, and I sent for Daniells the Pontman, who could speak Zulu a little, to interview him. Daniells had armed himself with Spalding's sword, which he flourished in so wild and eccentric a manner that the poor wretch thought his last hour had come. He professed to be friendly and to have escaped from Isandhlwana, and I sent him with a note to the Officer Commanding at Helpmakaar, explaining our situation, and asking for help; for now, although the men were in excellent spirits, and each man had a good supply of ammunition in his pouches, we had only about a box and a half left besides, and at this time we had no definite knowledge of what had happened, and I myself did not know that the part of the Column with Lord Chelmsford had taken any part in the action at Isandhlwana, or whether on the Camp being taken he had fallen back on Helpmakaar.

The enemy remained on the hill, and still more of them appeared, when about 8 a.m. the Column came in sight, and the enemy disappeared again. There were a great many of our Native Levies with the Column, and the number of red-coats seemed so few that at first we had grave doubts that the force approaching was the enemy. We improvised a flag, and our signals were soon replied to from the Column. The mounted men crossed the Drift and galloped up to us, headed by Major Cecil Russell and Lieut. Walsh, and were received by us with a hearty cheer. Lord Chelmsford, with his Staff, shortly after rode up and thanked us all with much emotion for the defence we had made. The Column arrived, crossing by the Ponts, and we then had a busy time in making a strong position for the night.

I was glad to seize an opportunity to wash my face in a muddy puddle, in company with Private Bush 24th, whose face was covered with blood from a wound in the nose caused by the bullet which had passed through and killed Private Cole 24th. With the politeness of a soldier, he lent me his towel, or, rather, a very dirty half of one, before using it himself, and I was very glad to accept it.

In wrecking the stores in my wagon, the Zulus had brought to light a forgotten bottle of beer, and Bromhead and I drank it with mutual congratulations on having come safely out of so much danger.

My wagon driver, a Cape (coloured) man, lost his courage on hearing the first firing around the hill. He let loose his mules and retreated, concealing himself in one of the caves of the Oscarberg. He saw the Zulus run by him and, to his horror, some of them entered the cave he was in, and lying down commenced firing at us. The poor wretch was crouching in the darkness, in the far depths of the cave, afraid to speak or move, and our bullets came into the cave, actually killing one of the Zulus. He did not know from whom he was in the most danger, friends or foes, and came down in the morning looking more dead than alive. The mules we recovered; they were quietly grazing by the riverside.

On my journey homewards, on arriving at the railway station, Durban, I asked a porter to get me some Kaffirs to carry my bags to the hotel. He sent several, and the first to come running up was my vorlooper boy who had taken me up to Rorke's Drift. He stopped short and looked very frightened, and I believe at first thought he saw my ghost. I seized him to prevent his running away, and when he saw that I was flesh and blood he became reassured. He said he thought I had been killed, and upon my asking him how he thought I got away, he said (the solution of the mystery just striking him), 'I know you rode away on the other horse.' As far as I could learn and according to his own story, the boy had taken the horse I rode up from the river to the Commissariat Store, and, wild with terror, had ridden it to Pietermaritzburg without stopping, where he gave it over to the Transport people, but having no certificate to say who he was, they took the horse from him but would not give him any employment.

During the fight there were some very narrow escapes from the burning Hospital. Private Waters, 24th Regiment, told me that he secreted himself in a cupboard in the room he was defending, and from it shot several Zulus inside the Hospital. He was wounded in the arm, and he remained in the cupboard until the heat and smoke were so great that they threatened to suffocate him. Wrapping himself in a cloak, or skirt of a dress he found in the cupboard, he rushed out into the darkness and made his way into the cook-house. The Zulus were occupying this, and firing at us from the wall nearest us. It was too late to retreat, so he crept softly to the fireplace and, standing up in the chimney, blacked his face and hands with the soot. He remained there until the Zulus left. He was very nearly shot in coming out, one of our men at the wall raising his rifle to do so at the sight of his black face and strange costume, but Waters cried out just in time to save himself. He produced the bullet that wounded him, with pardonable pride, and was very amusing in his admiring description of Dr. Reynolds's skill in extracting it.

Gunner Howard, R.A., ran out of the burning Hospital, through the enemy, and lay down on the upper side of the wall in front of our N. Parapet. The bodies of several horses that were killed early in the evening were lying here, and concealed by these and by Zulu bodies and the low grass and bushes, he remained unseen with the Zulus all around him until they left in the morning.

Private Beckett, 24th Regiment, escaped from the Hospital in the same direction, he was badly wounded with assegais in running through the enemy. He managed to get away and conceal himself in the ditch of the Garden, where we found him next morning. The poor fellow was so weak from loss of blood that he could not walk, and he died shortly afterwards.

Our mealie-bag walls were afterwards replaced by loop-holed walls of stone, the work making rapid progress upon the arrival of half the 5th Company R.E. with Lieut. Porter. As soon as the Sappers arrived we put a fence around, and a rough wood cross over, the graves of our poor men who were killed. This was afterwards replaced by a neat stone monument and inscription by the 24th, who remained to garrison the place.

I have already, in my report, said how gallantly all behaved, from Lieutenant Bromhead downwards, and I also mentioned those whom I had particularly noticed to have distinguished themselves.

On the day following, we buried 351 bodies of the enemy in graves not far from the Commissariat Buildings – many bodies were since discovered and buried, and when I was sick at Ladysmith one of our Sergeants, who came down there invalided from Rorke's Drift, where he had been employed in the construction of Fort Melvill, told me that many Zulu bodies were found in the caves and among the rocks, a long distance from the Mission house, when getting stone for that fort. As, in my report, I underestimated the number we killed, so I believe I also underestimated the number of the enemy that attacked us, and from what I have since learnt I believe the Zulus must have numbered at least 4,000.

As the Reverend George Smith said in a short account he wrote to a Natal paper – 'Whatever signs of approval may be conferred upon the defenders of Rorke's Drift, from high quarters, they will never cease to remember the kind and heartfelt expressions of gratitude which have fallen both from the columns of the Colonial Press and from so many of the Natal Colonists themselves.'

And to this may I add that they will ever remember with heartfelt gratitude the signs of approval that have been conferred upon them by their Sovereign and by the People and the Press of England.

JOHN R. M. CHARD,
January 1880.   Captain and Bt. Major, R.E.

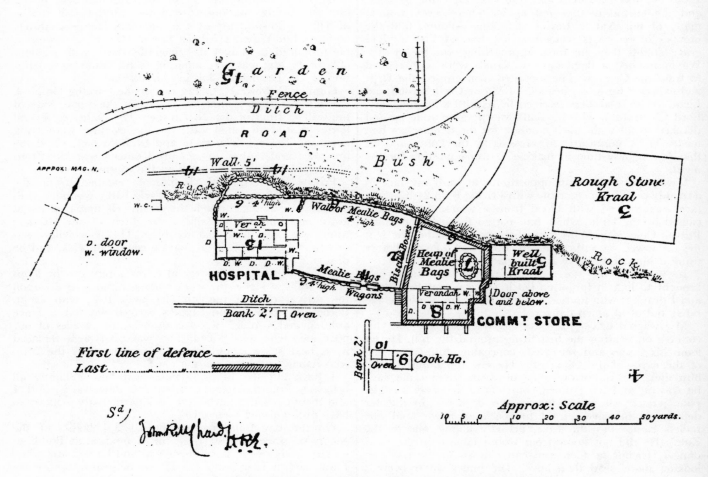

SKETCH SHOWING FIRST AND LAST LINE OF DEFENCE

(1)

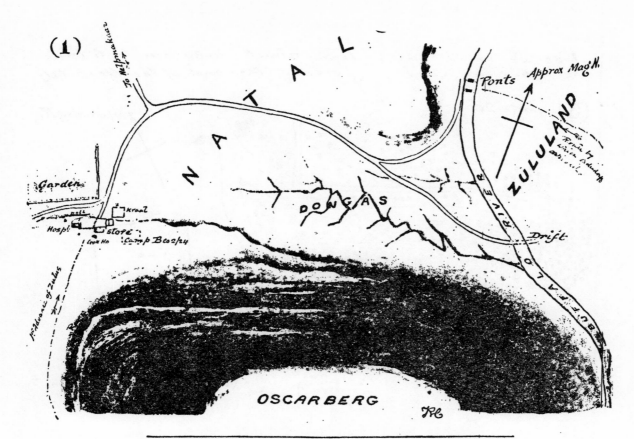

To Helpmakaar

NATAL

Garden

Kraal

Hospl.   Store

Cook Ho.   Camp B co 2/24

Retreat of Zulus

DONGAS

Ponts   Approx Mag. N.

ZULULAND

BUFFALO RIVER

Drift

OSCARBERG

This sketch is chiefly from memory, and therefore may not be quite correct – but it will give a fairly accurate impression of the relative positions of the Houses, Oscarberg, Drift &c –

---

(2) page 18

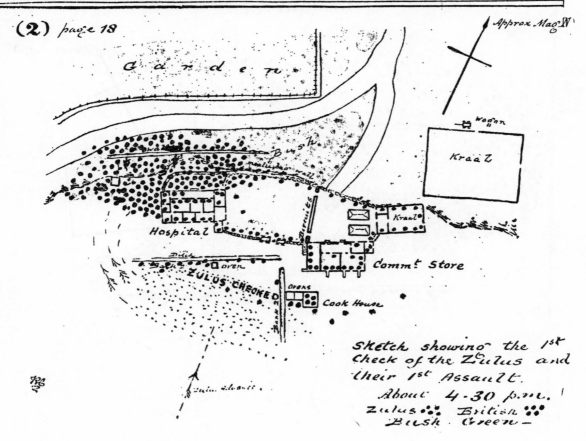

Approx Mag. N.

Garden

Bush

Waggn

Kraal

Hospital

Ditch   Oven

ZULUS CHECKED

Ovens

Cook House

Kraal

Commt Store

Sketch showing the 1st Check of the Zulus and their 1st Assault.
About 4.30 p.m.
Zulus ⋮ British ⋮
Bush. Green –

A series of Assaults from about 4-30 pm to 6 pm.
the Zulus at last, forcing the end of the Hospital

(3) page 20

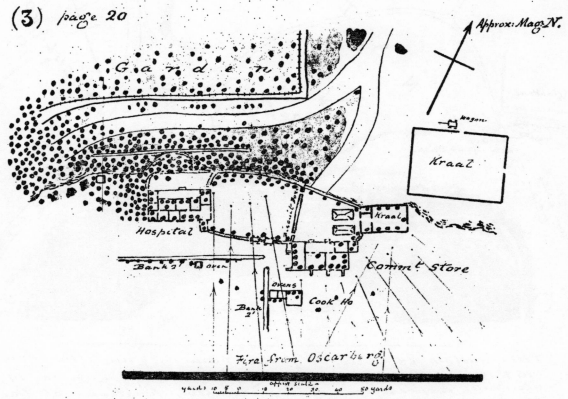

(4) page 22   About 6 pm. the enemy extend
their attack.

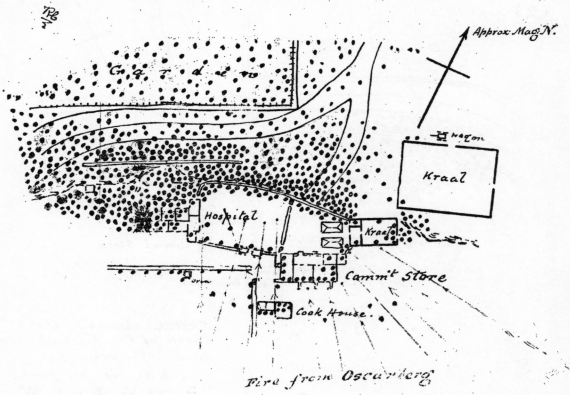

(5)

Darkness—Completely surrounded.

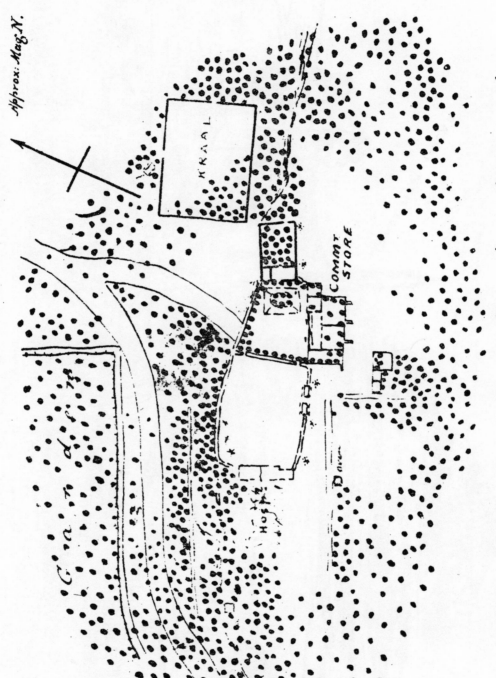

KRAAL

COMMᵗ STORE

HOSPᶧ

Door

G'n d'r'n

Approx: Mag. N.

✻ The flank fire from the store prevented
the Zulus from getting near these walls
in any number.

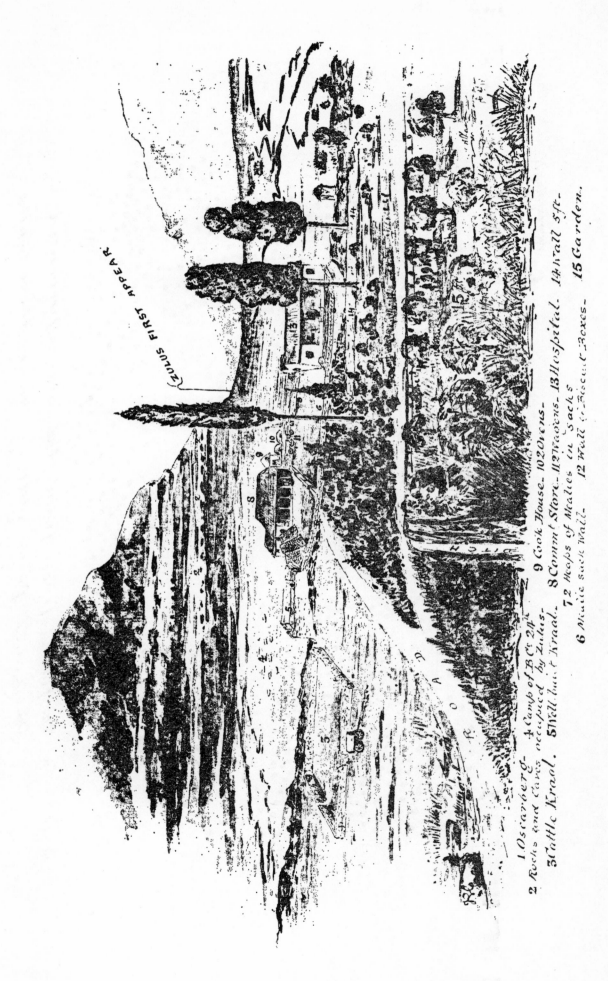

(ZULUS FIRST APPEAR)

1. Oscarberg — 4 Camp of B Co. 24 — 9 Cook House — 10 Oven —
2 Rocks and Caves occupied by Zulus — 8 Comm.t Store — 11 Waggons — 13 Hospital — 14 Wall 5 ft —
3 Cattle Kraal — 5 Well built Kraal — 7 2 Heaps of Mealies in Sacks — 15 Garden —
6 Mealie Sack Wall — 12 Wall of Biscuit Boxes —

CHARD'S PANORAMIC SKETCH OF AREA

An Account

by

447 Private J. WATERS, 1/24th Regiment.

Originally published in *The Cambrian* newspaper
for 13th June 1879.

I was special orderly at the hospital at Rorke's Drift, and at this time have seen twenty-one and a quarters years service. I was in the hospital when Private Evans rode into camp and reported that the Zulus had Massacred the whole column at Isandhlwana. We would hardly believe this at first, but very soon had reason to understand it was only too true. Between half past four and five, as near as I can remember, the Zulus came over the hill and I saw about fifty of them form a line in skirmishing order, just as British soldiers would do. Their main body was in their rear over the shoulder of the hill. They came about twenty yards, and then opened fire on the hospital. Some of them came in and set fire to it.

While I was there I took refuge in a cupboard, and Private Beckett, an invalid, came with me. As they were going out I killed many of them, and as I could not stay there long, the place being suffocating, I put on a black cloak which I found in the cupboard, and which must have belonged to Mr. Witt, and ran out in the long grass and lay down. The Zulus must have thought I was one of their dead comrades, as they were all round about me, and some trod on me. Beckett had gone out half an hour before me, and he, poor fellow, was assegaied right through his stomach, and went into laager next morning. Dr. Reynolds did all he could to save him, but did not succeed. I got up at daybreak, having expected every minute my life would be taken, and then saw my comrades on the top of the mealie sacks, and I said, 'Thank God, I have got my life.' I had been shot early in the engagement in the shoulder and knee, and here's the bullet, which was taken out next morning by Dr. Reynolds. I knew many poor fellows who fell at Isandhlwana. I saw Private Horrigan killed. Poor Beckett was buried next morning properly. Round the hospital dead Zulus were piled in heaps.

(See *The Red Soldier*)

An Account

by

Lieutenant-Colonel F. BOURNE, O.B.E., D.C.M.

In December 1872, when I was 18 years old, I enlisted in the 24th Regiment and received the princely pay of 6d. a day, of which 3½d. was deducted for messing and washing, leaving 1s. 5½d. a week – for luxuries. I went to bed every night hungry but quite happy, and it made a man of me.

The Regiment had just come home from India after fifteen years. Now the 'A' Company of any Regiment in those days was always called the Grenadier Company and was supposed to have the biggest men. I think the Sergeant-Major must have been a wee bit humorous, for he posted me to our 'A' Company although I stood only five foot six inches and was painfully thin.

After five years of home service, in February 1878 the Regiment received sudden orders to proceed to the Cape of Good Hope to take part in the Kaffir War. This was my first experience of active service, and shortly after, my Colonel promoted me Colour-Sergeant of 'B' Company – 100 strong. I was only twenty-three, very nervous, sensitive, and afraid of my new responsibilities. Several men of the Company were of my own age, others older, and some old enough to be my father, but after a few months I felt more secure and thought I was getting along quite well. I also found myself 'unpaid private secretary' to several men who could barely read and write, and I deciphered and answered their letters home, feeling quite happy in our relations. One day I heard a man named Wall ask my batman ' if the kid was in,' a day or two later I asked Partridge casually who 'the kid' was, and received the answer, ' Why, you are, of course.' My stock slumped at once. I think it does us all good to have our swollen heads reduced. But we were a very happy family. You can't live in tents, and on Mother Earth, for two years on Active Service without knowing your men intimately.

The Kaffir War ended in June 1878 and we were moved to Pietermaritzburg, Natal, to assist in raising the curtain on the Zulu drama. On January 11 we crossed the Buffalo River at Rorke's Drift – into the Zulu country. Our Commander-in-Chief was Lord Chelmsford. Our strength was four thousand five hundred men – including thirteen companies of my Regiment, the 24th, now the South Wales Borderers. One company was left behind at Rorke's Drift, to guard the hospital, stores, and the pontoons at the Drift on the Buffalo River. This was my company, and at the time I was bitterly disappointed. We saw the main column under Lord Chelmsford engaged the enemy at once, and I watched the action, along with my four sergeants, from a little hill by Rorke's Drift. Then we saw them move on again, and they disappeared.

And now I must tell you what happened to them during the next ten days.

They made their camp under a hill called Isandhlwana, about ten miles away. Then days later, on the twenty-first, Lord Chelmsford learned that the enemy was in force ahead of the camp, and he moved out on the morning of the twenty-second with nearly half his force to attack them. But as he advanced they disappeared, and in his absence his camp was attacked and overwhelmed by fourteen thousand Zulus. So swift was the disaster that the few survivors who got away could give no reliable account of it, but the evidence of the dead who were afterwards found and buried where they lay told the unvarying tale of groups of men fighting back to back until the last cartridge was fired. After the war, Zulu witnesses all told the same story. ' At first we could make no headway against the soldiers, but suddenly they ceased to fire, then we came round them and killed them with our assegais.' According to one account, the last survivor was a drummer boy who flung his short sword at a Zulu. This was the last occasion that Band or Drummer Boys were taken on Active Service, as it was also the last occasion that the Colours were carried into action.* Lieutenants Melvill and Coghill lost their lives that day trying to save the colours. Fully twelve hundred men were killed. And by half past one no white man was alive in Isandhlwana camp.

Of course, back at Rorke's Drift we knew nothing of this disaster, although my sergeants and I on our hill above it could hear the guns and see the puffs of smoke. But an hour later, at two o'clock, a few refugees arrived and warned us what to expect. One man whispered to me ' Not a fighting chance for you, young feller.' Up to that time we had done nothing to put our small post in a defensive

---

* This is incorrect. The last occasion that Colours were carried was at Majuba Hill on 27/2/81.

position, as our force in front was nearly five thousand strong and had six guns, and the last thing that we expected was that we should be the saviours of the remainder of that force. The strength of our small garrison at the Drift was two combatant and six departmental officers, and one hundred and thirty-three non-commissioned officers and men, thirty-six of whom were sick, leaving about one hundred fighting men. Remember that twelve hundred men had just been massacred at Isandhlwana. Can you then be surprised that, flushed with their success, the Zulus were making for our small post confident that we should be easy victims to their savagery? Having had the warning – but only two hours in advance, as it turned out – we set to work to loophole the two buildings and to connect the front of the hospital with a stone cattle kraal by sacks of Indian corn and oats, and to draw up two Boer transport wagons to join the front of the Commissariat Stores with the back of the hospital. These proved excellent barricades, but by no means impregnable.

The native has often been credited with deep cunning, but luckily for us if the Zulu possessed any he did not use it, for as the sacks connecting the hospital had to be laid on a slope of the ground he could safely have crept along, cut the sacks open with his assegais, the corn would have rolled out and he could have walked in and I should not now be telling the story. When Lieutenant Chard of the Royal Engineers joined us he approved of what we had done, but considered that our inner space was too big, and suggested a line of biscuit boxes. This was done and proved of great value when the enemy set the hospital on fire.

I was instructed to post men as look-out, in the hospital, at the most vulnerable points, and to take out and command a line of skirmishers. Shortly after 3.30 an officer commanding a troop of Natal Light Horse arrived, having got away from Isandhlwana, and asked Lieutenant Chard for instructions. He was ordered to send detachments to observe the drift and pontoons, and to place outposts in the direction of the enemy to check his advance.

About 4.15 the sound of firing was heard behind the hill on our front; the officer returned and reported the enemy close upon us. He also reported that his 100 men would not obey his orders and had ridden off. About the same time another detachment of 100 men belonging to the Natal native contingent bolted, including their officer himself. I am glad to say he was brought back some days later, court-marshalled and dismissed from the service. The desertion of these detachments of 200 men appeared at first sight to be a great loss, with only a hundred of us left, but the feeling afterwards was that we could not have trusted them, and also that our defences were too small to accommodate them anyhow.

We knew now that whatever might happen we had to fight it out alone, and about 4.30 the enemy, from 500 to 600 strong, came in sight round the hill to our south, and driving in my thin red line of skirmishers, made a rush at our south wall. They were met, and held, by a steady and deliberate fire for a short time, then, being reinforced by some hundreds, they made desperate and repeated attempts to break through our temporary defences, but were repulsed time and again. To show their fearlessness and their contempt for the red coats and small numbers, they tried to leap the parapet, and at times seized our bayonets, only to be shot down. Looking back, one cannot but admire their fanatical bravery.

About 7 o'clock they succeeded, after many attempts, in setting fire to the hospital. The small numbers we were able to spare defended it room by room, bringing out all the sick who could be moved before they retired. Privates Hook, R. Jones, W. Jones and J. Williams were the last to leave holding the door with the bayonet when all their ammunition was expended. The Victoria Cross was awarded to these men, and they fully deserved it.

The Zulus had collected the rifles from the men they had killed at Isandhlwana, and had captured the ammunition from the mules which had stampeded and threw their loads; so our own arms were used against us. In fact, this was the cause of every one of our casualties, killed and wounded, and we should have suffered many more if the enemy had known how to use a rifle. There was hardly a man even wounded by an assegai – their principal weapon.

The attack lasted from 4.30 p.m. on the twenty-second to 4.0 a.m. on the twenty-third – twelve exciting hours – and when daybreak occurred the enemy was out of sight. About 7 o'clock they appeared again to the south-west. But help was at hand; Lord Chelmsford with the other half of his original force was only an hour's march away. On the previous afternoon he had learned of the destruction of his camp at Isandhlwana. A certain Commandant Lonsdale had chanced to ride back to the camp and had been fired at by Zulus wearing our men's uniform. He escaped by a miracle and was able to report the news to Lord Chelmsford.

Lord Chelmsford at once addressed his men and said: ' Whilst we were skirmishing ahead the Zulus have taken our camp; there must be ten thousand in our rear, and twenty thousand in front, we must win back our camp tonight and cut our way back to Rorke's Drift tomorrow.' ' All right, sir, we'll do it.'

They got back to camp that night, but they found a grim and silent scene as they cautiously approached. The next day they resumed their march and appeared at Rorke's Drift, and our enemy retired.

In his dispatch afterwards, Lord Chelmsford said : ' To our intense relief the waving of hats was seen from the hastily erected entrenchments, and information soon reached me that the garrison . . . had for twelve hours made the most gallant resistance I have ever heard of against the determined attack of some 3,000 Zulus, 350 of whose dead bodies surrounded the post.' Our losses were 17 killed and 9 wounded, theirs 351 killed that we buried. Their wounded must have been between 400 and 500, which they removed under cover of the night.

There are two things which I think have made Rorke's Drift stand out so vividly after all these years. The first, that it took place on the same day as the terrible massacre at Isandhlwana, and the second, that Natal was saved from being overrun by a savage and victorious foe.

Seven V.C.s were awarded to this one company of the regiment which is now the South Wales Borderers. I have told you the names of four of the men who won the V.C.; the other three were Lieutenant Bromhead, Corporal Allen and Private F. Hitch. The Victoria Cross was also awarded to Lieutenant Chard, Royal Engineers, Surgeon Reynolds, and Corporal Scheiss, but not one, I regret to say, of those V.C.s is alive today . . .

Lieutenants Chard and Bromhead and the men received the thanks of Parliament, the officers being promoted to the rank of Major. I was awarded the Distinguished Conduct Medal with an annuity of £10 – the same as awarded to the Victoria Cross – and awarded a commission, but as I was the youngest of eight sons, and the family exchequer was empty, I had to refuse it that time.

Now just one word for the men who fought that night; I was moving about amongst them all the time, and not for one moment did they flinch, their courage and their bravery cannot be expressed in words : for me they were an example all my soldiering days.

The following year, Queen Victoria received at Windsor Castle a Colour Party of the Regiment, and decorated the

Queen's Colour with a silver wreath of immortelles in memory of Lieutenants Melvill and Coghill, 'for their devotion in trying to save the Colours of the twenty-second of January (that was at Isandhlwana) and for the noble defence of Rorke's Drift.' So if you ever have the great privilege of seeing the Colours of the South Wales Borderers uncased you will see the wreath. The original wreath presented by Her Majesty is now in the Regimental Chapel of Brecon Cathedral . . .

[From *The Listener*, 30th December 1936.]

An Account
by
1387 Sergeant G. SMITH, 2/24th Regiment.

Extracted from a letter written by George Smith on 24th January 1879 and addressed to his wife, who lived at Little Free Street, Brecon.

I am thankful at having been saved from the cruel slaughter and bloodshed that we had all gone through the last four days. I have some very bad news to tell you. Our regiment, that is the 2/24th, left here five days ago to go to Cetshwayo's kraal, to fight the Zulus. They had left my company at this place to protect the commissariat stores, and encamped about eight miles from here, and on the 22nd the troops went out reconnoitring the country, and had only left one company in camp to protect the ammunition and baggage. They went out about sixteen miles, and while they were out the camp was attacked by 6,000 of the enemy, and cut to pieces.

The 1st Battalion has lost seventeen officers killed and missing, and nearly all of the men. The Zulus got hold of four boys of the band 1/24th, and cut them up in bits, and destroyed everything they could lay their hands on, and our colours are missing, and all the ammunition is taken from us.

After destroying all they could, they made for Rorke's Drift, and at about two thirty p.m. on the same day we were attacked by about 3,000 of them, and had to build up a fort with bags of meal, oats and boxes of meat and biscuits. How we ever escaped I can hardly tell you. There were only about a hundred of us, all told. We kept up a continual firing for fifteen hours, from three p.m. on the 22nd until six a.m. on the 23rd when the two battalions of the 24th (what was left of them) came to our relief, and four guns of the Royal Artillery. We had thirteen men killed and about eight wounded. Amongst the former was poor Drummer Haydon, that lived at the top of John Street. He was stabbed in hospital in sixteen places, and his belly cut open right up in two places, and part of his cheek was cut off –. Corporal Allen was shot through the shoulder. It is only a flesh wound, and he is coming round very well –.

I myself had given up all hopes of escaping. My company was very highly praised for the noble stand they made in keeping the place, and the cool manner in which we defended it, and I heard the General say that the Colonel should take the two battalions home again after it was over, and that we were to be formed into one Regiment, and a new 2nd Battalion 24th Regiment was to be formed at home –.

One of our men was shot through the lungs, and he stuck to his post, and fired away for an hour, when he dropped down dead from loss of blood –. We have lost nearly everything that we had, and we have to return back to Pietermaritzburg to get a fresh supply of clothing, and everything else, for we have only got what we stand up in now. We have counted the number of the blacks that were killed and shot by my company, and they were over 800, so that they paid dearly for what they killed of our men.

(See *The Red Soldier*)

An Account
by
1112 Corporal J. LYONS, 2/24th Regiment

Originally published in *The Cambrian* newspaper for 13th June 1879.

I belong to B Company of the 2/24th, under Lieutenant Bromhead. I went up to Greytown with Private Hitch, who was one of the same company. We arrived at Rorke's Drift about 5 January. I saw Private Evans, of the Mounted Infantry, riding up at full gallop, without either coat or cap on, and I, of course, thought something was up.

Hitch had by this time reported that the Zulus were in sight, and we were scarcely finished before they were on us. We were told not to fire without orders. This, I suppose, was to make sure that the advancing force was really Zulus. Only a few seconds elapsed before the real character of it was made known to us. The Zulus did not shout, as they generally do; but, after extending and forming a half-moon, they steadily advanced and kept up a tremendous fire. I took up a position to check the fire from the enemy's right flank, as it was thought the crack shots would go up there. Corporal Allen and several men with me, and we all consider we did good service. Lieutenant Bromhead was on the right face, firing over the mealies with a Martini-Henry. Mr. Chard was also very busy, I only turned round once to see this, and in that brief interval I saw Private Cole shot, and he fell dead. Seeing this, I kept myself more over the bags, knowing that the shot which hit him had come over our heads, and I was determined to check this flank firing as much as possible. I became thus more exposed, and so did Corporal Allen. We fired many shots, and I said to my comrade, ' They (the Zulus) are falling fast over there,' and he replied ' Yes, we are giving it to them.' I saw many Zulus killed on the hill.

About half past seven, as near as I can tell, after we had been fighting between two and three hours, I received a shot through the right side of the neck. The ball lodged in the back, striking the spine, and was not extracted till five weeks afterwards. My right arm was partially disabled. I said, ' Give it to them, Allen. I am done; I am dying,' and he replied, ' All right, Jack '; and while I was speaking to him I saw a hole in the right sleeve of his jacket, and I said, ' Allen, you are shot,' and he replied, ' Yes, goodbye.' He walked away, with blood running from his arm, and he helped to serve ammunition all night. All I could do as I was lying on the ground was to encourage the men, and I did so as long as I was able to open my mouth. Every man fought dearly for his life, but we were all determined to sell our lives like soldiers, and to keep up the credit of our regiment. Mr. Dalton, who has since received a commission, deserved any amount of praise.

(See *The Red Soldier*)

An Account
by
1362 Private F. HITCH, V.C., 2/24th Regiment.

As I have been asked many times to give my illustration of Rorke's Drift, I cannot say it was a pleasure for me to do so and to think back to that terrible night of the 22nd January 1879. It was about 3.30 o'clock that we heard of that fatal disaster of Isandhlwana. I was cooking the tea for the Company. I tried to get it done before the Zulus attacked the little post at Rorke's Drift, which I managed; taking the tea and my rifle and ammunition and four kettles of tea. I just got into the fort when Bromhead asked me to try and get on top of the house. I at once mounted it. As soon as I got on the top I could see the Zulus had got as near to us as they could, without us seeing them. I told Bromhead that they were at the other side of the rise and was extending for attack. Mr. Bromhead asked me how many there were? I told him that I thought (they) numbered up to four to six thousand. A voice from below – 'Is that all; we can manage that lot very well for a few seconds.' There were different opinions. I stayed on the house watching the black mass extending into their fighting line. The same time a number of them creeping along under the rocks and took up cover in the caves, and keep trying to dismount me from the top of the house. Their direction was good but their elevation bad. A few minutes later one appeared on the top of the mountain; from the other side he could see us in the laager plain enough to count us.

I put myself in a lying position, but my shot fell short of him. He then moved steadily to the right and signalled with his arm – the main body at once began to advance. I told Mr. Bromhead that they would be all round us in a very short time. He at once told the Company to take up their post, the enemy making a right wheel, they attacked us in a shape of a bullock's horns, and in a few minutes was all round us.

I found as they got close to the laager I was out of the fighting, so I slid down the thatch roof, dropping into the laager, fixing my bayonet as I ran across the laager, taking up my position on a open space which we had not time to complete as the deadly work now commenced.

The Zulus pushing right up to the porch, it was not until the bayonet was freely used that they flinched the least bit. Had the Zulus taken the bayonet as freely as they took the bullets, we could not have stood more than fifteen minutes. They pushed right up to us and not only got up to the laager but got in with us, but they seemed to have a great dread of the bayonet, which stood to us from beginning to end. During that struggle there was a fine big Zulu see me shoot his mate down – he sprang forward, dropping his rifle and assegais, seizing hold of the muzzle of my rifle with his left hand and the right hand hold of the bayonet. Thinking to disarm me, he pulled and tried hard to get the rifle from me, but I had a firm hold of the small of the butt of my rifle with my left hand. My cartridges on the top of the mealie bags which enabled me to load my rifle and (I) shot the poor wretch whilst holding on to his grasp for some few moments. They dropped back into the garden, which served a great protection for them – had it not been for the garden, dead and wall, they could not have prolonged the engagement for thirteen hours as they did. Their next object was to get possession of the hospital, which they did by setting fire to it. The greatest task was in getting the sick and wounded out of the hospital, which the Zulus had busted open the doors and killed them in their beds. Whilst doing this, I noticed it was with great difficulty they were kept back. They keeping up a heavy fire from front and rear from which we suffered very much.

It was then about when Mr. Dalton was shot and Mr. Dunn. Mr. Dalton was very active up till he was wounded. We had to fall back to the second line of defence, and when the Zulus took possession of the hospital, Bromhead and myself and five others took up the position on the right of the second line of defence which we were exposed to the cross fire. Bromhead took the centre and was the only one that did not get wounded. There was four killed and two wounded, myself was the last of the six shot. Bromhead and myself had it to ourselves about an hour and a half, Bromhead using his rifle and revolver with deadly aim. Bromhead kept telling the men not to waste one round. About this time all was pressed very much, Bromhead was using his revolver with deadly aim. They seemed determined to move Bromhead and myself. We were so busy that one had (got) inside and was in the act of assegaiing Bromhead. Bromhead, not knowing he was there, I put my rifle on him knowing at the same time it was empty, instead of him delivering the assegai, which no doubt would have been fatal, he dodged down and hopped out of the laager.

Again this was just before they tried to fire the other building, they seemed to me as if they made up their minds to take Rorke's Drift with this rush. They rushed up madly not withstanding the heavy loss they had already suffered. It was in this struggle that I was shot. They pressed us very hard, several of them mounting the barricade. I knew this one had got his rifle presented at me, but at the same time I had got my hands full in front and I was at the present when he shot me through my right shoulder blade and passed through my shoulder which splintered the shoulder bone very much, as I have had in all 39 pieces of broken bone taken from my shoulder. I tried to keep my feet, but could not, he could have assegaied me had not Bromhead shot him with his revolver. Bromhead seemed sorry when he saw me down bleeding so freely, saying, 'Mate, I am very sorry to see you down.' I was not down more than a few minutes, stripping (to) my shirt sleeves with my waistbelt on and valise straps I put my wounded arm under my waist belt. I was able to make another stand, getting Bromhead's revolver, and with his assistance in loading it I managed very well with it. At this time we were fighting by the aid from the burning hospital, which was much to our advantage. Bromhead at this time was keeping a strict eye on the ammunition and telling the men not to waste one round as we were getting short. I was serving out ammunition myself when I became thirsty and faint. I got worse, a chum tore out the lining out of Mr. Dunn's coat and tied it round my shoulder. I got so thirsty that I could not do much, in fact we were all exhausted and the ammunition was being counted.

Deakin (Deacon), a comrade, said to me as I was leaning back against the biscuit boxes, 'Fred, when it comes to the last shall I shoot you?' I declined. 'No, they have very nearly done for me and they can finish me right out when it comes to the last.' I don't remember much after that. When I came to myself again, Lord Chelmsford had relieved us of our tasks. Bromhead brought his Lordship to see me, and his Lordship spoke very kindly to me and the doctor dressed my wound.

Bromhead was my principal visitor and nurse while I was at the Drift.

An Account

by

1373 Private A. H. HOOK, V.C., 2/24th Regiment.

[This narrative originally appeared in *The Royal Magazine*] for February 1905. The account, as supplied by Hook, was edited and transcribed for publication by Walter Wood, however it may be regarded as a verbatim rendering of Hook's recollections of the events.]

Everything was perfectly quiet at Rorke's Drift after the column (Durnford's force) had left, and every officer and man was going about his business as usual. Not a soul suspected that only a dozen miles away the very men that we had said 'Goodbye' and 'Good Luck' to were either dead or standing back-to-back in a last fierce fight with the Zulus. Our garrison consisted of 8 Company of the 2/24th under Lieutenant Bromhead, and details which brought the total number of us up to 139. Besides these, we had about 300 men of the Natal Native Contingent; but they didn't count, as they bolted in a body when the fight began. We were all knocking about, and I was making tea for the sick, as I was hospital cook at the time.

Suddenly there was a commotion in the camp, and we saw two men galloping towards us from the other side of the river, which was Zululand. Lieutenant Chard of the Engineers was protecting the ponts over the river and, as senior officer, was in command at the drift. The ponts were very simple affairs, one of them being supported on big barrels, and the other on boats. Lieutenant Bromhead was in the camp itself. The horsemen shouted and were brought across the river, and then we knew what had happened to our comrades. They had been butchered to a man. That was awful enough news, but worse was to follow, for we were told that the Zulus were coming straight on from Isandhlwana to attack us. At the same time, a note was received by Lieutenant Bromhead from the Column to say that the enemy was coming on and that the post was to be held at all costs.

For some little time we were all stunned, then everything changed from perfect quietness to intense excitement and energy. There was a general feeling that the only safe thing was to retire and try to join the troops at Helpmakaar. The horsemen had said that the Zulus would be up in two or three minutes; but luckily for us they did not show themselves for more than an hour. Lieutenant Chard rushed up from the river, about a quarter of a mile away, and saw Lieutenant Bromhead. Orders were given to strike the camp and make ready to go, and we actually loaded up two wagons. Then Mr. Dalton, of the Commissariat Department, came up and said that if we left the drift every man was certain to be killed. He had formerly been a sergeant-major in a line regiment and was one of the bravest men that ever lived. Lieutenants Chard and Bromhead held a consultation, short and earnest, and orders were given that we were to get the hospital and storehouse ready for defence, and that we were never to say die or surrender.

Not a minute was lost. Lieutenant Bromhead superintended the loopholing and barricading of the hospital and storehouse, and the making of a connection of the defences between the two buildings with walls of mealie-bags and wagons. The mealie-bags were good, big, heavy things, weighing about 200 pounds each, and during the fight many of them were burst open by assegais and bullets, and the mealies (Indian corn) were thickly spread about the ground.

The biscuit boxes contained ordinary biscuit. They were big, square wooden boxes, weighing about a hundred-weight each. The meat boxes, too, were very heavy, as they contained tinned meat. They were smaller than the biscuit boxes. While these precautions were being made, Lieutenant Chard went down to the river and brought in the pont guard of a sergeant and half-a-dozen men, with the wagons and gear. The two officers saw that every soldier was at his post, then we were ready for the Zulus when they cared to come.

They were not long. Just before half past four we heard firing behind the conical hill at the back of the drift, called Oskarsberg Hill, and suddenly about five or six hundred Zulus swept around, coming for us at a run. Instantly the natives – Kaffirs who had been very useful in making the barricade of wagons, mealie-bags and biscuit boxes around the camp – bolted towards Helpmakaar, and what was worse, their officer and a European sergeant went with them. To see them deserting like that was too much for some of us, and we fired after them. The sergeant was struck and killed. Half-a-dozen of us were stationed in the hospital, with orders to hold it and guard the sick. The ends of the building were of stone, the side walls of ordinary bricks, and the inside walls or partitions of sun-dried bricks of mud. These shoddy inside bricks proved our salvation, as you will see. It was a queer little one-storeyed building, which it is almost impossible to describe; but we were pinned like rats in a hole; because all the doorways except one had been barricaded with mealie-bags, and we had done the same with the windows. The interior was divided by means of partition walls into which were fitted some very slight doors. The patients' beds were simple, rough affairs of boards, raised only about half a foot above the floor. To talk of hospital and beds gives the idea of a big building, but as a matter of fact this hospital was a mere little shed or bungalow, divided up into rooms so small that you could hardly swing a bayonet in them. There were about nine men who could not move, but altogether there were about thirty. Most of these, however, could help to defend themselves.

As soon as our Kaffirs bolted, it was seen that the fort as we had first made it was too big to be held, so Lieutenant Chard instantly reduced the space by having a row of biscuit-boxes drawn across the middle, about four feet high. This was our inner entrenchment, and proved very valuable. The Zulus came on at a wild rush, and although many of them were shot down, they got to within about fifty yards of our south wall of mealie-bags and biscuit boxes and wagons. They were caught between two fires, that from the hospital and that from the storehouse, and were checked; but they gained the shelter of the cookhouse and ovens, and gave us many heavy volleys. During the fight they took advantage of every bit of cover there was, anthills, a tract of bush that we had not had time to clear away, a garden or sort of orchard which was near us, and a ledge of rock and some caves (on the Oscarsberg) which were only about a hundred yards away. They neglected nothing, and while they went on firing large bodies kept hurling themselves against our slender breastworks.

But it was the hospital they assaulted most fiercely. I had charge with a man that we called Old King Cole of a small room with only one patient in it. Cole kept with me for some time after the fight began, then he said he was not going to stay. He went outside and was instantly killed by the Zulus, so that I was left alone with the patient, a native whose leg was broken and who kept crying out, 'Take my bandage off, so that I can come.' But it was impossible to do anything except fight, and I blazed away as hard as I could. By this time I was the only defender of my room. Poor Old King Cole was lying dead outside and the helpless patient was crying and groaning near me. The Zulus were swarming around us, and there was an extraordinary rattle as the bullets struck the biscuit boxes, and queer thuds as they plumped into the bags of mealies. Then there was the whizz and rip of the assegais, of which I had experience during the Kaffir Campaign of 1877–8. We had plenty of ammunition, but we were told to save it and so we took careful aim at every shot, and hardly a cartridge was wasted. One of my comrades, Private Dunbar, shot no fewer than nine Zulus, one of them being a chief.

From the very first the enemy tried to rush the hospital, and at last they managed to set fire to the thick grass which formed the roof. This put us in a terrible plight, because it meant that we were either to be massacred or burned alive, or get out of the building. To get out seemed impossible; for if we left the hospital by the only door which had been left open, we should instantly fall into the midst of the Zulus. Besides, there were the helpless sick and wounded, and we could not leave them. My own little room communicated with another by means of a frail door like a bedroom door. Fire and dense choking smoke forced me to get out and go into the other room. It was impossible to take the native patient with me, and I had to leave him to an awful fate. But his death was, at any rate, a merciful one. I heard the Zulus asking him questions, and he tried to tear off his bandages and escape.

In the room where I now was there were nine sick men, and I alone to look after them for some time, still firing away, with the hospital burning. Suddenly in the thick smoke I saw John Williams, and above the din of battle and the cries of the wounded, I heard him shout, 'The Zulus are swarming all over the place. They've dragged Joseph Williams out and killed him.' John Williams had held the other room with Private William Horrigan for more than an hour, until they had not a cartridge left. The Zulus then burst in and dragged out Joseph Williams and two of the patients, and assegaied them. It was only because they were so busy with this slaughtering that John Williams and two of the patients were able to knock a hole in the partition and get into the room where I was posted. Horrigan was killed. What were we to do? We were pinned like rats in a hole. Already the Zulus were fiercely trying to burst in through the doorway. The only way of escape with the wall itself, by making a hole big enough for a man to crawl through into an adjoining room, and so on until we got to our inmost entrenchment outside. Williams worked desperately at the wall with the navvy's pick, which I had been using to make some of the loop-holes with.

All this time the Zulus were trying to get into the room. Their assegais kept whizzing towards us, and one struck me in front of the helmet. We were wearing the white tropical helmets then. But the helmet tilted back under the blow and made the spear lose its power so that I escaped with a scalp wound which did not trouble me much then, although it has often caused me illness since. Only one man at a time could get in at the door. A big Zulu sprang forward and seized my rifle, but I tore it free and, slipping a cartridge in, I shot him point-blank. Time after time the Zulus gripped the muzzle and tried to tear the rifle from my grasp, and time after time I wrenched it back, because I had a better grip than they had. All this time Williams was getting the sick through the hole into the next room, all except one, a soldier of the 24th named Conley, who could not move because of a broken leg. Watching for my chance, I dashed from the doorway and, grabbing Conley, I pulled him after me through the hole. His leg got broken again, but there was

no help for it. As soon as we left the room the Zulus burst in with furious cries of disappointment and rage.

Now there was a repetition of the work of holding the doorway, except that I had to stand by a hole instead of a door, while Williams picked away at the far wall to make an opening for escape into the next room. There was more desperate and almost hopeless fighting, as it seemed, but most of the poor fellow were got through the hole. Again I had to drag Conley through, a terrific task because he was a very heavy man. We were now all in a little room that gave upon the inner line of defence which had been made. We (Williams and Robert Jones and William Jones and myself) were the last men to leave the hospital, after most of the poor fellows were got through the hole. Again the small window and away from the burning building; but it was impossible to save a few of them, and they were butchered. Privates William Jones and Robert Jones during all this time were doing magnificent work in another ward which faced the hill. They kept at it with bullet and bayonet until six of the seven patients had been removed. They would have got the seventh, Sergeant Maxfield, out safely, but he was delirious with fever and, although they managed to dress him, he refused to move. Robert Jones made a last rush to try and get him away like the rest, but when he got back into the room he saw that Maxfield was being stabbed by the Zulus as he lay on his bed. Corporal Allen and Private Hitch helped greatly in keeping up communications with the hospital. They were both badly wounded, but when they could not fight any longer they served out ammunition to their comrades throughout the night.

As we got the sick and wounded out they were taken to a verandah in front of the storehouse, and Dr. Reynolds under a heavy fire and clouds of assegais, did everything he could for them. All this time, of course, the storehouse was being valiantly defended by the rest of the garrison. When we got into the inner fort, I took my post at a place where two men had been shot. While I was there another man was shot in the neck, I think by a bullet which came through the space between two biscuit boxes that were not quite close together. This was at about six o'clock in the evening, nearly two hours after the opening shot of the battle had been fired. Every now and then the Zulus would make a rush for it and get in. We had to charge them out. By this time it was dark, and the hospital was all in flames, but this gave us a splendid light to fight by. I believe it was this light that saved us. We could see them coming, and they could not rush us and take us by surprise from any point. They could not get at us, and so they went away and had ten or fifteen minutes of a war-dance. This roused them up again, and their excitement was so intense that the ground fairly seemed to shake. Then, when they were goaded to the highest pitch, they would hurl themselves at us again.

I need hardly say that we were using Martinis, and fine rifles they were, too. But we did so much firing that they became hot, and the brass of the cartridges softened, the result being that the barrels got very foul and the cartridge-chamber jammed. My own rifle was jammed several times, and I had to work away with the ramrod 'till I cleared it. We used the old three-sided bayonet, and the long, thin blade we called the 'lung' bayonet. They were very fine weapons, too, but some were very poor in quality, and either twisted or bent badly. Several were like that after the fight; but some terrible thrusts were given, and I saw dead Zulus who had been pinned to the ground by the bayonets going through them.

All this time the sick and wounded were crying for water. We had the water-cart full of water, but it was just by the deserted hospital and we could not hope to get it until the day broke, when the Zulus might begin to lose heart and to stop in their mad rushes. But we could not bear the cries any longer, and three or four of us jumped over the boxes and ran and fetched some water in.

The long night passed and the day broke. Then we looked around us to see what had happened, and there was not a living soul who was not thankful to find that the Zulus had had enough of it and were disappearing over the hill to the south-west. Orders were given to patrol the ground, collect the arms of the dead blacks, and make our position as strong as possible in case of fresh attacks.

One of the first things I did was to go up to the man who was still looking over our breastworks with his rifle presented to the spot where so many of the Zulus had been. I went up to him, and saw that he did not move, and that he looked very quiet. I went nearer and said 'Hello, what are you doing here?' He made no answer, and did not stir. I went still closer, and something in his appearance made me tilt his helmet back, as you sometimes tilt back a hat when you want to look closely into a face. As I did so I saw a bullet-mark in his forehead, and knew that he was dead.

I went away, and was walking up the dry bed of a little stream near the drift with my own rifle in my right hand and a bunch of assegais over my left shoulder. Suddenly I came across an unarmed Zulu lying on the ground, apparently dead but bleeding from the leg. Thinking it strange that a dead man should bleed, I hesitated, and wondered whether I should go on, as other Zulus might be lurking about. But I resumed my task. Just as I was passing, the supposed dead man seized the butt of my rifle and tried to drag it away. The bunch of assegais rattled to earth.

The Zulu suddenly released his grasp of the rifle with one hand, and with the other fiercely endeavoured to drag me down. The fight was short and sharp; but it ended by the Zulu being struck in the chest with the butt and knocked to the ground. The rest was quickly over. After that we were not allowed to go on with our task except in twos and threes. When we had done this work we went back to the inner line of defence, sad enough, even the most cheerful of us. But we had no time to dwell on the awful scenes about us. We did not know how soon another assault might be made, but we did know that if the Zulus kept on attacking us it was only a question of time before we were cut to pieces, as our comrades a dozen miles away had been destroyed.

The roof of the hospital had fallen in by this time, and only the storehouse was standing. We were ordered to put ropes through the loopholes of the wall of the hospital and pull them down. This we did, and the walls, which had already been weakened by our picks, partially collapsed. Then we tore away the thatch from the storehouse so that the Zulus could not, even if they wished, set fire to it, as they had fired the hospital. With the ruins of the walls we strengthened our little fort, and again waited for the Zulus – if they cared to come. But they had finished their attack.

We looked about us everywhere for signs of relief, but saw nothing, and our hearts sank. Then came an awful time of suspense. Two of our men had been on the roof of the storehouse signalling with flags when the Zulus meant to attack us. This gave us time to make ready for them. The signallers were still able to stand above the ground, so that they could be seen at a good distance. We saw their flags going wildly. What was it? Everbody was mad with anxiety to know whether it could be friends to relieve us, or more Zulus to destroy us. We watched the flags flapping, and then learnt that signals were being made in reply. We knew we were safe and that friends were marching up to us.

We broke into roar after roar of cheering, waving red coats and white helmets, and we cheered again and again when, at about six o'clock in the morning, Colonel Russell rode up with some mounted infantry. We saw them come in, and at the same time we saw that the Zulus had once more got ready to sweep around the mountain to attack us. But it was too late, and on seeing that we were reinforced they turned silently away, and only their dead and a few wounded were left with us.

Lord Chelmsford and what was left of the 3rd Column came up to Rorke's Drift soon after. There was no time to sit down and mope . . .'

(See *The Red Soldier*)

An Account

by

1061 Private J. JOBBINS, 2/24th Regiment.

[Extracted from a letter written by John Jobbins on 6th February 1879 and addressed to his father, who worked at the Crown Hotel, Pontypool.]

Before it was daylight the next morning those who were left of our poor soldiers had to retire upon the stores, where I was with about 120 men – our company and volunteers. The day before four men on horseback arrived at the stores, who escaped from the camp, and told us what had happened; this was about three o'clock in the afternoon of the 22nd January. We at once let our tents fall to the ground, and got inside the stores, and made a small fort with sacks filled with grain. Just as we had finished our fort we could see thousands of niggers coming down on our little body of men. At the end of the fort was a large house which had been turned into a hospital, the owners of which were Swedes, who fled as soon as the Zulus came in sight. There were a lot of sick men in the hospital at the time.

One, poor Sergeant Maxfield, was insane, and he was burnt alive, or killed and then burnt. Well, we fought hard from about three thirty p.m. till the following morning, when they retired, but they killed twelve of our men, but we killed at least 450 of them. All that night a minister was praying in the fort they would go away. God helped us and gave us the victory.

In the morning we could see in the distance a large body of men approaching. We did not at first recognise them, but after a bit we could see the welcome red coats retiring on us from the other unfortunate camp. Then we all gave a hearty cheer, as we felt safe when we were altogether.

(See *The Red Soldier*)

THE ROLL OF RORKE'S DRIFT DEFENDERS

THE SOURCES INVESTIGATED

The defenders of Rorke's Drift were comparatively few in number, and, furthermore, the garrison mainly consisted of soldiers belonging to one company of a particular regiment. On the basis of these facts the accurate identification of the individual men present during the action on 22nd/23rd January 1879 would appear to be a relatively simple task; however, such is not the case.

In order to establish the basis of this investigation it is necessary to refer to my initial researches, the results of which appeared in published form in 1971. The work had been undertaken throughout the period 1964–1971 and was based on the then known rolls of Rorke's Drift defenders attributed to Lieutenant Chard and Colour-Sergeant Bourne respectively. It was considered that the two documents represented the only authoritative sources of information, despite the fact that the lists failed to agree in a number of instances. In addition to the inaccuracies contained in both rolls, the fact that two such lists existed represented an anomaly. Neither roll was considered as being totally accurate, and in view of the conflicting information contained in each, a complete investigation was undertaken in respect of the men belonging to the 24th Regiment who were named in both rolls. Various documentary sources were again utilised in this work, which resulted in several names being amended and others removed from the rolls. The information obtained as a result of this evaluation represented a combination of the original lists by Chard and Bourne.

The original rolls of Rorke's Drift defenders were accepted with reservation in respect of a number of factors. I did not, for example, consider that Lieutenant Chard had personally undertaken the compilation of the roll bearing his name; however, the fact that he had apparently signed the document tended to impart a degree of authority. The roll is dated '3rd February 1879' and although this date may not be correct, it may be assumed that the document was compiled prior to the award of decorations for gallantry since the roll does not contain notes of these instances. The general acceptance of the origin and authenticity of this roll is clearly not without justification, and had there been no other source of comparison, then the contents would doubtless never have been disputed. A most important point relates to the fact that a large copy of the roll is mounted in a frame and displayed in the Regimental Museum of the 24th Foot. I was, of course, fully aware of this as a result of my visits to the Museum, and I had examined the document on several occasions. A facsimile of the roll was reproduced in *The South Wales Borderers, 24th Foot, 1689–1937* by C. T. Atkinson (published in 1937), to which I had permanent access. Having verified that the reproduction exactly equated with the roll in the Regimental Museum, it then became a matter of convenience to utilise the facsimile for the purpose of research. I considered it somewhat unusual for Atkinson to have included the roll in his book without making reference to it within the text of the work. *Historical Records of the 24th Regiment* by Paton, Glennie and Penn Symons (published in 1892) contains a list of casualties at Isandhlwana, yet Chard's roll of defenders of Rorke's Drift is neither included nor is it mentioned. It was impossible to account for the omission of this important roll, particularly in view of the fact that it had been in existence since 1879, and presumably would have been available to the authors of the book.

Similar problems exist in respect of the roll compiled by Frank Bourne. This document is dated '4th July 1910' and contains a footnote to the effect: ' By Special Request, and in order to preserve a record of those who took part in the Defence, this Roll was prepared by Major F. Bourne (late Colour-Sergeant 'B' Company) from the Regimental Pay List for January 1879, kindly placed at his disposal by the Public Record Office –'. As the former senior non-commissioned officer of 'B' Company, Bourne was eminently qualified to compile such a roll as he must necessarily have known many of the soldiers on a personal basis. In view of this knowledge, I considered it unusual that he had not been called upon to provide information, at least in respect of his own company, for inclusion in Chard's roll. It is evident that Bourne cannot have been consulted in this matter, otherwise he would surely not have undertaken to compile a second list of defenders as this would have represented a contradiction to information previously submitted by himself. Bourne's knowledge of at least some of his men is confirmed by his reference to 1524 Private Joseph Bromwich as 'Bromatch', which was undoubtedly the pronunciation used by the man himself when giving his name, as is verified by his service papers. Similarly, Bourne was aware when others were not, that 922 Private George Edwards had enlisted under an alias, his true name being Orchard. After a lapse of so many years it was thought unreasonable to assume that Bourne would have remembered each and every man belonging to 'B' Company. The pay list, which should have encompassed several months prior to January 1879, could only have provided him with slight assistance when preparing the roll. Bourne's list of defenders is far less comprehensive than that attributed to Chard, and this was thought to have been a contributing factor which caused Atkinson to include the latter roll in his book. Obviously the roll compiled by Bourne could not have been included in *Historical Records of the 24th Regiment* since this publication pre-dated the roll by some eighteen years. It proved impossible to determine the source of the 'Special Request' which prompted Bourne to prepare his list, and it was conjectured that the request may have been made as the result of dissatisfaction with the accuracy of the Chard roll.

On completion of my intial research, the above anomalies represented little more than a series of interesting problems. I made only a brief mention of these factors in my previous work, since any elaboration would have posed a number of questions for which I was unable to provide satisfactory answers. Having resolved to undertake further investigations regarding these matters, I commenced by endeavouring to establish the whereabouts of Chard's original roll. Preliminary investigations involved a re-examination of the Chard roll contained in the Regimental Museum. It was clearly necessary to establish the date on which this document had come into the possession of the Museum, and also the original source from which the roll had been acquired. The Regimental Accession Books, kindly placed at my disposal by Major Egerton, eventually yielded the following information in respect of the year 1935: 'Roll of all ranks, in manuscript, who were at Rorke's Drift (original and duplicate), from Mrs. Cantwell, 1935'. The hitherto unheard of duplicate of the roll was permanently displayed in the Officers Mess, and was obtained from there on my behalf. On examination the roll proved to be an exact duplicate of the one exhibited in the Museum, and it was understandably due to this fact that the copy was seldom referred to. The wooden frame in which the duplicate roll was contained bore a silver plaque on which was inscribed 'Presented by Mrs. Cantwell, widow of Bombardier Cantwell, R.A. – 1935'. The fact that the document had been presented during that year, although no precise month was indicated, offered two possible solutions as to why C. T. Atkinson had included the roll in his book, but failed to refer to it in the text. At the time in question the work must have been nearing completion and it would have been difficult for Atkinson to have inserted retrospective comments appropriate to the roll. Appropriately, being aware of the source of the roll, Atkinson may well have decided to refrain from attempting an explanation of the matter. Having formulated two possible solutions in respect of this problem, I was then confronted with the question of Cantwell being involved in the matter.

It is an undeniable fact that Bombardier (Wheeler) John Cantwell, R.A., was present at the defence of Rorke's Drift, since he was awarded the Medal for Distinguished Conduct in respect of the action. He was given as 'Wounded' in Chard's roll, but there is no evidence to support this statement.

John Cantwell was born at St. James's, Dublin, and was by trade a servant. He enlisted in the 9th Foot on 6th November 1868 at the age of twenty-three years six months. Cantwell transferred to the Royal Artillery on 1st April 1872, joining N Battery, 5th Brigade, R.A., on 1st July 1877. Having served for a time at St. Helena, he arrived at the Cape of Good Hope on 9th January 1878 and subsequently took part in the advance into Zululand. Promoted to the rank of Bombardier Wheeler on 29th July 1878, he reverted to the rank of Gunner on 21st January 1879, and was discharged at Woolwich on 19th July 1889 as being 'Medically unfit for further service'. His intended place of residence was 8 Loop Street, Pietermaritzburg, Natal, South Africa.

The Rorke's Drift roll of defenders, apparently authenticated by Lieutenant Chard and correctly addressed to Colonel Glyn, was regarded by many to be an official document. The discovery that Cantwell, or, to be more accurate, his widow, Caroline Margaret Cantwell, had been instrumental in providing the Regimental Museum with a copy of the roll, posed an extremely difficult problem. I resolved, however, to pursue the matter and began by attempting to establish the whereabouts of Chard's original roll. Being in possession of copies of all the official correspondence relating to the Zulu War, I was fully aware that no written request had been made for the submission of a list of those present at the defence of Rorke's Drift. Logic dictated that the Public Record Office was the obvious depository for such a document, and accordingly I engaged three professional researchers, each working independently, to undertake the necessary work on my behalf. After a lengthy interval of time, I was assured that the roll was not to be found within the Public Record Office. Having established this fact, a further series of investigations were carried out at the former Colonial Office, the Regimental Museum of the Royal Engineers, the War Office Library, the National Army Museum and the Royal Archives, but without success. A copy of the roll of Defenders of Rorke's Drift was finally located in the British Museum Library,

but this transpired to be Bourne's Roll, a fact which I considered to be of some significance; nothing was known of Chard's roll. Lieutenant-Colonel W. W. M. Chard and the late Mrs. D. Phillips, who possessed living memories of J. R. M. Chard, kindly responded to my request and searched through the papers formerly belonging to their forebear. There was neither trace nor mention of the Rorke's Drift roll.

As a result of these protracted investigations, it was plainly evident that Chard's roll was totally unknown, and in consequence of this fact I again scrutinized the roll contained in the Regimental Museum. After some time I was eventually able to formulate a number of conclusions regarding this document. To my untrained eye, the manuscript appeared to consist of two distinctive styles of handwriting. With three notable exceptions, the names of the garrison seemed to have been written in a conventional hand. A more ornate method of writing was employed in the heading and sub-headings of the roll and also in respect of the names of 'Lieutenant J. R. M. Chard (In Command)', 'Lieutenant Bromhead (Com'd B Comp)' and 'Bomb. J. Cantwell'. These three names, and no others, were made more distinctive by being underlined. In addition, it was also noted that the seventh name on the roll referred to 'Private Robson', R.E., who was Chard's batman. In his letter to Queen Victoria, Chard mentions Robson on two occasions, in both instances referring to him as 'Driver'. If Chard had in fact signed the roll, it is strange that he had not amended Robson's rank to that of Driver, or more conventionally Sapper, since the title had been in use from the time of the Crimean War. A number of documents which are known to have been written by Chard reveal that the rank of Sapper was correctly applied in all instances.

It had become increasingly evident to me that the roll and duplicate copy in the possession of the Regimental Museum represented the only examples of Chard's original list of Rorke's Drift defenders. The number and significance of the various anomalies associated with the document had engendered my suspicions regarding not only the source, but also the authenticity of the roll. In view of the documents having originated from the Cantwell family, it became a matter of necessity to confirm whether or not Lieutenant Chard had approved and signed the roll. Mr. Derek Davis, a Forensic Handwriting Expert, generously agreed to undertake an analysis of the roll in conjunction with a comparison of various samples of handwriting. An authenticated sample of Chard's handwriting, which included his signature, together with a photocopy of the Rorke's Drift roll, were submitted for examination. I considered the possibility that Lieutenant Bromhead may have been responsible for compiling the roll, and, accordingly, an authenticated sample of his handwriting was also submitted. In view of my previous comments regarding Colour-Sergeant Bourne, I did not consider it necessary to include an example of his writing. I did not, unfortunately, possess an authenticated sample of Bombardier Cantwell's handwriting. Precise information and specific instructions regarding the work were submitted as follows:

'Written instructions to examine photostat copies of historical documents relating to the defence of Rorke's Drift. To compare the handwriting on these documents and offer opinions as to authorship'.

In due course, Mr. Davis produced a comprehensive report in which he stated:

'The handwriting in each document was examined and notes made of the personal handwriting habits, tendencies and formations found. Examination of all notes allowed opinions to be formed as to specific authorship of the documents. In my considered opinion, one person wrote the whole of the Roll, including the headings and the signature of Lieutenant Chard. This includes the names which visually appear to be a different writing. The only clue that I can offer as to the production of the roll is that it is possible that a man from the 2/24th Regiment produced it – Due to the use of first names in that regiment. The only name that shows as carefully written is that of Private Michael Kiley, although this may be coincidence. The numbers of the men are mentioned in the 1st and 2nd/24th Regiment but omitted from others'.

As a result of the conclusions contained in the report, it is obvious that Lieutenant Chard did not sign the document, neither did Lieutenant Bromhead contribute to any part of the roll. My attention was then given to the right-hand portion of the document which contains a return enumerating the strength and composition of the garrison, together with notes referring to those killed, wounded and died of wounds. This information, with the figures slightly amended, was reproduced in Lieutenant Chard's dispatch dated 12th February 1879, which was correctly addressed to 'Colonel Glyn, C.B.' It was evident that this was the only part of the roll of defenders which had been transmitted to higher authority. Assuming that Chard had ordered that the information be obtained for inclusion in his dispatch, then the person undertaking the task would presumably have first compiled a list of names sub-divided into regiments and corps, etc. It would then have become a comparatively simple matter to extract the required information which could then be presented in numerical form. The evidence for this is contained in the fact that each name appearing in the roll is numbered sequentially from '1' to '141', which represents the figure given as the total strength of the garrison. It is a matter of conjecture as to the identity of the man who actually compiled the roll of Rorke's Drift defenders. Whoever this person was, he for some unknown reason provided Cantwell with a high degree of prominence in the roll, perhaps in the knowledge that once having been used for its intended purpose, the document then became no longer of use. It is equally impossible to determine the sources from which the roll was compiled; as previously stated, Colour-Sergeant Bourne was obviously not consulted in respect of men belonging to B Company. It is my personal opinion that the degree of authority attributed to 'Lieutenant Chard's' roll of Rorke's Drift defenders is not substantiated by the evidence, as described in the foregoing.

The list of defenders compiled by Major Bourne was totally unrelated to the 'Chard' roll and therefore represented an independent means of verifying a portion of the information contained in the latter document. I considered the individuals named in both rolls as having been present at the action; however, the numerous instances of names appearing in one roll but not in the other constituted a number of anomalies. During the course of my investigations a fortunate coincidence revealed the whereabouts of Mrs. Mary F. Whitby, youngest daughter of Lieutenant-Colonel Frank Bourne, formerly Colour-Sergeant of 'B' Company 2/24th Regiment. Major Egerton kindly provided me with the necessary assistance in communicating with Mrs. Whitby, and as a result I was able to obtain from her a considerable amount of valuable and hitherto unknown information.

The most important single aspect of this information concerned the fact that Frank Bourne had amended his personal copy of the roll previously compiled by himself, these amendments having been undertaken after the publication of Atkinson's book containing the 'Chard' roll. An examination of the amended roll revealed that the work was in Bourne's own handwriting, as confirmed by his daughter, and that each name had been examined and duly marked. In addition, Bourne had added most but not all the names previously omitted from his original roll, and his failure to include certain individuals from the 'Chard' roll disclosed his obvious lack of agreement regarding their presence at the action.

Of equal significance was the fact that Bourne had not deleted one single name from his original roll, and there are indications that in part this may well have been justified. For example, the 'Chard' roll fails to include 1005 Private John Smith who was undeniably present at the defence of Rorke's Drift as he was slightly wounded in the battle, a fact which is confirmed by his service papers. In view of the amendments undertaken by Bourne, I considered that there now existed a closer relationship between his amended roll and the 'Chard' roll, and this provided a far greater degree of confirmation in respect of the majority of individuals named in both documents. I was obviously aware that the names contained in Bourne's amended roll, together with those which he had not included from the 'Chard' roll of defenders, represented 'B' Company as being above average company strength. At least four men, and there may well have been others, belonging to 'B' Company were killed at Isandhlwana. Two men who served in 'B' Company at the defence of Rorke's Drift had items of equipment lost, and in one case later recovered at Isandhlwana. It is not unusual to discover items of field service equipment at one camp whilst the owners of the material were elsewhere, and this may indicate that the men concerned were by chance present at Rorke's Drift at the time of the Zulu attack. Inter-company transfers were not at all uncommon and at the time in question 'B' Company appears to have been a somewhat fragmented unit. It is possible that this may have been the principal factor which contributed to the omissions and errors contained in Bourne's original roll. The importance of the amendments undertaken by Lieutenant-Colonel Bourne is contained in the fact that the 'Chard' roll had finally been examined by a known and extremely well qualified authority.

During the final stage of the investigation I learned of the existence of yet another roll of Rorke's Drift defenders. F. W. David Jackson, author of 'Isandhlwana, 1879 : the sources re-examined, (*Journal of the Society for Army Historical Research,* 1965), kindly informed me that a roll signed by Major Dunbar had appeared in *The Natal Colonist* for 15th January 1880. Having obtained a photostat of the newspaper, I discovered that the roll had been specially prepared in connection with the 'Presentation of an Address by the Mayor of Durban', a copy of which had been presented to each individual soldier. This roll of defenders was clearly based on the 'Chard' roll and I concluded that the unknown compiler of the 'Chard' roll was possibly present with the battalion, or, alternatively, he had provided the information for Dunbar. Major Dunbar, who was then commanding the 2nd Battalion 24th Regiment, had signed the list of defenders which related exclusively to the survivors of 'B' Company. No mention was made of men belonging to the 1st Battalion 24th Regiment and those men who had served in other regiments and corps, both Imperial and Colonial, were similarly excluded. The honour conferred upon the garrison by the people of Durban was somewhat unfairly reserved for members of 'B' Company.

After assessing the four rolls of defenders and taking into consideration not only their contents but also the evidence regarding the source of each document, I saw no reason to amend my former evaluation of those present at the defence of Rorke's Drift. This evaluation was based on a provisional acceptance of all the names appearing in the various rolls, research then being undertaken in each individual case. Very few soldiers' papers refer specifically to the defence of Rorke's Drift and therefore alternative documentary sources were consulted. These included the relevant pay and credits (muster) rolls, medal casualty and effects rolls, together with reports, official and otherwise, and various documents and narratives relating to the battle. The results of this work indicated that a number of individuals named in one or more of the original rolls were not present at the defence of Rorke's Drift and in consequence their names were excluded from my roll. In certain instances, where entries in service papers were obviously confused, there must remain an element of doubt as to whether or not the individual was present at the action, and notes appropriate to these cases have been included in this work. The following details relate to those soldiers who, as a result of my own researches, are considered as not having been present at the defence of Rorke's Drift.

2–24/981 Private Charles Bromwich, 'B' Company, 2/24th Foot. Charles Bromwich was born at St. Nicholas's, Warwick, and was by trade a labourer. He served in the 2nd Warwickshire Militia (No. 3926) from 11th October 1858 until attesting for the 24th Regiment at Plymouth on 22nd March 1859; he was then aged 18 years. Bromwich re-engaged at Preston on 20th August 1869 and subsequently served at Mauritius, the East Indies and South Africa, arriving there on 10th March 1878. The pay roll for the period 1st October 1878 – 31st March 1879 clearly states that he was sent 'To the General Depot at Pietermaritzburg on 31st October 1878'. His pay via the Service Companies of the 24th Regiment ceased with effect from this date and there is no record of him returning to his company during the period concerned. Bromwich was sent to Cape Town and subsequently transferred to the 91st Highlanders (595) on 30th November 1879. On 19th May 1880 he was attached to the Royal Welch Fusiliers (58B/2739) for the purpose of discharge. Charles Bromwich was discharged from the army on 9th June 1880, his intended place of residence being given as 12 Brook Street, Warwick. 981 Private Charles Bromwich is named in the 'Chard' roll as having been present at the defence of Rorke's Drift; his name also appears in Dunbar's list, but this is hardly surprising as the list was based on the 'Chard' roll. Bourne omits 981 Charles Bromwich from his roll, but names 1524 Private Joseph Bromwich as being present at the action. In the light of the evidence provided by the pay roll, this would seem to be correct.

1402 Private W. Buck, 2420 Private P. Caine and 1060 Private T. Williams, all of whom served in 'B' Company, were sent to the General Depot at Pietermaritzburg on 31/10/78. Their pay via the Service Companies of the 24th Regiment ceased with effect from this date and there is no record of them returning to their company during the period concerned. These men are named in Bourne's original roll, but do not appear in the 'Chard' roll, and in consequence neither are they given in Dunbar's list.

1374 Private J. Williams appears in Bourne's original roll as serving in 'B' Company at the defence of Rorke's Drift. The pay roll confirms that this man was sentenced to 112 days imprisonment, being confined on 1/10/78, tried on 9/10/78, and sent to prison on 13/10/78. He was transferred to the General Depot prison on 1/11/78 and released on 1/2/79, shortly after which he deserted from the regiment. He could not, therefore, have been present at the action on 22nd January 1879.

1083 Private Watkin Jenkins (1st Battalion) is given in the 'Chard' roll as a survivor of the action at Rorke's Drift. This man was frequently mis-named as 'Matthew Jenkins' and Bourne in his rolls lists him as 'M. Jenkins – killed in action'. He was in fact killed at Isandhlwana and not Rorke's Drift and it would appear that Bourne has confused him with 841 Private James Jenkins, who was killed at the latter battle. It is not unreasonable to assume that had the 'Chard' roll been correct, then 1083 Jenkins would have been included in Dunbar's list, which he was not.

25B/953 Private Frederick Evans (Mounted Infantry), 'H' Company. At the time of my original research it proved impossible to identify this individual, who was one of ten soldiers named Evans then serving in the 2nd Battalion. He is named in the 'Chard' roll and also in Bourne's amended roll, but no mention is made of his service number or the initial of his first name. Fortunately the list signed by Major Dunbar includes a 'Frederick Evans' and it therefore became possible to establish the correct identity of this man. Evans is mentioned in a number of statements written by men present at the defence of Rorke's Drift. Corporal Lyons and Private Waters refer to him, and a letter by Private Hitch (page 136 The Red Soldier by Frank Emery) contains the following : 'The first news I had of what had happened at Isandhlwana was when one of the mounted infantry, named Evans, came galloping up to the mission house, and said that a part of the camp across the river had been destroyed by the Zulus, that two guns had been taken as well as all the ammunition, and that the enemy were advancing in force to attack Rorke's Drift'. Evans himelf, in a letter written in Welsh to his wife, then living at Tonypandy, South Wales, mentions that he 'was at Rorke's Drift' but does not elaborate further on the action. It is unusual that a soldier who had not only survived the annihilation of his comrades at Isandhlwana, but had also ridden to warn the garrison at Rorke's Drift and then remained to assist in the defence, should make so brief a mention of his experiences. In his letter to Queen Victoria, Lieutenant Chard states, ' A letter describing what had happened (at Isandhlwana) had been sent by Bromhead, by two men of the Mounted Infantry, who had arrived fugitives from Isandhlwana, to the Officer Commanding at Helpmakaar.' Chard continues, ' Several fugitives from the Camp arrived, and tried to impress upon us the madness of an attempt to defend the place. They proved the truth of their belief in what they said, by leaving us to our fate, and in the state of mind they were in, I think our little garrison was as well without them. As far as I know, but one of the fugitives remained with us – Lieutenant Adendorff whom I have before mentioned.' Despite the fact that Evans was one of the men who carried the news of Isandhlwana to Rorke's Drift, as confirmed by the three eye-witnesses, there is no mention whatsoever of his participation in the defence, and in view of Lieutenant Chard's comments I consider that there is insufficient evidence to support the inclusion of Evans in the Rorke's Drift roll of defenders. The fact that Evans received a copy of the Address from the Mayor of Durban does not, in any way, prove his presence at the battle.

The evidence in respect of the four varying rolls of Rorke's Drift defenders obviously cannot be regarded as being complete, and consequently a number of important questions must necessarily remain unanswered. In the final analysis, the identification of those present at the defence of Rorke's Drift can only be achieved by the means employed in this work, that is by utilising the original rolls together with additional documentary sources. The results of such a comparison make it possible to determine the majority of the individual soldiers who were present, or likely to have been present at the action, and it is only in a very few instances that an element of doubt must continue to exist.

The individuals named in the Rorke's Drift roll contained in this work are related to the original rolls by means of the following references:

'C'   The 'Chard' roll.

'B'   Bourne's original roll.

'Ba'   Bourne's amended roll.

'D'   The list signed by Major Dunbar.

THE 'CHARD' ROLL

2nd Battalion ⊕ "24th Regiment."

ROLL OF "B" COMPANY who defended "RORKE'S DRIFT" against the Zulu attack on the night of the 22nd-23rd January, 1879

Reg. No.	Rank	Name	Remarks	Reg. No.	Rank	Name	Remarks
	Lieutenant	BROMHEAD, GONVILLE (V.C.)	Mentioned in Despatches Awarded the Victoria Cross	24.9	Private	GEE, E	Mentioned in Despatches Awarded the Victoria Cross
2459	Color-Sergt.	BOURNE, F.	Mentioned in Despatches Awarded the Distinguished Conduct Medal	1362	Private	HITCH, F. V.C.	
735	Sergeant	WINDRIDGE, J. L.	Mentioned in Despatches	1373	Private	HOOK, H. A.	Mentioned in Despatches Awarded the Victoria Cross
81	Sergeant	GALLAGHER, H. L.		1061	Private	JOBBINS, J.	
1387	Sergeant	SMITH, G.		1428	Private	JONES, E.	
440	Sergeant	SAXTY, A.		970	Private	JONES, J.	
1328	Lce.Sergt.	WILLIAMS, T.	Mentioned in Despatches Died of Wounds 23rd Jan. 1879	3179	Private	JONES, J.	
				716	Private	JONES, R. V.C.	Mentioned in Despatches Awarded the Victoria Cross
62	Corporal	TAYLOR, J.		593	Private	JONES, W. V.C.	Mentioned in Despatches Awarded the Victoria Cross
1240	Corporal	ALLAN, W. W. (V.C.)	Wounded Severely. Awarded the Victoria Cross	2437	Private	JUDGE, P.	
562	Corporal	FRENCH, J.		972	Private	KEARS, P.	
2350	Corporal	BUSH, J.		1386	Private	KILEY, M	
1298	Lce.Corpl.	HALLEY, J.		963	Private	LEWIS, D	
1287	Lce.Corpl.	BISSELL, W.		1409	Private	LLOYD, D.	
2389	Lce.Corpl.	KEY, J.		1304	Private	LODGE, J.	
1418	Lce.Corpl.	SHERMAN, C.		942	Private	LYNCH, T.	
2067	Drummer	HAYES, P.		7-6	Private	MARTIN, H	
2381	Drummer	KEEFE, J.		1204	Private	MASON, C.	
912	Private	ASHTON, J.		1527	Private	MINEHAN, M.	
1381	Private	BARRY, T.		968	Private	MOFFATT, T.	
918	Private	BENNETT, W.		525	Private	MORRIS, F.	
2427	Private	BLY, J.		1342	Private	MORRIS, A.	
1403	Private	BUCK, W.		1371	Private	MORRISON, T.	
1104	Private	BUCKLEY, T.		1257	Private	MORRIS, R.	
1220	Private	BURKE, P.		1480	Private	OSBORNE, W.	
9403	Private	CAINE, P.		1399	Private	PARRY, S	
1181	Private	CAINE, W. N.		1286	Private	ROBINSON, T	
1241	Private	CHESTER, T.		1065	Private	RUCK, J	
766	Private	CLAYTON, P.		914	Private	SHERGOLD,	
801	Private	COLE, T.	Killed 22nd January, 1879.	1005	Private	SMITH, J	
1396	Private	COLLINS, T.		1812	Private	TASKER, W.	
1395	Private	CONNORS, T.		973	Private	TAYLOR, F.	
2310	Private	CONNORS, H.		869	Private	TAYLOR, T.	
470	Private	DAVIES, G.		879	Private	TOBIN, M.	
1363	Private	DAVIES, W. H.		1281	Private	TODD, W. G.	
1178	Private	DAW, T.		1315	Private	TONGUE, R	
1467	Private	DEACON, G.		1497	Private	WALL, J	
1357	Private	DEANE, W.		977	Private	WHITTON, A.	
1697	Private	DICKS, W.		1187	Private	WILCOX, W.	
571	Private	DRISCOLL, T.		1395	Private	WILLIAMS, J. (V.C.)	Mentioned in Despatches Awarded the Victoria Cross
1421	Private	DUNBAR, J.		1374	Private	WILLIAMS, J.	
922	Private	EDWARDS, G.		1398	Private	WILLIAMS, J.	Killed 2nd January, 1879
969	Private	FAGAN, J.	Killed 22nd January, 1879.	1398	Private	WILLIAMS, T.	

The following Officers and N. C. Officers were attached to the Company

1st Battalion, 24th Regiment.

Private W. BECKETT	..	Killed H
Private W. HARRIGAN	..	Killed H.
Private H. JENKINS	..	Killed H
Private W. NICHOLAS	..	Killed H
Private J. WILLIAMS	..	Killed H
Private ROY	..	Mentioned in Despatches

2nd Battalion, 24th Regiment.

Sergeant H. MAXFIELD	..	Killed H
Private R. ADAMS	..	Killed H
Private J. CHICK	..	Killed H
Private W. HAYDEN	..	Killed H
Private J. SCANLON	..	Killed H

Royal Artillery.

Bombardier LEWIS .. .. H.

Royal Engineers.

Lieutenant JOHN R. M. CHARD (V.C.)
Mentioned in Despatches
Awarded the Victoria Cross

The Buffs

Sergeant MILNE.

Commissariat Department

Asst. Commissary DUNNE.
Mentioned in Despatches

Acting Commsst. Officer DALTON.
Mentioned in Despatches

Acting Store keeper BYRNE
Mentioned in Despatches

Corporal ATTWOOD
Awarded the Distinguished Conduct Medal

Army Hospital Corps.

Surgeon REYNOLDS V.C.
Mentioned in Despatches
Awarded the Victoria Cross

Private McMAHON
Mentioned in Despatches

Natal Mounted Police

Trooper HUNTER	..	H
Trooper GREEN	..	H

Natal Native Contingent

Corpl. SCHIESS V.C.
Mentioned in Despatches
Awarded the Victoria Cross

Corporal MAYER .. H
Corporal SCAMMELL.

Chaplain's Department

Revd G. SMITH Acting Chaplain.

Civilian — Mr. DANIELS.

N.B. Those Officers and Men marked with an H were wounded, they were patients in Hospital.

BOURNE'S ORIGINAL ROLL

2nd Battalion "24th Regiment."

ROLL OF "B" COMPANY who defended "RORKE'S DRIFT" against the Zulu attack on the night of the 22nd-23rd January, 1879.

Regtl. No.	Rank.	Name.	Remarks.	Regtl. No.	Rank.	Name.	Remarks.
	Lieutenant	BROMHEAD, GONVILLE (V.C.)	Mentioned in Dispatches. Awarded the Victoria Cross.	2429	Private	GEE, E.	
2459	Color-Sergt.	BOURNE, F.	Mentioned in Dispatches. Awarded the Distinguished Conduct Medal.	1362	Private	HITCH, F. (V.C.)	Wounded Severely. Awarded the Victoria Cross.
735	Sergeant	WINDRIDGE, J. L.	Mentioned in Dispatches.	1373	Private	HOOK, H. (V.C.)	Mentioned in Dispatches. Awarded the Victoria Cross.
81	Sergeant	GALLAGHER, H. L.		1061	Private	JOBBINS, J.	
1387	Sergeant	SMITH, G.		1428	Private	JONES, E.	
849	Sergeant	SAXTY, A.		970	Private	JONES, J.	
1328	Lce.Sergt.	WILLIAMS, T.	Mentioned in Dispatches. Died of Wounds 23rd Jan., 1879.	1179	Private	JONES, J.	
				716	Private	JONES, R. (V.C.)	Mentioned in Dispatches. Awarded the Victoria Cross.
82	Corporal	TAYLOR, J.		593	Private	JONES, W. (V.C.)	Mentioned in Dispatches. Awarded the Victoria Cross.
1240	Corporal	ALLAN, W. W. (V.C.)	Wounded Severely. Awarded the Victoria Cross.	2437	Private	JUDGE, P.	
582	Corporal	FRENCH, J.		972	Private	KEARS, P.	
2350	Corporal	BUSH, J.		1386	Private	KILEY, M.	
1282	Lce.Corpl.	HALLEY, J.		963	Private	LEWIS, D.	
1287	Lce.Corpl.	BISSELL, W.		1409	Private	LLOYD, D.	
2389	Lce.Corpl.	KEY, J.		1304	Private	LODGE, J.	
1618	Lce.Corpl.	SHERMAN, G.		942	Private	LYNCH, T.	
2067	Drummer	HAYES, P		756	Private	MARTIN, H.	
2381	Drummer	KEEFE, J.		1284	Private	MASON, C.	
912	Private	ASHTON, J.		1527	Private	MINEHAN, M.	
1381	Private	BARRY, T.		968	Private	MOFFATT, T.	
918	Private	BENNETT, W.		525	Private	MORRIS, F.	
2427	Private	BLY, J.		1342	Private	MORRIS, A.	
1402	Private	BUCK, W.		1371	Private	MORRISON, T.	
1184	Private	BUCKLEY, T.		1257	Private	NORRIS, H.	
1220	Private	BURKE, T.		1480	Private	OSBORNE, W.	
2420	Private	CAINE, P.		1399	Private	PARRY, S.	
1181	Private	CAMP, W. H.		1286	Private	ROBINSON, T.	
1241	Private	CHESTER, T.		1065	Private	RUCK, J.	
755	Private	CLAYTON, F.		914	Private	SHERGOLD, J.	
801	Private	COLE, T.	Killed 22nd January, 1879.	1005	Private	SMITH, J.	
1396	Private	COLLINS, T.		1812	Private	TASKER, W.	
1323	Private	CONNORS, T.		973	Private	TAYLOR, F.	
2310	Private	CONNORS, R.		889	Private	TAYLOR, T.	
470	Private	DAVIES, G.		879	Private	TOBIN, M.	
1363	Private	DAVIES, W. H.		1281	Private	TODD, W. G.	
1178	Private	DAW, T.		1315	Private	TONGUE, R.	
1467	Private	DEACON, G.		1497	Private	WALL, J.	
1357	Private	DEANE, W.		977	Private	WHITTON, A.	
1697	Private	DICKS, W.		1187	Private	WILCOX, W.	
971	Private	DRISCOLL, T.		1395	Private	WILLIAMS, J. (V.C.)	Mentioned in Dispatches. Awarded the Victoria Cross.
1421	Private	DUNBAR, J.		1374	Private	WILLIAMS, J.	
922	Private	EDWARDS, G.		1398	Private	WILLIAMS, J.	Killed 22nd January, 1879.
969	Private	FAGAN, J.	Killed 22nd January, 1879.	1060	Private	WILLIAMS, T.	

BOURNE'S AMENDED ROLL (Part I)

The following Officers and N.C. Officers were attached to above Company.

1st Battalion, 24th Regiment.

Private W. BECKETT .. .. Killed—H.
Private W. HARRIGAN .. .. Killed—H.
Private M. JENKINS .. .. Killed—H.
Private W. NICHOLAS .. .. Killed—H.
Private J. WILLIAMS .. .. Killed—H.
Private ROY Mentioned in Dispatches.

[handwritten: DAVIES, TURNER & WATERS]

2nd Battalion, 24th Regiment.

Sergeant R. MAXFIELD .. .. Killed—H.
Private R. ADAMS .. .. Killed—H.
Private J. CHICK .. .. Killed—H.
Private G. HAYDEN .. .. Killed—H.
Private J. SCANLON .. .. Killed—H.

Royal Artillery.

Bombardier LEWIS *[handwritten: & CANTWELL]*
[handwritten: GUNNER EVANS & HOWARD]

Royal Engineers.

Lieutenant JOHN R. M. CHARD (V.C.),
Mentioned in Dispatches.
Awarded the Victoria Cross.
[handwritten: ROBSON]

The Buffs.

Sergeant MILNE.

Commissariat Department.

Asst. Commissary DUNNE,
Mentioned in Dispatches.
Acting Commst. Officer DALTON,
Severely Wounded.
Mentioned in Dispatches.
Acting Store-keeper BYRNE .. Killed.
Mentioned in Dispatches.
Corporal ATTWOOD.
Awarded the Distinguished
Conduct Medal.

Army Hospital Corps.

Surgeon REYNOLDS (V.C.).
Mentioned in Dispatches.
[handwritten: CORPL MILLER] Awarded the Victoria Cross.
[handwritten: LUDDINGTON]
Private McMAHON. Mentioned in Dispatches.
[handwritten: GN ELLIOTT IN COL GRAHAM]

Natal Mounted Police.

Trooper HUNTER .. .. Killed—H.
Trooper GREEN .. .. Killed—H.

Natal Native Contingent.

Corporal SCHIESS (V.C.) Severely Wounded.
Mentioned in Dispatches.
Awarded the Victoria Cross.

Corporal MAYER .. .. .. H.
Corporal SCAMMELL.
[handwritten: LIEUT MAYNARDS C. DOUGHTY, ADENDORFF & WILSON]

Chaplain's Department.

Revd. C. SMITH .. Acting Chaplain.
[handwritten]

Civilian .. Mr. DANIELS.

Note.—Those N. C. Officers and Men marked
with an "H" indicate they were
patients in Hospital.

By Special Request, and in order to preserve a record of those who took part in the Defence, this Roll was prepared
by Major F. Bourne (late Color-Sergeant "B" Company) from the Regimental Pay List for January, 1879, kindly placed at his
disposal by the Public Record Office, Chancery Lane, London.

BECKENHAM, KENT,
4th July, 1910.

[handwritten: P.T.O. for other Names]

BOURNE'S AMENDED ROLL (Part II)

List of Rorke's Drift Defenders

Signed by Brevet Lieutenant-Colonel and Major W. M. Dunbar, 2/24th Regiment

2nd BATTALION 24th REGIMENT

Nominal roll of officers, non-commissioned officers, and men of the above battalion who took part in the defence of Rorke's Drift Post on the 22nd January 1879, and who are now serving with the battalion.

Brevet-Major Gonville Bromhead, V.C., Colour-Sergeant Bourne, Sergeants Henry Gallagher, George Smith, James Taylor, Alfred Saxty, Drummers Patrick Hayes, James Keefe, Patrick Galgey, Patrick Meehan, Privates William Bessell, James Bromwich, Thomas Buckley, James Bush, William Camp, Thomas Chester, Thomas Collins, Robert Cole, Timothy Connors, Anthony Connors, William Cooper, Michael Deane, William Dicks, Thomas Driscoll, James Dunbar, George Edwards, Frederick Evans, Edward Gee, James Hogan, William Halley, John Harris, John Jobbins, Robert Jones, V.C., John Jones, John Jones, Evan Jones, Peter Judge, Michael Kiley, Henry Lines, Thomas Lockhart, David Lloyd, Joshua Lodge, James Marshall, Henry Martin, Charles Mason, Michael Minihan, Thomas Moffat, Frederick Morris, Augustus Morris, Thomas Morrison, James Murphy, William Neville, William Osborne, Samuel Pitt, Thomas Robinson, George Sherman, Thomas Stevens, William Tasker, Thomas Taylor, John Thomas, John Thompson, Patrick Tobin, William J. Todd, Robert Tongue, John Wall, Alfred Whetton, John Williams, V.C., William Wilcox, Caleb Woods, John Momley,* George Partridge, Arthur Sears, and Joseph Windridge.

(*Signed*) W. M. DUNBAR,

Brevet-Lieutenant-Colonel and Major,

Commanding 2/24th Regiment.

In addition to those present, there were a number who had already left the colony, and to these, enumerated below, Major Bromhead, V.C., undertook to convey the copies of the Address which had been prepared for them.

2nd BATTALLION 24th REGIMENT

Nominal roll of men of the above battalion who took part in the defence of Rorke's Drift, but who have since proceeded to England, &c., to be addressed to 25 Brigade Depot, Brecon, South Wales.

Pinetown, Natal,

January 1880.

Corporals William Allen, V.C., and John Lyons, invalided to England; Private James Ashton, on colonial leave, Pietermaritzburg; Private Charles Bromwich, transferred to 91st Highlanders; Private Frederick Hitch, V.C., invalided to England; Private John French, Capetown; Private Henry Hooke, V.C., Gibraltar; Privates William Jones, V.C., Patrick Kears, Edward Savage, John Lyons, John Connolly, invalided to England.

(*Signed*) W. M. DUNBAR,

Brevet-Lieutenant-Colonel and Major,

Commanding 2/24th Regiment.

* John Manley

1st Battalion

24th Regiment of Foot

List of Officer, Non-commissioned Officers and Men present at the
Defence of the Mission Station at Rorke's Drift,
22nd - 23rd January 1879

25B/56 Sergeant WILSON Edward
Born at Peshawur, India; trade – labourer. Religion: C/E. Attested at Kingston on 28/1/74, aged 18 years 4 months. Previously served in 3rd Surrey Militia. Description: 5′ 6″ tall, fresh complexion, hazel eyes, brown hair. Married Mary Ann Evans at Gosport on 13/5/80. Children: Irene Mary (b. not recorded), Francis George (b. 16/5/81), Thomas Gilbert John (b. 22/2/82). Promoted Corporal 5/7/75, Appointed Lance-Sergeant 16/5/77, Promoted Sergeant 12/1/78. (Followed by several demotions and promotions.) Final rank: Sergeant on 18/1/89. Served in South Africa from 25/11/74 to 2/10/79. Engaged for South Wales Borderers at Brecon on 22/1/86, as permanent staff – 3rd Battalion. Died of hypotrophy of heart on 19/9/91. Medal for South Africa with clasp '1877–8–9'. (Ref. 'C' and 'Ba' rolls).

25B/135 Private BECKETT William
Attested at Manchester on 14/4/74, aged 18 years 3 months. Posted to 2/24th on 17/6/74, transferred to 1/24th on 25/11/74. Served in South Africa and sent with reinforcement to Komgha in 1877. He was a patient in the hospital at Rorke's Drift and during the battle was dangerously wounded by an assegai penetrating his abdomen. Died of wound on 23/1/79. (Appendix A.) Mentioned in Lieutenant Chard's letter to Queen Victoria, also in a letter by Private Waters. Effects claimed by his relatives. He is buried in the cemetery at Rorke's Drift and his name appears on the monument. Medal for South Africa with clasp '1877-8-9'. (Ref. 'B' and 'C' rolls, the latter gives his number incorrectly as '129' and names him as 'R. Bekett'.)

25B/568 Private DESMOND Patrick
Attested at Fort Hubberstone on 27/3/75, aged 18 years. Posted to 2/24th on 15/4/75, transferred to 1/24th on 15/7/76. Received 18 fines for drunkenness between July and October 1878, also imprisoned by Civil Power. Wounded in action at Rorke's Drift. (Appendix A.) Discharged on 15/11/80 as a 'worthless character'. Medal for South Africa with clasp '1877–8–9'. Medal forfeited on 19/6/06 (68/24/623), however there is no trace of the medal having been returned. (Ref. 'C' and 'Ba' rolls.)

1–24/1861 Private HORRIGAN William
Attested on 12/11/63, aged 14 years 7 months. Re-engaged at Gibraltar on 16/12/73. Served in South Africa and was at East London in August-September 1877. He was a patient in the hospital at Rorke's Drift and assisted in the defence of the building. Killed in action. (Appendix A.) Effects claimed by next of kin. Mentioned in Lieutenant Chard's letter to Queen Victoria, also in accounts by Privates Hook and Waters. Mentioned in the citations for the award of the Victoria Cross to Privates Hook and Williams. He is buried in the cemetery at Rorke's Drift and his name appears on the monument. Medal for South Africa with clasp '1877–8–9'. (Ref. 'C' roll but incorrectly named as 'Harrigan' on 'B' roll.)

25B/841 Private JENKINS James
Attested at Monmouth on 18/7/76, aged 22 years 4 months. Sent with a draft to join battalion on 2/8/77. He was a patient in the hospital at Rorke's Drift and assisted in the defence. Killed in action. (Appendix A.) Effects claimed by his father. Mentioned in Lieutenant Chard's letter to Queen Victoria. He is buried in the cemetery at Rorke's Drift and his name appears on the monument. Medal for South Africa with clasp '1879'. (Ref. 'C' roll which also incorrectly list 1083 Pte. Jenkins as surviving the action; 'B' roll gives 1083 Pte. M. Jenkins as killed but omits 841 Pte. James Jenkins. In fact 1083 Matthew (real name Watkin) Jenkins was killed at Isandhlwana.)

25B/625 Private NICHOLAS Edward
Attested at Newport on 30/7/75, aged 18 years. Sent with a drift to join battalion on 2/8/77. He was a patient in the hospital at Rorke's Drift and assisted in the defence. Killed in action. (Appendix A.) Effects claimed by next of kin. Mentioned in an account by Private Hitch. He is buried in the cemetery at Rorke's Drift and his name appears on the monument. Medal for South Africa with clasp '1877–8–9'. (Ref. 'C' roll gives his name as E. Nicholls, this error being repeated in the Regimental History where he is shown as a casualty twice, once under 'Nicholls' and again under 'Nicholas'. 'B' roll names him as W. Nicholas. The error regarding his name is reflected throughout the regimental documents; one pay roll gives him as 'Nicholls', this latter being amended to his correct name 'Nicholas'.)

25B/372   Private   PAYTON Thomas
Attested at Manchester on 13/7/74, aged 21 years. Posted to 1/24th on 11/10/74. Served in South Africa and was at East London during August/September 1877. Discharged at Gosport on 2/1/80; to Army Reserve, AGL 103. Intended place of residence 7 Planet St., off Cross St., Stafford. Medal for South Africa with clasp '1877–8–9'. (Ref. 'C' and 'Ba' roll in both instances shown named as 'Paton'.)

1–24/1542   Private   ROY William D.C.M.
Born at Edinburgh, Midlothian; trade – baker. Attested for 32nd Light Infantry at Edinburgh Castle on 8/8/70, aged 17 years. Transferred to 1/24th Foot on 4/12/77. Description: 5' 5½" tall, fresh complexion, brown eyes, red hair. Served in Mauritius and South Africa. He contracted malaria and was frequently admitted to hospital as a result of this. Present at the defence of Rorke's Drift, mentioned in dispatches and awarded the Silver Medal for Distinguished Conduct in the Field. Appointed Lance-Corporal on 22/8/79, Corporal 24/11/79. A specific disease, acquired at King William's Town in January 1876, seriously affected his vision. Following a medical examination at Haslar, Gosport, on 2/10/79, he was found unfit for further service and was discharged on 7/12/80, having served for 8 years, 303 days. Intended place of residence, Post Office, Gosport. Medal for South Africa with clasp '1877–8–9'. (Ref. 'C' gives incorrect number '1522' and name 'R. Joy'. Details correct on 'B' roll.)

25B/104   Private   TURNER Henry
Born at Ball Bridge, Dublin, also given as Bassbridge and Killeatty, Wexford; trade – bricklayer. Attested at Aldershot on 27/3/74, aged 23 years. Religion: C/E. Description: 6' 1" tall, fresh complexion, light hazel eyes, brown hair. Posted to 2/24th on 31/3/74, transferred to 1/24th on 26/11/74. He was struck over the left ear by a black bottle when on picquet duty in 1876, the wound scar being evident. Since that time he suffered epilepsy, the first attack being at Simm's Town, Cape Colony, in 1876. He was examined by a medical board at Pietermaritz-

burg on 9/9/79 and found to be unfit for further service. On arrival in England he was sent to Netley, having suffered two further epileptic attacks, one of which was on the ship bringing him home. Medical opinion considered his disability to be permanent and that he 'may not be able to struggle for a precarious livelihood'. Discharged as unfit for further service on 9/2/80. Medal for South Africa with clasp '1877–8–9'. (Ref. 'C' and 'Ba' rolls.)

1–24/447   Private   WATERS John
Born at Lichfield, Staffordshire; trade – clerk. Attested at Westminster on 8/3/58, aged 18 years 2 months. Re-engaged at Malta on 9/9/67. Description: 5' 5" tall, fresh complexion, hazel eyes, brown hair. Served in the Mediterranean and in South Africa. Promoted Corporal 10/1/71. Reduced to Private 2/3/75. Served as special orderly at the hospital at Rorke's Drift, where he was wounded in action. (Appendix A.) Mentioned in Lieutenant Chard's letter to Queen Victoria, see also his own account of the battle. Due to the severity of the shoulder wound, there is no mention of a knee wound, Waters was examined by a medical board at Pietermaritzburg on 14/7/79. The wound was described as having been caused by a 'bullet entering outer side of arm, six inches from joint of shoulder, and lodging'. 'It was cut out behind shoulder 12 hours after – distance travelled through fleshy part of arm – 4 inches'. 'The joint not injured – bone uninjured'. 'He has fair power of motion of the injured arm in all directions, but complains of pain in the track of the wound and shoulder when exerting himself'. 'From length of service and wound, his capacity to earn a living will be considerably impaired'. Waters was found unfit for further service and discharged on 27/10/79. Intended place of residence, 12 Courtfield Gardens, Kensington, London. Medal for South Africa with clasp '1877–8–9'. The medal roll originally gave his initial as 'G' and entitlement to the clasp with dates '1877–8–9'. This was later corrected under 68/124/211 and the medal with the initial J and the clasp dated '1877–8–9' was handed to him on 15/10/80. (Ref. 'C' and 'Ba' rolls.)

2nd Battalion

24th Regiment of Foot

List of Officer, Non-commissioned Officers and Men present at the
Defence of the Mission Station at Rorke's Drift,
22nd - 23rd January 1879

Gonville BROMHEAD, V.C.

(Lieutenant)

Born on Friday, 29th August 1845, at Versailles, France, he was the third son of Edmund de Gonville Bromhead, 3rd Baronet, and his wife Judith Christine Cahill, daughter of James Wood of Woodville, County Sligo. The family home was Thurlby Hall at Newark. He was educated at Magnus Grammar School, Newark. Entered the 24th Foot as an Ensign, by purchase, on 20/4/67. Promoted by selection to Lieutenant on 28/10/71. Posted to South Africa and embarked at Plymouth on 2/2/78. Served in the Kaffir War 1878; Zulu War 1879 and commanded 'B' Company 2nd/24th Foot at the defence of Rorke's Drift. Mentioned in dispatches, brevet of Major and awarded the Victoria Cross for his conduct on that occasion. Mentioned by Lieutenant Chard in his letter to Queen Victoria. (See also reference by Private Hitch in his letter.) Lieutenant Bromhead received his Victoria Cross from Sir Garnet Wolseley at Utrecht on 22/8/79, the citation (L.G. 2/5/79) reading: 'For gallant conduct at the defence of Rorke's Drift, 22nd and 23rd January 1879. The lieutenant general reports that had it not been for the firm example and excellent behaviour of Lieutenants Chard, Royal Engineers, and Bromhead, 24th Regiment, the defence of Rorke's Drift would not have been conducted with the intelligence and tenacity which so eminently characterised it. The lieutenant general adds, that the success must in a great measure be attributable to the two young officers who exercised the chief command on the occasion in question'. Promoted Captain and Brevet-Major on 23/1/79; Major on 4/4/83. Posted from South Africa to Gibraltar, where he served until August 1880, then to East Indies until March 1881. On being posted home, he attended the School of Musketry, Hythe, from 1/10/82 to 5/12/82, gaining a First Class Extra Certificate. Embarked at Portsmouth in the *Serapis* on 2/1/83 to join the 2nd South Wales Borderers at Secunderabad, India. Served in Burma from 27/10/86 to 24/5/88 (medal with clasps 'Burma 1885-7 and Burma 1887-9'), returning to East Indies. Died of enteric fever on 9/2/91, aged 46 years, at Camp Dabhaura, Allahabad, India. He was unmarried. Bromhead received and address and a revolver presented to him by the tenants of Thurlby Hall. (He must have treasured the revolver, for it remained with him for the next twelve years.) The people of Lincoln gave him a sword, and Queen Victoria a photograph of herself. On 7/11/91, in his will, originally drawn up at Taunton, Somerset, in 1869, he left these items, together with his Victoria Cross and a watch belonging to his late father, to his brother, Colonel Charles J. Bromhead. The residue of his estate went to his sisters Alice Margaret and Elizabeth Frances Pocklington. He left no written report, official or otherwise, concerning Rorke's Drift.

Medal for South Africa with clasp '1877-8-9'.
(Ref. 'C' and 'B' rolls, also 'D' list.)

2-24/2459 Colour-Sergeant BOURNE Frank D.C.M.

Born on 27th April 1854 at Balcombe, Cuckfield, Sussex; no trade. Attested at Reigate on 18/12/72, aged 18 years 8 months. Finally approved at Chatham on 24/12/72. (His father, a farmer, attempted to prevent him from enlisting, but was prevailed upon not to do so.) Description: 5' 5½" tall, dark complexion, grey eyes, brown hair. Posted to 2/24th in January 1873. Promoted Corporal 11/4/75. Appointed Lance-Sergeant 7/4/78. Promoted Sergeant 15/4/78. Appointed Colour-Sergeant 27/4/78. Served in South Africa, Mediterranean, India and Burma (medal and clasp 'Burma 1887-9'). Served in 'B' Company at the defence of Rorke's Drift. Mentioned in Lieutenant Chard's report of the action and also in a letter by Private Hitch. Wrote and broadcast his own account of the battle. Awarded the Silver Medal for Distinguished Conduct in the Field, with a £10 annuity. He was also offered a commission but had to refuse as he could not afford the expense involved as an officer. His wife, Eliza Mary, was included on the married roll on 27/9/82. Promoted Quarter-Master Sergeant to his battalion, he transferred to the South Wales Borderers (SWB 1141) on 26/3/84. He was promoted Honorary Lieutenant and Quartermaster on 21/5/90. On 15/11/93 he was appointed Adjutant at the School of Musketry, Hythe, where Mary Frances, the youngest of his five children, was born. He continued in this post for 14½ years until his retirement under the age limit in 1907. For some years he assisted Lord Roberts in the work of the Society of Miniature Rifle Clubs in London. On the outbreak of the Great War he again offered his services and was appointed Adjutant to the School of Musketry, Dublin, a position which he held for over four years. Promoted Lieutenant-Colonel and awarded the O.B.E. in recognition of his services. Attended the Northern Command Tattoo, held at Gateshead in 1934, and appeared in the arena with Sergeant Saxty and Privates Cooper, Jobbins and Woods, former comrades from Rorke's Drift. In December 1936 he broadcast on radio in the 'I Was There' programme and as a result received over 350 letters, to which he replied personally in every instance. In response to a 'Special Request', he compiled a roll of the defenders of Rorke's Drift, which is dated 4/7/10. Lieutenant-Colonel Bourne was an extremely modest man who, when asked about the defence of Rorke's Drift, invariably replied that he 'Considered myself lucky to have been there'. The anniversary of the battle was always commemorated by a family dinner held at his home. He died on 8/5/45, aged 91 years, and is buried at Elmers End, Kent, and it is believed that he was the last surviving member of the Rorke's Drift garrison. Medal for South Africa with clasp '1877–8–9'. (Ref. 'C' and 'B' rolls, also 'D' list.)

25B/81 Sergeant GALLAGHER Henry

Born at Killendale, Thurles, Tipperary; trade – clerk. Attested at Liverpool on 13/3/74, aged 19 years. Religion: R.C. Description: 5' 6¼" tall, fresh complexion, amber eyes, dark-brown hair. Promoted Corporal 11/3/75. Appointed Lance-Sergeant 17/1/77. Promoted Sergeant 9/10/77. Served in South Africa, Gibraltar, India and Burma (medal and clasp 'Burma 1887–9'). Served in 'B' Company at the defence of Rorke's Drift. Married Caroline Maria Stanley at Dover on 7/4/77. Children: Caroline Lillian Gertrude (b. 4/9/81 at Brecon), Henry Edward (b. 8/7/83 at Secunderabad), William Alfred (b. 11/11/85 at Madras), Violet Elizabeth (b. 19/2/88 at Toungov), Daisy Dorothea (b. 9/3/90 at Raniket), Lawrence Stanley (b. 10/7/95 at Cosham). Service extended on 27/4/80 to complete 12 years with the colours. Appointed Colour-Sergeant on 26/1/81. Re-engaged for the South Wales Borderers (SWB/1590) at Madras on 28/7/85. Promoted to Warrant Officer as Sergeant-Major on 9/1/89. Permitted to continue in the service beyond 21 years, by authority dated 28/2/95. Appointed to Army Staff as Garrison Sergeant-Major on 10/8/95. Discharged from South Wales Borderers (Staff) on 10/5/97. In addition to his pension, he also received, for a limited period, a pension for services as Barrack Warden. Payment of his pension appears to have ceased in 1929. He died at Drayton, Hants., and was buried at Christchurch, Portsdown Hill, Hants. Medal for South Africa with clasp '1877–8–9'. (Ref. 'C' and 'B' rolls, also 'D' list.)

25B/623 Sergeant MAXFIELD Robert

Attested at Newport on 30/7/75, aged 18 years 3 months. (He allegedly came from Cinderhill Street, Newport.) Posted to 2/24th on 18/8/75. Appointed Lance-Corporal 25/5/76, Promoted Corporal 11/11/76, Sergeant 1/2/78. Awarded a 'good shooting' prize in 1878. He served in 'G' Company and was a patient in the hospital at Rorke's Drift. Killed in the hospital when the Zulus broke into the building. (Appendix 'A'.) Effects claimed by his mother, brothers and sisters. Mentioned in Lieutenant Chard's letter to Queen Victoria, and also in accounts by Privates Hook and Jobbins. He is buried in the cemetery at Rorke's Drift and his name

appears on the monument. Medal for South Africa with clasp '1877–8–9' issued on 29/3/82, AGL 105. (Ref. 'C' and 'B' rolls.)

2-24/1387 Sergeant SMITH George

Born at Islington, London; trade – labourer. Attested at Finsbury on 29/5/60, aged 18 years. Previously served for 6 weeks in Royal London Militia. Description: 5' 4" tall, sallow complexion, grey eyes, brown hair. Served in Mauritius, East Indies, South Africa and Gibraltar. Re-engaged at Rangoon on 10/1/68. Promoted Corporal 4/8/71. Appointed Lance-Sergeant 1/4/76. Promoted Sergeant 1/2/78. Married Fanny Martin at the Wesleyan Chapel, Brecon, on 30/6/77. Served in 'B' Company at the defence of Rorke's Drift. (See letter, dated 24/1/79, to his wife, then living in Little Free Street, Brecon. Transferred from 'B' to 'A' Company, in rank of Sergeant, on 4/2/79. Permitted to continue in the service beyond 21 years, by authority dated 22/8/81. Transferred to permanent staff – 3rd South Wales Borderers – on 28/12/81. Discharged on 31/7/83 – not passed to reserve. Medal for South Africa with clasp '1877–8–9'. (Ref. 'B' and 'B' rolls, also 'D' list.)

2-24/735 Sergeant WINDRIDGE Joseph

Born at Birmingham, Warwickshire; trade – carpenter. Attested at Birmingham on 26/1/59, aged 18 years 4 months. Description: 5' 10½" tall, fresh complexion, hazel eyes, brown hair. Served in Mauritius, East Indies, South Africa and Gibraltar. Promoted Corporal 6/5/61, Sergeant 2/3/62, Quarter-Master Sergeant 21/12/63. He was demoted and promoted several times and again achieved the rank of Sergeant on 27/4/77. Re-engaged at Rangoon on 3/9/68 to complete 21 years service. Married Helena Catherine Rawlinson at Holy Trinity, Dover, on 14/6/77. Served in 'B' Company at the defence of Rorke's Drift. Mentioned in Lieutenant Chard's report of the action and also in his letter to Queen Victoria. Windridge suffered from dyspepsia. He was reduced to Private on 20/11/79. Appointed Lance-Corporal 3/9/80. Promoted Corporal 6/10/80, transferring to the South Wales Borderers in that rank on 1/7/81. Promoted Sergeant 31/3/82. Discharged at Gosport on 7/8/83, having completed his service. Medal for South Africa with clasp '1877–8–9'. (Ref. 'C' and 'B' rolls, also on 'D' list.)

25B/82 Lance-Sergeant TAYLOR James

Born at Meltham, Halifax, Yorkshire; trade – clerk. Attested on 13/3/74 at Manchester, aged 19 years. Religion: C/E. Description: 5' 8½" tall, fresh complexion, blue eyes, brown hair. Served in South Africa, Mediterranean, India and Burma (Medal with clasp 'Burma 1887–9'). Promoted Corporal 3/3/75. Reduced to Private 27/5/75. Appointed Lance-Corporal 10/1/76. Promoted Corporal 4/8/76. Appointed

Lance-Sergeant 26/10/77. Reverted to Corporal 25/11/77. Appointed Lance-Sergeant 11/7/78. Served in 'E' Company at the defence of Rorke's Drift. Promoted Sergeant on 23/1/79, in 'E' Company, vice Cuthbert. Reduced to Private 20/3/80. Extended his army service on 27/4/80. Promoted Corporal 16/9/83. Appointed Lance-Sergeant 3/9/84. Re-engaged in the South Wales Borderers (SWB 1682) at Madras on 23/11/85. Again promoted, eventually becoming Orderly-room Sergeant on 5/6/91. Presumably discharged after 8/3/94. Next-of-kin, Mother – Mrs. S. Taylor, 33 Parkfield Road, Rusholme, Manchester. Medal for South Africa with clasp '1877–8–9'. (Ref. 'C' roll, 'B' roll gives his rank incorrectly as Corporal, also on 'D' list.)

25B/1328 Lance-Sergeant   WILLIAMS Thomas
Attested at Brecon on 6/3/77. Posted to 2/24th on 13/12/77. Appointed Lance-Corporal 8/1/78. Promoted Corporal 1/2/78. Date of appointment to Lance-Sergeant not recorded and it is possible that this may have been a local appointment. Served in 'B' Company at the defence of Rorke's Drift. Wounded in action and died of wound on 23/1/79. (Appendix A.) Mentioned in Lieutenant Chard's report and also in his letter to Queen Victoria. He is buried in the cemetery at Rorke's Drift and his name appears on the monument. Medal for South Africa with clasp '1877–8–9'. The medal roll gives his initial incorrectly as 'J'. (Ref. 'C' and 'B' rolls.)

2–24/1240 Corporal   ALLEN William Wilson V.C.
Born in 1844. Attested at York on 27/10/59, aged 15 years 8 months. Description : 5′ 4″ tall. Joined the regiment at Aldershot on 31/10/59. He is known to have served in Mauritius and South Africa. During his early service career he was confined in cells Oct.-Nov. 1860, July-Sept. 1861, Jan.-March 1861, July, Aug., Sept. 1864, Oct.-Nov. 1864. Re-engaged in 1873. Posted to Regimental Depot on 21/4/74. Appointed Lance-Corporal 18/5/76. Promoted Corporal 6/7/77. Appointed Assistant Schoolmaster whilst at the depot, receiving an additional 6d. per day. Returned to 2/24th on 26/1/78. Appointed Lance-Sergeant 22/5/78. Reverted to Corporal on 21/10/78. Awarded good shooting and judging distance prize in 1878. His wife, Sarah Ann, who appears on the married roll at Brecon in 1879, received from him a monthly allowance of £3. Children born circa May 1877, July 1878, August 1880, April 1882 (twins). The twins seem to have died about 1883. Served in 'B' Company and wounded in action at Rorke's Drift. (Appendix A.) Mentioned in Lieutenant Chard's report on the action, and also in his letter to Queen Victoria. Corporal Allen was awarded the Victoria Cross for his gallant conduct at

Rorke's Drift and received his decoration from Queen Victoria at Windsor Castle on 9/12/79, the citation (L.G. 2/5/79) reading : 'William Allen, Corporal, and Frederick Hitch, Private, 2nd Battalion, 24th Regiment. It was chiefly due to the courageous conduct of these men at Rorke's Drift that communication was kept up with the hospital at all. Holding together, at all cost, a most dangerous post, raked in reverse by the enemy's fire from the hill, they were both severely wounded; but their determined conduct enabled the patients to be withdrawn from the hospital, and when incapacitated by their wounds from fighting, they continued, as soon as their wounds had been dressed, to serve out ammunition to their comrades through the night'. Following the action at Rorke's Drift, he was sent to Pietermaritzburg and from there to England on 26/8/79. He was serving with the 3rd South Wales Borderers Militia at Brecon by 8/11/79 and later served with the Provisional Battalion at Colchester. Appointed Sergeant Instructor of Musketry (date not traced). Died on 12/3/90 aged 46 years at 85 Monnow Street, Monmouth, and was buried at Monmouth. Medal for South Africa with clasp '1877–8–9'. (Ref. 'C' and 'B' rolls, also on 'D' list.)

2–24/582 Corporal   FRENCH George
Born at Kensington, London; trade – groom. Attested at Westminster on 16/12/59, aged 18 years. Description : 5′ 4″ tall, fair complexion, blue eyes, brown hair. Promoted Corporal 8/11/60. (Followed by several demotions and promotions.) He gained extra pay as a fencing and gymnastics instructor. Promoted Corporal 16/7/71. His wife, Mary, appears on the married roll in 1873; by 1877 they had two children. Served in 'B' Company at the defence of Rorke's Drift. Promoted Sergeant in 'B' Company 23/1/79. Later transferred to 'G' Company and reduced to Private on 28/6/79. Promoted Corporal 9/2/81. Reduced to Private 3/8/81. Discharged on 3/1/82 on completion of his service (22 years 11 days). Intended place of residence, 8 Hillaire Street, London. Medal for South Africa with clasp '1877–8–9'. (Ref. 'C' and 'B' rolls, also on 'D' list.)

2–24/2389 Corporal   KEY John
Attested on 28/8/71 at Secunderabad, India. Appointed Drummer in 1873. Reduced to Private 25/9/77. Appointed Lance-Corporal 3/5/78. Promoted Corporal 13/7/78. Served in 'B' Company at the defence of Rorke's Drift. Appointed Lance-Sergeant 31/3/79 in 'H' Company, vice Jones. Promoted Sergeant 20/3/80. To unattached list 1/3/84, while at Secunderabad, which suggests he settled at the same place as he enlisted. Medal for South Africa with clasp '1877–8–9'. (Ref. 'B' roll where his rank is incorrectly given as Lance-Corporal.)

25B/1112 Corporal LYONS John

Attested on 28/1/77. Posted to 1/24th, transferred to 2/24th on 22/2/77. Appointed Lance-Corporal 13/1/77. Promoted Corporal 26/11/77. Served in 'B' Company at the defence of Rorke's Drift, where he was wounded in action. (Appendix A.) Mentioned in Lieutenant Chard's letter to Queen Victoria, see also his own account of the battle. He was sent to the depot at Pietermaritzburg on 1/3/79. Date of discharge not traced. Died on 1/5/03. The bullet which had caused his wound was extracted and given to him as a memento. Lyons had the bullet mounted on a silver watch chain, which he evidently wore on his person. The bullet and chain are on display in the Regimental Museum. Medal for South Africa with clasp '1877–8–9' issued on 5/9/81. A search of the medal roll was made on 4/5/23 (18878/AGL). (Ref. 'C' and 'Ba' rolls, neither of which list him as wounded, also on 'D' list.)

25B/849 Corporal SAXTY Alfred

Born at Buckland Dinham, Somerset; trade – labourer. Attested at Newport on 18/9/76, aged 19 years. Religion: R/C. Description: 5' 7½" tall, fresh complexion, blue eyes, light brown hair. Served in South Africa, Mediterranean, India and Burma (medal and clasp 'Burma 1885–7'). Appointed Lance-Corporal 24/4/77. Promoted Corporal 23/8/77. Appointed Lance-Sergeant 1/2/78. Reverted to Corporal 11/7/78. Served in 'B' Company at the defence of Rorke's Drift. Promoted Sergeant 23/1/79. Reduced to Private 18/5/81. (Followed by several promotions and demotions.) Married Mary Copeland at Madras on 30/12/85. Children: Albert (b. 20/5/87 at Wellington). Following the death of his first wife, he married Mary Cole at Wellington, Madras. Children: Wilfred (b. 2/11/90 at Secunderabad), Leo (b. 20/12/94 at Rangoon). He re-engaged at Wellington, Madras, on 1/1/88 into the 2nd Battalion, Bedfordshire Regiment, to complete 21 years service. On 30/11/91 he transferred to the 2nd Royal Inniskilling Fusiliers in the rank of Sergeant. Discharged at his own request at Thayetmyo, Burma, on 28/2/95 as a Corporal with 18 years 170 days service. Admitted as an In-Pensioner at the Royal Military Hospital, Chelsea, on 12/6/1930. Died on 11/7/36, of myocarditis and senility, at Woolaston House Infirmary, Newport. Medal for South Africa with clasp '1877–8–9'. Two replacement medals (for South Africa and Burma) issued under 68/GEN/5160. (Ref. 'C' and 'B' rolls, the latter giving his rank incorrectly as Sergeant, also on 'D' list.)

25B/1287 Lance-Corporal BESSELL William

Born at Bethnal Green, London; trade – porter. Attested at Bow Street, London, on 26/2/77, aged 20 years 11 months. Religion: C/E. Description: fresh complexion, hazel eyes, brown hair. Served in South Africa, Gibraltar and India. Served in 'B' Company at the defence of Rorke's Drift. Appointed Lance-Corporal 26/11/78. Promoted Corporal 23/1/79, in 'B' Company, vice Jones. Reduced to Private 25/11/79. Transferred to Army Reserve on 28/6/83. Discharged 26/2/89. Medal for South Africa with clasp '1877–8–9'. (Ref. 'C' roll and 'B' roll which shows his name incorrectly as Bissell, also on 'D' list.)

25B/1282 Lance-Corporal HALLEY William

Attested on 3/3/77. Posted to 1/24th, transferred to 2/24th on 13/12/77. Served in South Africa, India and Burma. Appointed Lance-Corporal 17/7/78. Served in 'B' Company at the defence of Rorke's Drift. Promoted Corporal 23/1/79 in 'B' Company vice French. Reduced to Private 2/8/79. Appointed Lance-Corporal 21/2/80. Reduced to Private 10/1/82. Died on 30/4/87 at Thayetmyo, Burma. Medal for South Africa with clasp '1877–8–9'. Medal returned to mint on 23/11/97. (Ref. 'C' and 'B' rolls, also on 'D' list.)

2–24/1713 Drummer GALGEY Patrick

Attested at Cork on 12/3/65, aged 14 years. Description: 4' 7½" tall. Appointed Drummer 1/2/66. Joined the regiment in India on 5/4/69. Reduced to Private 1/7/70. Appointed Drummer 23/2/72. Served in 'D' Company at the defence of Rorke's Drift. Reduced to Private 1/2/80. Discharged (date not known) under AGL 89. Medal for South Africa with clasp '1877–8–9' issued on 17/6/81. (Ref. 'C' and 'Ba' rolls, also 'D' list.)

2–24/2067 Drummer HAYES Patrick

Born at Newmarket, Co. Clare; trade – labourer. Attested at Ennis on 8/9/68, aged 14 years. Description: 4' 8¼" tall, fresh complexion, grey eyes, light brown hair. Appointed Drummer (boy) on 8/12/69. Reverted to Boy 8/11/70. Appointed Private 9/9/71. Appointed Drummer 1/4/73. Served in India, South Africa, Mediterranean and Burma. Served in 'B' Company at the defence of Rorke's Drift. Re-engaged on 22/11/79. Appointed Lance-Corporal 28/4/84. Promoted Corporal 22/9/85. Reverted to Private 10/9/87. Appointed Bandsman 7/10/87. Permitted to continue in the service beyond 21 years by authority dated 29/10/89. Discharged on 30/11/92. Following his discharge he became a civilian workman at the barracks at Brecon, remaining in this capacity until well past 60 years of age. On retirement he lived at a house in Riverhall Street, Wandsworth Road, London. Medal for South Africa with clasp '1877–8–9'. (Ref. 'C' and 'B' rolls, also 'D' list.)

2–24/2381 Drummer KEEFE James
Born at St. Andrew's, London; trade – none. Religion: C/E. Attested at Marlborough Police Court on 3/3/71, aged 14 years 10 months. Description: 4′ 7½″ tall, fresh complexion, grey eyes, brown hair. Private 4/3/73. Appointed Drummer 21/8/74. Served in South Africa, Mediterranean, India and Burma. Served in 'B' Company at the defence of Rorke's Drift. Re-engaged at Secunderabad on 18/12/79, to complete 21 years service. Reverted to Private 6/4/83. (Followed by several promotions and demotions.) Transferred to South Wales Borderers (SWB 2311), as a Private, on 10/10/87. Sent to depot and promoted Corporal 28/11/89. Married Margaret Ellis at Brecon Registry Office on 17/4/89. (His son, also named James, served in the South Wales Borderers.) Transferred to 3rd Battalion, South Wales Borderers, as permanent staff on 16/4/90, having been promoted Sergeant on 15/4/90. To 3rd Volunteer Battalion – permanent staff – on 22/9/91. Permitted to continue in the service beyond 21 years, by authority dated 10/3/92. Appointed Lance-Sergeant 4/3/92. Died on 18/9/93. Medal for South Africa with clasp '1877–8–9'. (Ref. 'C' and 'B' rolls, also 'D' list.)

2–24/2383 Drummer MEEHAN John
Date of attestation not traced. He appears on the muster roll for 1/1/73, at Warley, as a 'Private from the depot'. Appointed Drummer 7/8/76. Awarded 42 days hard labour, of which 11 days were remitted, in June 1877 – yet still retained his rank. He was awarded a Good Shooting prize in 1878. Served in 'A' Company at the defence of Rorke's Drift. Posted from India to England, for discharge, on 29/1/83. Medal for South Africa with clasp '1877–8–9'. (Ref. 'C' roll, which names him incorrectly as Pat Meeham, and 'Ba' roll which appears to name him as T. Meehan, also on 'D' list.)

25B/987 Private ADAMS Robert
Attested on 21/12/76. Previously served in East Middlesex Militia. Posted to 2/24th on 22/1/77. Sent to General Depot on 1/11/78, returning on 21/12/78. He served in 'D' Company and was a patient in the hospital at Rorke's Drift. Killed in action. (Appendix A.) Effects claimed under E/78649/4 AGL 77. He is buried in the cemetery at Rorke's Drift and his name appears on the monument. Medal for South Africa with clasp '1877–8–9'. (Ref. 'C' and 'B' rolls.)

2–24/913 Private ASHTON James
Born at St. Mary's, Liverpool; trade – groom. Religion: C/E. Attested at Cork on 3/3/59, aged 17 years 9 months. Description: 5′ 5½″ tall, fresh complexion, hazel eyes, dark brown hair. Served in Mauritius, East Indies and South Africa. Served in 'B' Company at the defence of Rorke's Drift. There is a report that on the 23rd January, after the Zulus

had been repulsed at Rorke's Drift, Private Ashton appeared with a Zulu prisoner. No one in authority had time to spare for either soldier or his prisoner, and he was told to dispose of the captive. It was later discovered that Ashton had taken this in a literal sense and had hanged the Zulu. Colour-Sergeant Bourne stated that Ashton had told him: 'I took him (the Zulu) to Lieutenant Bromhead and he told me to get the hell out of here with him – and I did.' Similar confirmation is provided by Lieutenant Smith-Dorien who had ridden to Rorke's Drift on the day following the battle and was shocked to discover two Zulus hanging from the gallows he had erected to stretch hides. Private Ashton was discharged on 29/3/81, on completion of his service (21 years 110 days). Medal for South Africa with clasp '1877–8–9'. (Ref. 'C' and 'B' rolls, the latter giving his number incorrectly as 912, also on 'D' list.)

25B/1381 Private BARRY Thomas
Attested at Newport on 6/4/77. Posted to 2/24th on 11/5/77. Served in South Africa and India. Served in 'B' Company at the defence of Rorke's Drift. Returned to England from India on 26/4/83. Medal for South Africa with clasp '1877–8–9'. (Ref. 'B' roll only.)

25B/918 Private BENNETT William
Attested at Brecon on 22/11/76. Posted to 2/24th on 15/12/76. Confined in cells from 29/10/78 to 5/11/78. Served in 'B' Company at the defence of Rorke's Drift. Deserted on 21/12/79 at Pinetown, Natal. Did not, therefore, receive his medal for South Africa with clasp '1877–8–9'. (Ref. 'C' and 'B' rolls.)

2–24/2427 Private BLY John
Date of attestation not known. Posted to 2/24th on 1/1/73. Served in 'B' Company at the defence of Rorke's Drift. Sent to Netley on 1/2/80, and from there discharged to Army Reserve (AGL 149). Medal for South Africa with clasp '1877–8–9'. (Ref. 'B' roll only.)

25B/1524 Private BROMWICH Joseph
Born at St. Mary's, Warwick; trade – porter. Religion: C/E. Attested for the 6th Regiment, 28 Brigade (28B/1028), at Warwick on 27/8/77, aged 18 years. (His attestation papers originally gave his name as 'Bromage', this latter being amended in all instances to his correct name. See note below re 'B' roll. Description: 5′ 5½″ tall, fair complexion, brown eyes, dark brown hair. Next of kin, Mother, Mrs. M. Bromwich, 12 Brook Street, Warwick. Transferred as a Private to 2/24th Regiment on 24/1/78. Served in South Africa, India and Mauritius. Served in 'B' Company at the defence of Rorke's Drift. Transferred from 'B' Company to 'A' Company on 29/1/79. Transferred to South Wales Borderers on 1/7/81. As a result of his military service and the climate, he developed chronic hepatitis resulting in a

chronically damaged liver. Following a medical examination at Netley on 1/7/82, his disability was found to be permanent and 'Will for some 12 months impair his power of earning a living.' He was invalided from the service on 25/7/82. Medal for South Africa with clasp '1877–8–9'. (Ref. 'C' roll and 'Ba' roll, which show him as Bromatch, also on 'D' list.)

25B/1184 Private   BUCKLEY Thomas
Attested on 15/2/77. Posted to 2/24th on 23/2/77. Served in South Africa, India and Burma (medal with clasps 'Burma 1885–7' and 'Burma 1887–9'). Served in 'B' Company at the defence of Rorke's Drift. Served in the South Wales Borderers, but did not transfer to the regiment. Appointed Lance-Corporal 2/10/82. Promoted Corporal 1/8/83. Reduced to Private on 6/10/83. Returned to England on 12/1/89. He is known to have been alive in 1932. Medal for South Africa with clasp '1877–8–9'. Two replacement medals (for South Africa and Burma) were issued to him on 5/7/24, under AG10/19689 and IV475/AG10 respectively. (Ref. 'C' and 'B' rolls, on 'D' list.)

25B/1220 Private   BURKE Thomas
Born at Liverpool, Lancashire; trade – labourer. Religion: R/C. Attested at Liverpool on 14/2/77, aged 18 years. Previously served in 2nd Royal Lancashire Militia. Description: 5' 4⅝" tall, fresh complexion, blue eyes, brown hair. Served in South Africa, Mediterranean, India and Burma (medal with clasp 'Burma 1885–7'). Served in 'B' Company at the defence of Rorke's Drift. Appointed Lance-Corporal 24/11/80. Promoted Corporal 1/11/81. Served in South Wales Borderers, but did not transfer to the Regiment. To Army Reserve on 21/6/83. Rejoined in 1st Liverpool Regiment on 19/10/84. Re-engaged at Fyzabad on 20/8/88, to complete 21 years service. (Followed by several demotions and promotions.) Discharged at his own request on 15/10/97, as a Sergeant, after 18 years service. Medal for South Africa with clasp '1877–8–9'. (Ref. 'B' roll only.)

2–24/2350 Private   BUSHE James
Born at St. John's, Dublin; trade – tailor. Religion: C/E. Attested at Dublin on 14/9/70, aged 18 years. Description: 5' 5⅛" tall, fresh complexion, grey eyes, black hair. Served in India, South Africa, Mediterranean and Burma (medal with clasp 'Burma 1887–9'). Promoted Corporal 20/11/75. Reduced to Private 17/5/77. Served in 'B' Company at the defence of Rorke's Drift. Injured in action. (Appendix A.) Mentioned in Lieutenant Chard's letter to Queen Victoria. Appointed Lance-Corporal 10/2/79 and transferred from 'B' to 'F' Company, vice Haslam. Promoted Corporal 28/11/79. Appointed Lance-Sergeant 24/11/80. Served in South Wales Borderers, but did not transfer to the regiment. Re-engaged at Secunder-

abad on 2/12/80, to complete 21 years service. Reverted to Private, at own request, on 2/11/81. Appointed Lance-Corporal 1/6/83. Promoted Corporal 27/4/87. Discharged on 10/10/91. Medal for South Africa with clasp '1877–8–9'. (Ref. 'C' and 'B' rolls, in both instances incorrectly shown as Bush. 'B' roll also gives his rank as Corporal, on 'D' list.)

25B/1181 Private   CAMP William Henry
Born at Camberwell, Surrey; trade – clerk. Attested at Liverpool on 8/2/77, aged 23 years. Description: 5' 8½" tall, sallow complexion, hazel eyes, dark brown hair. Served in 'B' Company at the defence of Rorke's Drift. Embarked at Bombay, for England, in H.M. Troopship *Malabar* on 28/10/81. Following a medical examination at Netley on 25/11/81, he was found to be suffering from melancholia caused by an 'heriditary predisposition and aggravated by self-abuse'. His illness was found to be permanent and he would be unable to contribute to his own support. He was declared insane and discharged unfit for further service on 27/12/81. Intended place of residence: c/o Union Authorities, Camberwell, Surrey. Medal for South Africa with clasp '1877–8–9'. (Ref. 'C' and 'B' rolls, also 'D' list.)

25B/1241 Private   CHESTER Thomas
Born at Calthorpe, Leicester; trade – labourer. Religion: C/E. Attested at Bow Street Police Court on 19/2/77, aged 24 years 7 months. Description: 5' 10¼" tall, fair complexion, blue eyes, brown hair. Served in South Africa, Mediterranean and India. Appointed Lance-Corporal 16/2/78. Reverted to Private 25/6/78. Served in 'B' Company at the defence of Rorke's Drift. Returned to England, from India, on 28/5/83. Married Ellen Cave at Cheltenham on 9/12/83. Served in South Wales Borderers but did not transfer to the regiment. Discharged to Army Reserve on 21/6/83, having served 6 years 121 days. Medal for South Africa with clasp '1877–8–9'. (Ref. 'C' and 'B' rolls, also 'D' list.)

25B/1335 Private   CHICK James
Attested on 8/3/77. Posted to 2/24th on 11/5/77. Acted as assistant schoolmaster during 1877. He served in 'D' Company, and despite being a patient in the hospital at Rorke's Drift, he assisted in the defence. Killed in action. (Appendix A.) Mentioned in Lieutenant Chard's official report on the action. He is buried in the cemetery at Rorke's Drift and his name appears on the monument. Medal for South Africa with clasp '1877–8–9'. (Ref. 'C' and 'B' rolls.)

25B/755 Private   CLAYTON Thomas
Born at Leominster, Herefordshire; trade – labourer. Attested at Monmouth on 9/2/76, aged 20 years 8 months. Posted to 2/24th on 10/3/76. Served in 'B' Company at the defence of Rorke's Drift. Died of disease at

Helpmakaar on 5/4/79. (He left the sum of £10–18s–3d.) Medal for South Africa with clasp '1877–8–9'. (Ref. 'C' and 'B' rolls, the latter gives his initial incorrectly as 'F').

25B/1459 Private   COLE Robert
Born at Chatham, Kent; trade – gunmaker. Religion : C/E. Attested at Brecon on 29/10/77, aged 19 years. Description : 5' 6" tall, fresh complexion, grey eyes, brown hair. Posted to 2/24th on 13/12/77. Served in South Africa, Gibraltar and India. He served in 'F' Company and was, presumably, a patient in the hospital at Rorke's Drift. (Corporal Michael McMahon, Army Hospital Corps, was awarded the Distinguished Conduct Medal for rescuing Private Cole from the Zulus at Rorke's Drift.) Posted from India to England on 1/12/83. Married Elizabeth Gibelin at St. Bartholomew's Church, Birmingham, on 20/4/84. To South Wales Borderers on 1/7/81, but did not transfer to the regiment. Discharged to Army Reserve at Brecon on 8/12/83. Medal for South Africa with clasp '1877–8–9'. (Ref. 'C' and 'Ba' rolls, also 'D' list.)

25B/801 Private   COLE Thomas
Attested at Monmouth on 23/3/76, aged 20 years 10 months. Posted to 2/24th on 20/6/76. Served in 'B' Company at the defence of Rorke's Drift. Killed in action. (Appendix A.) Mentioned in Lieutenant Chard's official report on the action, also in letters by Private Hook and Corporal Lyons. He is buried in the cemetery at Rorke's Drift and his name appears on the monument. Medal for South Africa with clasp '1877–8–9'. (Ref. 'C' and 'B' rolls.)

25B/1396 Private   COLLINS Thomas
Born at Camrose, Haverfordwest, Pembroke; trade – labourer. Religion : C/E. Attested at Monmouth on 22/5/77, aged 22 years. Previously served in the Monmouth Militia. Description : 5' 6½" tall, fresh complexion, grey eyes, light brown hair. Served in South Africa, Mediterranean, India and Burma (medal and clasps 'Burma 1885–7 and 1887–9'). Served in 'B' Company at the defence of Rorke's Drift. Re-engaged for the South Wales Borderers (SWB 28) at Ranikhet, Bengal, on 19/8/89. As a result of his service and the climate, he suffered from rheumatism, and following a medical examination at Netley he was invalided as 'unfit for further service' on 16/6/91. Medal for South Africa with clasp '1877–8–9'. (Ref. 'C' and 'B' rolls, also 'D' list.)

25B/906 Private   CONNOLLY John
Born at Trevethin, Monmouth; trade – labourer. Religion : R/C. Attested at Newport on 20/11/76, aged 20 years 8 months. Description : 5' 6½" tall, fresh complexion, blue eyes, light brown hair. Previously served in Monmouth Militia. Posted to 2/24th on 25/11/76. He served in 'C' Company and was a patient in the hospital at Rorke's Drift.

Mentioned in an account by Private Hook – wrongly named as Conley and injury incorrectly described as a 'broken leg'. In actual fact, Connolly was suffering from synovitis due to a partial dislocation of the left knee, caused whilst loading a wagon at the Lower Tugela River. He was brought before an Invaliding Board in Natal on 11/3/79, and recommended for return to this country. Following an examination by a medical board at Netley he was found unfit for further service and invalided from the army on 25/8/79. Medal for South Africa clasp '1877–8–9'. (Ref. 'C' roll which gives his number as '106', and 'Ba' roll, also 'D' list.)

2-24/2310 Private   CONNORS Anthony
Date of attestation not traced. He arrived in India to join the 2/24th on 28/12/71. In July 1873 he was sentenced to 168 days hard labour at Millbank Prison. Served in 'B' Company at the defence of Rorke's Drift. Sent to Netley on 18/7/80. No trace of date of discharge. Medal for South Africa with clasp '1877–8–9'. (Ref. 'C' roll which gives his name incorrectly as 'Arthur', also on 'B' roll with wrong initial 'H' amended to 'A' on 'Ba' roll, also on 'D' list.)

2-24/1323 Private   CONNORS Timothy
Born at Killeaty, Co. Cork; trade – labourer. Attested at Bandon on 15/3/60. Description : 5' 4¾" tall, fair complexion, blue eyes, dark brown hair. Served in India, Mauritius, South Africa and Gibraltar. Served in 'B' Company at the defence of Rorke's Drift. Re-enlisted at Rangoon on 26/7/67. He was discharged at Colchester on 2/5/82, having served 21 years 7 months (L.S.G.C. medal). Intended place of residence: Lough, near Bandon, Co. Cork. Medal for South Africa with clasp '1877–8–9'. (Ref. 'C' and 'B' rolls, also 'D' list.)

2-24/2453 Private   COOPER William
Date of attestation not traced. Posted to 2/24th in January 1873 when stationed at Warley. Served in 'F' Company at the defence of Rorke's Drift. Sent to Netley on 1/2/80 and subsequently discharged to the Army Reserve. Medal for South Africa with clasp '1877–8–9' issued on 17/6/81. (Ref. 'C' and 'Ba' rolls, also 'D' list.)

25B/470 Private   DAVIES George
Attested at Wrexham on 15/10/74, aged 21 years. Posted to 2/24th on 4/12/74. Served in 'B' Company at the defence of Rorke's Drift. There is no trace of his name in the regimental records after 4/3/81, and it is presumed that he was discharged on or about this date. Medal for South Africa with clasp '1877–8–9'. (Ref. 'B' roll only.)

25B/1363 Private   DAVIS William Henry
Born at St. Bartholomew's, London; trade – porter. Religion : C/E. Attested at Bow Street Police Court on 26/2/77, aged 24 years.

Description: 5′ 4½″ tall, dark complexion, hazel eyes, dark brown hair. Served in South Africa, Mediterranean and India. Served in 'B' Company in the defence of Rorke's Drift. Transferred to Army Reserve on 21/1/83. Discharged on 10/8/89. Medal for South Africa with clasp '1877–8–9'. (Ref. 'B' roll only.)

25B/1178 Private DAW Thomas
Born at Merriott, Somerset; trade–labourer. Religion: C/E. Attested at Crewkerne on 5/2/77, aged 18 years 6 months. Description: 5′ 4½″ tall, florid complexion, grey eyes, brown hair. Served in South Africa, India and Mediterranean. Served in 'B' Company at the defence of Rorke's Drift. Served in South Wales Borderers from 1/8/81 but did not transfer to regiment. Discharged to Army Reserve on 31/5/83. Medal for South Africa with clasp '1877–8–9'. (Ref. 'B' roll only.)

25B/1467 Private DEACON George
Born at Bank; trade – clerk. Attested at Chatham on 10/11/77, aged 19 years. Confined in cells from 12th to 18th March 1878. Served in 'B' Company at the defence of Rorke's Drift. Mentioned in an account by Private Hitch, who names him incorrectly as 'Deakin'. Confined in cells from 11th to 24th February 1879 for 'Failing to obey an order'. Deserted at Pietermaritzburg on 9/9/79. Medal for South Africa with clasp '1877–8–9'. Medal rolls searched on 6/1/20 under 19/Inf/239 and 2177. (Ref. 'C' and 'B' rolls.)

25B/1357 Private DEANE Michael
Attested on 10/3/77. Posted to 2/24th on 26/1/78. Served in 'B' Company at the defence of Rorke's Drift. Deserted at Gibraltar on 22/7/80. Did not, therefore, receive his campaign medal for South Africa with clasp '1877–8–9'. (Ref. 'C' and 'B' rolls, the latter giving his initial incorrectly as W, also on 'D' list.)

2–24/1697 Private DICK James
Born at Island Magee, Co. Antrim; trade – labourer. Attested at Belfast on 3/2/65, aged 18 years. Description: 5′ 7″ tall, fresh complexion, grey eyes, curly brown hair. Served in India, South Africa and Mediterranean. May have served in 'B' Company at the defence of Rorke's Drift. Re-engaged at Secunderabad on 18/11/71. Discharged at his own request on 20/2/89, having completed 24 years 15 days service. (L.S. and G.C. Medal.) Medal for South Africa with clasp '1877–8–9'. Incorrectly named on medal rolls as W Dicks (see next entry). (Ref. 'B' roll only named as 1697 W. Dicks.) In view of the confusion regarding this man and 1634 Pte. William Dicks, it is impossible to determine whether either or both were present at the defence of Rorke's Drift. James Dick was illiterate and therefore may not have been aware of the confusion regarding his true name.

2–24/1634 Private DICKS William
Born at Islington, London; trade–labourer. Attested at Westminster Police Court on 26/11/64, aged 17 years. Description: 5′ 6″ tall, fresh complexion, brown eyes, brown hair. Transferred from 1/24th to 2/24th on 31/1/65. Served in India, South Africa and Mediterranean. Re-engaged at Secunderabad on 6/8/72. Appointed Lance-Corporal 17/9/77. Promoted Corporal 14/11/77. Appointed Lance-Sergeant 3/5/78. Reduced to Private on 19/9/78. May have served in 'B' Company at the defence of Rorke's Drift. Served in South Wales Borderers from 1/7/81, but did not transfer to regiment. Next of kin: Sister, Mrs. A. Framplar, 42 Havelock Street, London. Discharged on 9/2/86, having completed 21 years 65 days service. Medal for South Africa with clasp '1877–8–9'. (Ref. 'C' roll only.) The official records frequently confuse him with James ('William') Dick (see previous entry). For example, his medical history sheet originally bore James Dick's number 1697, which was later amended to the correct number 1634, also on 'D' list.)

25B/971 Private DRISCOLL Thomas
Attested on 15/12/76. Posted to 2/24th on 22/1/77. Served in South Africa and India. Served in 'B' Company at the defence of Rorke's Drift. Transferred from 'B' to 'A' Company on 29/1/79. Served in South Wales Borderers but did not transfer to regiment. Date of discharge not traced. Medal for South Africa with clasp '1877–8–9'. (Ref. 'C' and 'B' rolls, also on 'D' list.)

25B/1421 Private DUNBAR James
Attested at Newport on 20/6/77. Posted to 2/24th on 13/12/77. Appointed Lance-Corporal 1/2/78. Promoted Corporal 15/3/78. Reduced to Private and awarded 28 days hard labour on 22/7/78. Served in 'B' Company at the defence of Rorke's Drift. Mentioned in Lieutenant Chard's letter to Queen Victoria, also in an account by Private Hook. Served in India and returned to England on 11/4/83. Discharged to Army Reserve on 9/10/83. Intended place of residence: Newport. Medal for South Africa with clasp '1877–8–9'. (Ref. 'C' and 'B' rolls, also on 'D' list.)

25B/972 Private EDWARDS George
(Alias George Edward Orchard.) Born at Charles Street, St. James's, Bristol, in 1855. His real name being George Edward Orchard. He worked as a shoemaker's apprentice and in the building trade before enlistment. Attested at Newport on 24/11/76, aged 21 years. To 2/24th on 15/12/76. Served in 'B' Company at the defence of Rorke's Drift. Confined to cells for 10 days during June 1880. Served in India and returned to England on 29/1/83. Discharged in 1889. Intended place of residence: Withy Mill, Paulton, Somerset. Married (Wife – Rena, Elizabeth), and had 10 children. Lived at New Pit, Paulton, Somerset, and worked in a

boat factory. Died on 14/2/04 and is buried at Paulton Cemetery. Medal for South Africa with clasp '1877–8–9'. Donated to Brecon Museum. (Ref. 'C' and 'B' rolls, also on 'D' list.)

25B/969   Private   FAGAN John
Attested on 13/12/76. Posted to 2/24th on 22/1/77. Convicted by Civil Power to 5 days imprisonment on 7/11/78. Served in 'B' Company at the defence of Rorke's Drift. Killed in action. (Appendix A.) Effects claimed under E/77478/? Mentioned by Lieutenant Chard in his report on the action. He is buried in the cemetery at Rorke's Drift and his name appears on the monument. Medal for South Africa with clasp '1877–8–9'. (Ref. 'C' and 'B' rolls.)

2–24/2429   Private   GEE Edward
Attested in November 1872. Transferred from 1/24th to 2/24th on 1/1/73. Served in 'B' Company at the defence of Rorke's Drift. Sent to Netley on 1/2/80. Transferred to Army Reserve under AGL 120, date of transfer not recorded. Medal for South Africa with clasp '1877–8–9'. (Ref. 'C' and 'B' rolls, also on 'D' list.)

25B/798   Private   HAGAN James
Born at Neenagh, Co. Tipperary; trade – labourer. Religion : R/C. Attested at Monmouth on 23/3/76, aged 18 years 7 months. Previously served in Royal Monmouth Militia. Description : 5' 6½" tall, grey eyes, brown hair, fresh complexion. Next of kin (originally given as sister) Mary Ann Martland, N.E. America. Served in South Africa, Gibraltar and India. Served in 'B' Company at the defence of Rorke's Drift. To South Wales Borderers Depot on 25/11/81. Transferred to Army Reserve on 24/3/82. Recalled to army service at Salford, Lancashire, on 3/8/82. Re-transferred to Army Reserve on 8/2/83. Married Catherine Barry at Treforrest, Glamorgan, on 8/7/72. Discharged from Army Reserve on 23/3/88. Medal for South Africa with clasp '1877–8–9'. (Ref. 'C' roll only, also on 'D' list incorrectly named as 'Hogan'.)

25B/1062   Private   HARRIS John
Born at Crickhowell, Breconshire; trade – labourer. Religion : Wesleyan. Attested at Brecon on 15/1/77, aged 19 years. Previously served in the Royal South Wales Borderers Militia Rifles. Description : 5' 6" tall, sallow complexion, grey eyes, light brown hair. Posted to 2/24th on 31/1/77. Served in India, South Africa and Gibraltar. Served in 'B' Company at the defence of Rorke's Drift. (Confirmed by entries in his service documents, 'Present at Defence of Rorke's Drift' and 'Compensation – loss of kit at defence of Rorke's Drift'. He was brought before a medical board at Gibraltar on 16/7/80 and invalided from the service as a result of chronic osteo-arthritis. Sent to Netley on 24/7/80 and discharged as unfit for further

service on 14/2/80. Intended place of residence : Wandsworth, Surrey. Medal for South Africa with clasp '1877–8–9'. (Ref. 'C' and 'Ba' rolls, also 'D' list.)

2–24/1769   Private   HAYDEN Garret
Attested at Dublin on 9/12/65, aged 18 years. Description : 5' 5" tall. Joined the battalion at Port Blair on 11/7/67. Appointed Drummer on 1/10/68. Reduced to Private on 10/9/75. He served in 'D' Company and was a patient in the hospital at Rorke's Drift. He was mutilated and killed by the Zulus when they broke into the hospital. (Appendix A.) Mentioned in Lieutenant Chard's official report on the action, also mentioned in letters by Private Probert, Private Price and Sergeant George Smith (pages 98, 99, 139 *The Red Soldier*). At the time of his death Hayden's home was in John Street, Brecon. Effects claimed by his father. He is buried in the cemetery at Rorke's Drift and his name appears on the monument. Medal for South Africa with clasp '1879'. (Ref. 'C' and 'B' rolls.)

25B/1362   Private   HITCH Frederick V.C.
Born at Edmonton, London, on 28/11/56. Religion : C/E. Attested at Westminster Police Court on 7/3/77; trade – bricklayer's labourer. Age given as 20 years 3 months. (He was illiterate at the time of his enlistment.) Description : 5' 8¾" tall, fresh complexion, hazel eyes, brown hair. Posted to 2/24th on 11/5/77. Served in 'B' Company and wounded in action at Rorke's Drift. (Appendix A.) Mentioned in Lieutenant Chard's report on the action, also in his letter to Queen Victoria. Hitch wrote an account of his part in the battle, and he is also mentioned in a narrative by Private Hook. Private Hitch was awarded the Victoria Cross for his gallant conduct at Rorke's Drift, and received his decoration from Queen Victoria at Netley on 12/8/79, the citation (L.G. 2/5) reading : 'William Allen, Corporal, and Frederick Hitch, Private, 2nd Battalion, 24th Regiment. It was chiefly due to the courageous conduct of these men at Rorke's Drive that communication was kept up with the hospital at all. Holding together, at all costs, a most dangerous post, raked in reverse by the enemy's fire from the hill, they were both severely wounded; but their determined conduct enabled the patients to be withdrawn from the hospital, and when incapacitated by their wounds from fighting they continued, as soon as their wounds had been dressed, to serve out ammunition to their comrades through the night.' Hitch was sent to Netley on 10/6/79, and following examination by a medical board on 28/7/79, he was invalided from the service on 25/8/79. Intended place of residence : Southgate, Middlesex. He obtained employment as a commissionaire at the Royal United Services Institute, Whitehall, and whilst there his V.C. was stolen from his coat. A replacement V.C. was ordered by King Edward VII and this was

presented to him in 1908. In later years Hitch became a cab driver in London, and resided at 62 Cranbrook Road, Chiswick. He died on 7/1/13, and was buried at Chiswick cemetery on 11/1/13. Medal for South Africa with clasp '1877–8–9', issued on 23/5/81. (Ref. 'C' and 'B' rolls, also 'D' list.)

25B/1373 Private   HOOK Alfred Henry V.C.

Born at Churcham, Gloucestershire, in May 1850. Attested at Monmouth on 13/3/77; trade – farm labourer. Previously served in the Monmouth Militia for a period of five years. (He was a married man and enlisted in the regular army as the result of a foreclosure on a mortgage. Posted to 2/24th on 11/5/77. Served in 'B' Company and slightly wounded whilst defending the hospital at Rorke's Drift. (Appendix A.) Mentioned in Lieutenant Chard's report on the action and also in his letter to Queen Victoria. Hook wrote two accounts of his experiences during the battle. Transferred from 'B' to 'G' Company on 29/1/79, and appointed servant to Major Black. Private Hook was awarded the Victoria Cross and received his decoration from Sir Garnet Wolseley at Rorke's Drift on 3/8/79, the citation (L.G. 2/5/79) reading: 'Private John Williams was posted with Private Joseph Williams and Private William Horrigan, 1st Battalion, 24th Regiment, in a distant room of the hospital, which they held for more than an hour, so long as they had a round of ammunition left. As communication was for the time cut off, the Zulus were able to advance and burst open the door; dragged out Private Joseph Williams, with two of the patients, and assegaied them. Whilst the Zulus were occupied with the slaughter of these men, a lull took place during which Private John Williams, who with two patients, were the only men left alive in this ward, succeeded in knocking a hole in the partition, and in taking the patients into the next ward, where he found Private Hook. These two men together, one man working whilst the other fought and held the enemy with his bayonet, broke through three more partitions, and were thus enabled to bring out eight patients through a small window into the inner line of defence.' Hook purchased his discharge for £18 on 25/6/80. On returning to his home at Churcham he discovered his property had been sold and his wife, who believed he had been killed, had re-married. He moved to Sydenham Hill, London, and on 26/12/81 he commenced employment as a labourer at the British Museum, later becoming a cloakroom attendant in the reading room. He married Ada Taylor at Islington on 10/4/97. Hook suffered from ill-health, but despite this he served for many years as a Sergeant in the 1st Vol. Battalion, Royal Fusiliers. His health continued to deteriorate and he was advised to retire, which he did on 31/12/04. Harry (as he preferred to be called) Hook returned to Gloucester and died of pulmonary tuberculosis on 12/3/05 at 2 Osborn Villas,

Roseberry Avenue, Gloucester. He was buried in the churchyard at Churcham. Medal for South Africa with clasp '1877–8–9'. (Ref. 'C' and 'B' rolls, also on 'D' list.)

25B/1061 Private   JOBBINS John

Attested at Pontypool on 12/1/76. Previously served in Monmouth Militia. Posted to 2/24th on 31/1/77. Served in 'B' Company at the defence of Rorke's Drift. Described the battle in a letter to his father who was then working at the Crown Hotel, Pontypool. Returned to England from India on 29/1/83. Discharge not traced. Died at Pontnewenydd, Monmouthshire, in December 1934, aged 79 years. Medal for South Africa with clasp '1877–8–9'. (Ref. 'C' and 'B' roll, also on 'D' list.)

25B/1428 Private   JONES Evan

Born at Ebbw Vale, Monmouthshire; trade – labourer. Attested at Brecon on 20/7/77, aged 18 years 4 months. Previously served in Royal Monmouth Engineers. Description: 5' 4½" tall, fresh complexion, grey eyes, light brown hair. Religion: R/C. Posted to 2/24th on 26/1/78. Served in South Africa, Mediterranean, India and Burma (Medal with clasp 'Burma 1887–9'). Served in 'B' Company at the defence of Rorke's Drift. Appointed Drummer 8/8/80. Reverted Private 31/10/84. Appointed Drummer 17/12/87. Served in South Wales Borderers from 21/7/89, but did not transfer to the regiment. Re-engaged at Ranikhet on 24/8/89. Transferred to Gloucester Regiment 30/9/89, to then unattached list on 10/10/89. Transferred to South Wales Borderers (SWB 2835) on 31/12/92. Reverted to Private on 16/12/93. Appointed Lance-Corporal 13/7/94. Appointed Drummer 25/9/95. To South Wales Borderers at Brecon on 27/5/96 as permanent staff – 4th Battalion. Allowed to continue in the service beyond 21 years. Claimed discharge on 17/10/99. Married Alice Evans (widow) at Welshpool Registry Office on 15/10/98. Attested at Welshpool on 17/3/00 for Royal Northern Reserve Battalion (1226); trade – musician. Discharged on 16/3/01. Served in Montgomery Yeomanry, dates of service not traced. (Territorial Long Service Medal.) Attested at Aberystwyth on 15/4/15 for 2nd/7th Royal Welch Fusiliers (291067). Appointed Drummer 9/5/15. Appointed Lance-Corporal 29/8/15, Acting Corporal 24/8/16, Acting Lance-Sergeant 7/8/17. Discharged on 15/2/19. Attested at Wrexham on 12/8/19 as a Private in the Northumberland Fusiliers (99052). Discharged on 10/2/20. Intended place of residence: 18 Union Street, Welshpool. (At the time of his discharge he had served for 43 years. Died in 1931 aged 72 years and was buried at Welshpool. Medal for South Africa with clasp '1877–8–9'. (Ref. 'C' roll which shows him incorrectly as Evan Jordes, and 'B' roll which names him correctly, also on 'D' list.)

25B/970   Private   JONES John

Attested on 13/12/76. Posted to 2/24th on 22/1/77. Served in 'B' Company at the defence of Rorke's Drift. Served in South Wales Borderers but did not transfer to the regiment. Returned to England from India on 29/1/83. Date of discharge not traced. Medal for South Africa with clasp '1877–8–9'. (Ref. 'C' and 'B' rolls, also on 'D' list.)

25B/1179   Private   JONES John

Born at Merthyr, Glamorgan; trade – labourer. Attested at Tredegar on 2/2/77, aged 24 years. Previously served in Cardiff Militia. Description : 5′ 5½″ tall, dark complexion, blue eyes, brown hair. Religion : C/E. Posted to 2/24th on 23/2/77. Served in South Africa, Gibraltar and India. Served in 'B' Company at the defence of Rorke's Drift. To South Wales Borderers on 1/7/81, but did not transfer to regiment. Next of kin, cousin, D. Morgan, High Street, Merthyr Tydfil. Transferred to Army Reserve on 28/6/83. Discharged on 6/2/89. Medal for South Africa with clasp '1877–8–9'. (Ref. 'C' and 'B' rolls, on 'D' list.)

25B/716   Private   JONES Robert V.C.

Born at Penrose, Raglan, Monmouth; trade – labourer. Attested at Monmouth on 10/1/76, aged 18 years 5 months. Description : 5′ 7½″ tall, fresh complexion, grey eyes, brown hair. Religion : C/E. Posted to 2/24th on 28/1/76. Served in South Africa, Gibraltar and India. Served in 'B' Company and slightly wounded whilst defending the hospital at Rorke's Drift. (Appendix A.) Mentioned in Lieutenant Chard's report on the action and also in his letter to Queen Victoria. He is also mentioned in an account by Private Hook. Private Jones was awarded the Victoria Cross for his gallant conduct at Rorke's Drift, and received his decoration from Sir Garnet Wolseley at Utrecht on 11/9/79, the citation (L.G. 2/5/79) reading: 'In another ward facing the hill, at Rorke's Drift, on 22nd and 23rd January 1879, Privates William Jones and Robert Jones defended the post until six out of the seven patients it contained had been removed. The seventh, Lance-Sergeant Maxfield, 2/24th Foot, was delirious with fever. Although they had previously dressed him, they were unable to induce him to move. When Private Robert Jones volunteered to endeavour to carry him away, he found that he had been stabbed by the Zulus as he lay on his bed.' To South Wales Borderers but did not transfer to regiment. Served at the Depot from 1/7/81 to 26/1/82, then to Army Reserve. Recalled on 2/8/82 and re-transferred to Reserve on 7/2/83. Discharged on 26/1/88. Married Elizabeth Hopkins at Llantilio on 7/1/85. Died on 6/9/98 and is buried at Peterchurch, Hereford. Medal for South Africa with clasp '1877–8–9'. (Ref. 'C' and 'B' rolls, on 'D' list.)

2–24/593   Private   JONES William V.C.

Born at Evesham, Worcester; trade – shoemaker. Attested at Birmingham on 21/12/58, aged 19 years. Description : 5′ 5″ tall, sallow complexion, brown eyes, brown hair. Served in Mauritius, East Indies and South Africa. Promoted Corporal 1/9/59. Reduced to Private 4/9/60. Re-engaged at Rangoon on 10/1/68, to complete 21 years service. An unconfirmed story published in the *Natal Mercury* on Wednesday, 18th June 1879 states : 'When he (Jones) came here with his regiment his wife came with him, but after he had been at the front some time she became dangerously ill, and he obtained leave of absence to come down to attend to her. Jones took a little room in a house facing the St. George's Hotel Tap, and there, by working night and day repairing boots and shoes, he managed to earn many comforts for his then dying wife. He was a steady, plodding fellow, but his wife was beyond recovery, and he remained with her until she died. The next day he buried her remains, and at once started off to join his regiment . . . ' Served in 'B' Company and assisted in the defence of the hospital at Rorke's Drift. Mentioned in Lieutenant Chard's report on the action, and also in his letter to Queen Victoria. Mentioned in an account by Private Hook. Jones was awarded the Victoria Cross and received his decoration from the Queen at Windsor Castle on 13/1/80, the citation reading : 'In another ward facing the hill, at Rorke's Drift, on 22nd and 23rd January 1879, Privates William Jones and Robert Jones defended the post until six out of the seven patients it contained had been removed. Lance-Sergeant Maxfield, 2/24th Foot, was delirious with fever. Although they had previously dressed him, they were unable to induce him to move. When Private Robert Jones volunteered to endeavour to carry him away he found that he had been stabbed by the Zulus as he lay on his bed.' Jones was examined by a medical board at Pietermaritzburg on 3/9/79 and was found to be suffering from chronic rheumatism. Invalided to England, he was sent to Netley and discharged on 2/2/80 as 'unfit for further service due to chronic rheumatism of the joints'. Intended place of residence, 174 Lupin Street, Birmingham. Jones, having re-married, later moved to Rutland Street, Chorlton, Manchester. In 1912 he was found wandering the streets, and although able to identify himself, he could give no address. He was taken to Bridge St. Workhouse, where, later, having been identified by his wife, he was returned to his home. Jones was found to be ill and in an impoverished state. He had been forced to sell his V.C. some twenty years previously when out of work and unable to provide for his family. He died at 6 Brampton Street, Ardwick, Manchester, on 15/4/13. He was buried on 21/4/13 in a public grave at Phillip Park Cemetery (Bradford Ward), Manchester. Medal for South Africa with clasp '1877–8–9' issued on 5/9/81. (Ref. 'C' and 'B' rolls, also on 'D' list.)

2–24/2437 Private   JUDGE Peter

Date of attestation not traced. Posted to 2/24th in January 1873. Awarded a good shooting prize in 1878. Served in 'B' Company at the defence of Rorke's Drift. Returned to England from India on 29/1/83. Discharged to Army Reserve (AGL 105), date not traced. Medal for South Africa with clasp '1877–8–9' issued on 28/3/82. (The medal roll gives his initial incorrectly as 'T'.) (Ref. 'C' and 'B' rolls, also 'D' list.)

25B/972   Private   KEARS Patrick

Born at Liverpool, Lancashire; trade – labourer. Attested at Liverpool on 6/12/76, aged 19 years. Previously served in 2nd Royal Lancashire Militia. Description : 5' 4¾" tall, fresh complexion, blue eyes, brown hair. Religion : R/C. Served in South Africa from 1/2/78 to 1/10/79. Served in 'B' Company at the defence of Rorke's Drift. (Confirmed by an entry on his service documents 'Took part in the Defence of Rorke's Drift'.) Examined by a medical board at Pietermaritzburg on 23/7/79 as a result of debility, and recommended for a 'change of climate'. Sent to Netley on 3/10/79 and then to Depot at Brecon on 17/10/79. Married Annie Lewis at Brecon on 16/11/80. Transferred to Army Reserve on 1/2/83 and discharged on 8/12/88. Medal for South Africa with clasp '1877–8–9'. (Ref. 'C' and 'B' rolls, also 'D' list.)

25B/1386 Private   KILEY Michael

Attested at Brecon on 24/4/77. Posted to 2/24th on 11/5/77. Confined by Civil Power on 7/10/78 and sentenced to 5 days hard labour. Served in 'B' Company at the defence of Rorke's Drift. Confined on 11/3/79, tried by Courts Martial for insubordination on 17/3/79, sentenced to receive 50 lashes and to be fined £1. Again confined by Civil Power on 26/9/79. On release he was sent to the General Depot on 1/1/80 and appears to have been struck off the strength. He made remittances to Helen Kiley and Mary Sullivan. Transferred from 'B' to 'G' Company on 29/1/79. Medal for South Africa with clasp '1877–8–9'. (Ref. 'C' roll which names him incorrectly as Riley. Correctly named on 'B' list, also 'D' list.)

25B/963   Private   LEWIS David

Attested at Brecon on 9/12/76. Posted to 2/24th on 22/1/77. Served in 'B' Company at the defence of Rorke's Drift. No trace of his further service or date of discharge found. He made a pay allowance to Miss Emma Owens. Medal for South Africa with clasp '1877–8–9'. A search of the medal roll (for the Royal Hospital, Chelsea) was made on 7/5/28 under 68/L/261. (Ref. 'B' roll only.)

2–24/1528 Private   LINES Henry

Attested at Birmingham on 11/1064, aged 18 years. Description : 5' 5" tall. Served in Mauritius, South Africa and India. Promoted Corporal 4/7/68, Sergeant 12/8/69. Reduced to Private 14/1/70. Attended a course at the School of Musketry, Hythe, in 1874. Served in 'B' Company at the defence of Rorke's Drift. Appointed Lance-Corporal 2/11/81. Promoted Corporal 31/1/82. Reduced to Private on 6/3/83. Returned to England from India in October 1883. Date of discharge not traced. He died at Horden, near West Hartlepool, in 1922 at the age of 76 years. Medal for South Africa with clasp '1877–8–9'. (Ref. 'C' and 'Ba' rolls, also 'D' list.)

25B/1409 Private   LLOYD David

Born at Dowlais, Merthyr, Glamorgan; trade – collier. Attested at Brecon on 5/6/77, aged 19 years 1 month. Previously served in Royal South Wales Borderers. Description : 5' 4½" tall, fresh complexion, grey eyes, brown hair. Religion : C/E. Posted to 2/24th on 3/8/77. Served in South Africa, Mediterranean and India. Served in 'B' Company at the defence of Rorke's Drift. Returned to England from India on 30/11/83. Transferred to Army Reserve on 13/12/83. Discharged on 5/6/89. Married Mary Price at Merthyr Tydfil on 21/1/85. Medal for South Africa with clasp '1877–8–9'. (Ref. 'C' and 'B' rolls, also 'D' list.)

25B/1176 Private   LOCKHART Thomas

Born at St. Michael's, Manchester; trade – fitter. Attested at Derby on 6/2/77, aged 19 years. Description : 5' 9¼" tall, fresh complexion, dark grey eyes, brown hair. Religion : C/E. Posted to 2/24th on 23/2/77. Served in South Africa and Gibraltar. Served in 'B' Company at the defence of Rorke's Drift. He returned to England from Gibraltar on 11/8/80. In September 1881, whilst at Colchester, he was attacked by other soldiers and received a blow on the head which caused him to suffer from epilepsy. Following an examination by an invaliding board at Colchester on 30/1/82 his epilepsy was found to be of a 'permanent nature', being 'induced by an injury to the head received at the hands of soldiers of the Colchester Garrison who waylaid and maliciously illtreated him without provocation and notice – causing a fracture of the orbit and displacement of certain other bones'. It was considered that his disability would 'very seriously interfere with his powers of supporting himself'. He was found unfit for further service and discharged on 6/2/82. Intended place of residence, 41 Butler Street, Manchester. Medal for South Africa with clasp '1877–8–9'. (Ref. 'C' and 'Ba' rolls, on 'D' list.)

25B/1304 Private   LODGE Joshua

Attested on 4/3/77. Posted to 2/24th on 16/1/78. Served in 'B' Company at the defence of Rorke's Drift. Appointed Lance-Corporal 1/11/81. Promoted Corporal 1/1/82. Reduced to Private on 21/7/82. Served in South Wales Borderers but did not transfer to regiment. Returned to England from India on 1/5/83. Date of discharge not traced. Medal for South Africa with clasp '1877–8–9'. (Ref. 'C' and 'B' rolls, on 'D' list.)

25B/942   Private   LYNCH Thomas Michael

Born at Limerick, Co. Limerick; trade – letter sorter. Attested at London on 10/11/76, aged 18 years 2 months. Description: 5′ 4¼″ tall, fresh complexion, blue eyes, brown hair. Religion: R/C. Served in South Africa, India and Gibraltar. Served in 'B' Company at the defence of Rorke's Drift. Appointed Drummer 1/6/82. Transferred to Army Reserve on 30/3/83. Rejoined the Colours on 16/10/84 and posted to the Cameron Highlanders. Transferred to permanent staff, as a Drummer, 4th Battalion, Argyll and Sutherland Highlanders, on 14/1/85. Convicted of 'Felony' by Civil Power on 9/3/88 and in consequence discharged from the service on 17/4/88, at Stirling. Next of kin: Mother – Covent Garden, London. Medal for South Africa with clasp '1877–8–9'. (Ref. 'B' roll only.)

2–24/1441   Private   LYONS John

Born in Killaloe, O'Brien's Bridge, Co. Clare; trade – labourer. Attested for the 87th Foot at Ennis on 31/3/59, aged 22 years. Description: 5′ 7¾″ tall, fresh complexion, grey eyes, red hair. Transferred to 2/24th Foot 1/7/61. Served in Mauritius, East Indies and South Africa. Served in 'A' Company and was a patient in the hospital at Rorke's Drift at the time of the Zulu attack. Awarded the medal for Long Service and Good Conduct with gratuity of £5. Sent from South Africa to England and admitted to Netley on 10/6/79. Examined by a medical board at Netley on 16/7/79 and found to be suffering from 'General debility at the Cape 1879. Treated for supposed Bright's Disease referable to exposure to wet and cold – after 10 days treatment at Rorke's Drift was transferred to other hospitals. A very clear and honest case of a worn-out old soldier – scarcely able to earn anything for his family'. Discharged as unfit for further service on 4/8/79. Intended place of residence, Manchester. Medal for South Africa with clasp '1877–8–9'. (Ref. 'C' and 'Ba' rolls, on 'D' list.)

2–24/1731   Private   MANLEY John

Attested at Cork on 17/4/65, aged 15 years 3 months. Description: 5′ 1″ tall. Appointed Drummer on 1/12/66. Served at the Depot until posted to 2/24th about December 1868. Reduced to Private on 14/7/68. Appointed Drummer 1/1/69. Reduced to Private 7/8/76. Served in 'A' Company and was a patient in the hospital at Rorke's Drift at the time of the Zulu attack. Sent to Netley on 1/2/80. Date of discharge not traced. Medal for South Africa with clasp '1877–8–9' issued on 17/6/81. (Ref. 'C' and 'Ba' rolls, on 'D' list wrongly named as Momley.)

25B/964   Private   MARSHALL James

Born at Hitchin, Hertfordshire; trade – chimney sweep. Attested at London on 4/12/76, aged 20 years 9 months. Description: 5′ 6″ tall, fresh complexion, hazel eyes, brown hair. Religion: C/E. Served in South Africa, India and Gibraltar. Confined on 1/8/77, tried and convicted of 'Fraudulent enlistment' on 3/9/77, released on 25/11/77. Re-convicted on 22/10/78, released on 11/11/78. Served in 'B' Company at the defence of Rorke's Drift. Served in South Wales Borderers but did not transfer to regiment. Transferred to Army Reserve on 28/6/83. Discharged at Brecon on 4/12/88. Medal for South Africa with clasp '1877–8–9'. (Ref. 'C' roll only, also on 'D' list.)

25B/756   Private   MARTIN Henry

Born at Binegar, Somerset; trade – quarryman. Attested at Newport on 10/2/76, aged 19 years. Posted to 2/24th on 10/3/76. Served in 'B' Company at the defence of Rorke's Drift. Returned to England from India on 28/10/81. Date of discharge not traced. Married (Wife – Polly), no children. Died in 1937 and was buried at Binegar Parish Church. A memorial was erected in 1965. Medal for South Africa with clasp '1877–8–9'. (Ref. 'C' and 'B' rolls, also on 'D' list.)

25B/1284   Private   MASON Charles

Born at Aldgate, London; trade – solder maker. Attested at London on 26/2/77, aged 22 years 5 months. Description: 5′ 6¼″ tall, fresh complexion, hazel eyes, brown hair. Religion: C/E. Served in South Africa, Gibraltar and India. Served in 'B' Company at the defence of Rorke's Drift. Transferred to Army Reserve on 28/6/83. Recalled to 1st South Wales Borderers on 30/10/84. Discharged on 26/2/89. Medal for South Africa with clasp '1877–8–9'. (Ref. 'C' and 'B' rolls, also on 'D' list.)

2–24/1527   Private   MINEHAN Michael

Born at Castlehaven, Co. Cork; trade – groom. Attested at Bandon on 14/10/64, aged 19 years. Description: 5′ 9¾″ tall, fair complexion, blue eyes, brown hair. Found to have joined West Coast Artillery Militia on 9/5/64. Allowed to continue in 2/24th Foot. Served in India, South Africa and Mediterranean. Re-engaged at Secunderabad on 7/10/71. Served in 'B' Company at the defence of Rorke's Drift. Penn-Symons wrote: 'Minehan was a great pal of mine; he was right-hand man, front rank of 'B' Company, who knew his drill well and had often kept me straight.' At one stage of the battle at Rorke's Drift, Minehan had been posted in the kraal. The day after the fight he was unable to speak as a result of exhaustion, but had taken Penn-Symons to the corner of the kraal at which he had been stationed. By means of gesticulation he indicated the body of a Zulu, partly hidden under the straw. It appeared that during the battle the

Zulu had crawled under the straw and grabbed Minehan by the leg. Minehan had 'prodded' the straw with his bayonet and one such thrust had penetrated the Zulu's body, killing him instantly. Private Minehan was again posted to India on 12/8/80 and whilst there contracted cholera on 15/4/84. He was invalided to England on 30/4/84, and following his examination by a medical board at Netley on 29/6/84 he was found unfit for further service and discharged on 2/9/84. Next of kin: sister, M. Regan, Castletown, Co. Cork. Minehan was apparently highly regarded by his officers and received a testimonial from Lieutenant Bromhead on 24/3/84. Medal for South Africa with clasp '1877–8–9'. He is named incorrectly in the medal roll as 'Minshaw'. (Ref. 'C' roll which gives his name incorrectly as 'Michan', and 'B' roll which names him correctly, also on 'D' list.)

25B/968   Private   MOFFATT Thomas
Attested on 13/12/76. Posted to 2/24th on 22/1/77. Served in 'B' Company at the defence of Rorke's Drift. Transferred from 'B' to 'G' Company on 29/1/79. Served in India and returned to England on 27/1/83. Date of discharge not recorded. Died at Runcorn, Cheshire, aged 80 years. Medal for South Afrct with clasp '1877–8–9'. (Ref. 'C' and 'B' rolls, on 'D' list.)

25B/1342   Private   MORRIS Augustus
Born at Dublin, Co. Dublin; trade – labourer. Attested at Liverpool on 3/3/77, aged 20 years. Description: 5' 7" tall, fresh complexion, grey eyes, red hair. Religion: R/C. Served in South Africa, Gibraltar, India and Burma (medal with clasp 'Burma 1885–7'). Served in 'B' Company at the defence of Rorke's Drift. Appointed Lance-Corporal on 5/2/79. Reverted to Private on 21/10/79. Served in South Wales Borderers but did not transfer to regiment. Appointed Lance-Corporal 12/6/86. Transferred to Army Reserve on 18/12/87. Discharged on 5/3/89. Next of kin, sister – Mrs. Hughes, 46 Oliver Street, Bootle, Liverpool. Medal for South Africa with clasp '1877–8–9'. (Ref. 'C' and 'B' rolls, on 'D' list.)

25B/525   Private   MORRIS Frederick
Attested at Liverpool on 4/12/74, aged 19 years. Posted to 2/24th on 13/12/76. Served in 'B' Company at the defence of Rorke's Drift. Posted to India and died of disease at Secunderabad on 26/9/83. Medal for South Africa with clasp '1877–8–9'. (Ref. 'C' and 'B' rolls, on 'D' list.)

25B/1371   Private   MORRISON Thomas
Attested on 8/3/77. Posted to 2/24th on 11/5/77. Served in 'B' Company at the defence of Rorke's Drift. Served in India and returned to England on 26/4/83. Date of discharge not recorded. Medal for South Africa with clasp '1877–8–9'. (Ref. 'C' and 'B' rolls, on 'D' list.)

25B/662   Private   MURPHY John
Attested at Tredegar on 22/11/75, aged 19 years. Posted to 2/24th on 6/1/76. Name amended from John to James in various documents. Confined on 11/2/78 and sentenced to receive 25 lashes. Served in 'B' Company at the defence of Rorke's Drift. Returned to England from India on 28/10/83. Date of discharge not recorded. Medal for South Africa with clasp '1877–8–9'. (Ref. 'C' roll where his name is given as James, and 'Ba' roll, on list.)

25B/1279   Private   NEVILLE William
Born at Wigan, Lancashire; trade – collier. Attested at Liverpool on 23/2/77, aged 19 years. Description: 5' 5¼" tall, fresh complexion, hazel eyes, brown hair. Religion: C/E. Served in South Africa, Gibraltar and India. Served in 'B' Company at the defence of Rorke's Drift. Transferred to Army Reserve on 21/6/83. Married Sarah Elizabeth Graham at Ince-in-Makerfield on 1/6/80. Confined by Civil Power on 30/11/85, tried and convicted of assault and sentenced to 12 months imprisonment with hard labour. Released from prison on 18/5/87, he then completed his service in the Army Reserve and was discharged on 25/2/89. (He signed his service documents 'William Nevil' which may be the correct spelling of surname). Medal for South Africa with clasp '1877–8–9'. (Ref. 'C' and 'Ba' rolls, on 'D' list.)

25B/1257   Private   NORRIS Robert
Born at Liverpool, Lancashire; trade – labourer. Attested at Liverpool on 22/2/77, aged 19 years 2 months. Description: 5' 7¼" tall, fresh complexion, grey eyes, brown hair. Religion C/E. Served in South Africa, India and Mediterranean. Served in 'B' Company at the defence of Rorke's Drift. Transferred to Army Reserve on 28/6/83. Rejoined for army service in the Royal Sussex Regiment (1922) on 5/5/85. Appointed Lance-Corporal 18/8/86. Promoted Corporal 17/12/86. Reverted to Private on 27/7/87. Re-engaged on 29/2/88. Transferred to Corps of Military Foot Police (301) on 1/8/88. He was admitted to hospital at the Curragh on 14/9/89 suffering from the effects of a specific disease he had acquired in India in 1882. Following examination by a medical board at the Curragh Camp, Ireland, on 13/6/89, it was found that the disease had affected his heart. He was declared unfit for further service and invalided from the army on 17/7/89. Next-of-kin, uncle, J. Norris, 15 Hind Street, Edge Hill, Liverpool. Medal for South Africa with clasp '1877–8–9'. (Ref. 'B' roll only.)

25B/1480   Private   OSBORNE William
Attested at Pontypool on 28/11/77. Posted to 2/24th on 26/1/78. Served in 'B' Company at the defence of Rorke's Drift. Posted to India and returned to England in October 1883. Date of discharge not recorded. Medal for South Africa with clasp '1877–8–9'. (Ref. 'C' and 'B' rolls, on 'D' list.)

25B/1399 Private   PARRY Samuel

Born at Sirhowy, Tredegar; trade – labourer. Attested at Monmouth on 23/5/77, aged 20 years. Previously served in Monmouthshire Militia. Description: 5′ 5½″ tall, fresh complexion, grey eyes, light hair. Religion: C/E. Served in South Africa. Served in 'B' Company at the defence of Rorke's Drift. Following an attack of fever in January 1879 he was examined by a medical board at Pinetown on 29/1/80 and recommended to be returned to England. On arrival at Netley he was again examined by a medical board and found to be suffering from chronic rheumatism, which had originally been manifested at Rorke's Drift in 1879. The cause of his disability was attributed to the climate and military service, as 'His regiment underwent exposure'. He was found unfit for further service and invalided from the army on 25/5/80. Medal for South Africa with clasp '1877–8–9'. (Ref. 'B' roll.)

25B/1410 Private   PARTRIDGE William

Born at St. Paul's, Ross, Hereford; trade – labourer. Attested at Newport on 5/6/77, aged 20 years. Previously served in Monmouthshire Militia. Description 5′ 6¼″ tall, fresh complexion, grey eyes, brown hair. Religion: C/E. Served in South Africa and Gibraltar. Served in 'G' Company at the defence of Rorke's Drift. (In his letter Bourne, then Colour-Sergeant of 'B' Company in 1878, mentions that his batman was named Partridge. William Partridge may possibly have been this man, having been transferred to 'G' Company prior to the action at Rorke's Drift; however, it is strange that Bourne failed to include him in his original 'Roll of Defenders'). He served in the South Wales Borderers but did not transfer to the regiment. Married to Mary Letitia at Brecon on 15/11/80. Discharged at Davenport on 11/11/81, as unfit for further service, and awarded a 12 months conditional pension of 7d. per diem. Medal for South Africa with clasp '1879'. (Ref. 'C' and 'Ba' rolls, also on 'D' list.)

25B/1186 Private   PITTS Samuel

Attested on 14/2/77. Posted to 2/24th on 22/2/77. Served in 'B' Company at the defence of Rorke's Drift. Posted to India and returned to England on 26/4/83. Date of discharge not traced. Medal for South Africa with clasp '1877–8–9'. (Ref. 'C' roll and 'D' list, incorrectly named as Pitt in both.)

25B/1286 Private   ROBINSON Thomas

Born at St. Patrick's, Dublin, Co. Dublin; trade – none. Attested at Bow Street Police Court, London, on 23/2/77, aged 24 years. Description: 5′ 9″ tall, fresh complexion, grey eyes, brown hair. Served in South Africa, Gibraltar and India. Confined on 24/4/78, convicted of disgraceful conduct 'In losing a pair of boots' and imprisoned on 27/4/78. Released on 29/7/78. Served in 'B' Company at the defence of Rorke's Drift. Served in

South Wales Borderers from 1/7/81 but did not transfer to regiment. Transferred to Army Reserve on 21/6/83, discharged on 25/2/89. Medal for South Africa with clasp '1877–8–9'. (Ref. 'C' and 'B' rolls, also on 'D' list.)

25B/1065 Private   RUCK James

Attested on 18/1/77. Posted to 2/24th on 31/1/77. Promoted Corporal 12/1/78. Reduced to Private 17/7/78. Served in South Africa and India. Served in 'B' Company at the defence of Rorke's Drift. Appointed Lance-Corporal 23/1/79. Transferred to 'G' Company on 14/3/79. Promoted Corporal 30/4/79. Reduced to Private on 13/10/79. Promoted Corporal 15/5/81. Reduced to Private 14/3/82. Placed on unattached list on 28/11/86 whilst serving at Madras, India. Medal for South Africa with clasp '1877–8–9'. (Ref. 'B' roll only.)

25B/1185 Private   SAVAGE Edward

Born at St. Woolas, Newport, Monmouth; trade – labourer. Attested at Cardiff on 8/2/77, aged 19 years. Previously served in Monmouthshire Militia. Description: 5′ 4¾″ tall, fresh complexion, blue eyes, light brown hair. Religion: R/C. Served in South Africa only. Served in 'B' Company at the defence of Rorke's Drift. Transferred from 'B' to 'G' Company on 29/1/79. Served in South Wales Borderers from 1/7/81 but did not transfer to regiment. Married Joanna McCarthy on 26/3/83. Transferred to Army Reserve on 11/2/83. Whilst serving at Gosport in 1880 he acquired a specific disease which eventually rendered him unfit for further service. He was discharged from the Army Reserve on 20/6/92, having been admitted to Glamorgan County Asylum. A medical certificate dated 6/6/92 was provided by the institution and sent to the Regimental Headquarters at Brecon, together with a letter written at 137 Wellington Street, Canton, Cardiff. The letter is signed 'Mary Savage, Wife' and it can only be presumed he had re-married. Medal for South Africa with clasp '1877–8–9'. (Ref. 'C' roll and 'D' list.)

25B/1051 Private   SCANLON John

Attested on 16/1/77. Posted to 2/24th on 31/1/77. He served in 'A' Company and was a patient in the hospital at Rorke's Drift. Killed in action. (Appendix A.) Effects claimed by his mother. Mentioned in Lieutenant Chard's official report on the action. He is buried in the cemetery at Rorke's Drift and his name appears on the monument. Medal for South Africa with clasp '1877–8–9'. (Ref. 'C' and 'B' rolls.)

2-24/2404 Private   SEARS Arthur

Born at Sunbury, Kingston, Middlesex; trade – labourer. Attested at Little Warley on 14/2/73, aged 19 years. Description: 5′ 9″ tall, fresh complexion, grey eyes, light brown hair. Religion: C/E. Served in South Africa, Mediterranean, India and Burma. Was at Kneller Hall School of Military

Music in 1874-5. Appointed Bandsman 4/2/78. Served in 'A' Company and was presumably a patient in the hospital at the defence of Rorke's Drift. Transferred to South Wales Borderers (SWB 1404) on 1/7/81. Promoted Corporal 6/3/83, Sergeant 1/4/84. Served in Burma (medal and clasp 'Burma 1887–9'). Re-engaged at Madras on 30/1/85. Married Emma Patrick at Secunderabad on 14/8/82. Children : Mildred Clara (14/9/83), Arthur John (12/9/85), Alice Emma (4/1/89). Awarded L.S.G.C. Medal on 4/10/92. Discharged on 14/2/94. Medal for South Africa with clasp '1877–8–9'. (Ref. 'C' roll incorrectly shows as Pears, given correctly on 'Ba' roll and on 'D' list.)

2–24/1618 Private   SHEARMAN George
Born at Hayes, Middlesex; trade – labourer. Attested at Westminster on 4/11/64, aged 17 years. Description : 5′ 5½″ tall, fresh complexion, grey eyes, brown hair. Served in India, South Africa, Mediterranean and Burma. Re-engaged at Secunderabad on 6/7/72. Promoted Corporal 2/6/74. Reduced to Private 11/7/74. Served in 'B' Company at the defence of Rorke's Drift. Appointed Lance-Corporal 5/2/79. Reduced to Private on 18/11/79. (Followed by several promotions and demotions.) Served in South Wales Borderers but did not transfer to regiment. Discharged at Gosport on 14/12/86. Medal for South Africa with clasp '1877–8–9'. (Ref. 'C' roll only, incorrectly named as Sherman, as he is in medal roll, also on 'D' list.)

2–24/914 Private   SHERGOLD John
Born at St. George's, London; trade – labourer. Attested at Coventry on 1/3/59, aged 18 years 3 months. Description : 5′ 5¾″ tall, fresh complexion, hazel eyes, light brown hair. Served in Mauritius, India and South Africa. Re-engaged at Rangoon on 26/3/68. Served in 'B' Company at the defence of Rorke's Drift. (He claimed compensation for his field kit, 'lost at Isandhlwana'. Examined by a medical board at Pinetown on 15/11/79 and recommended for return to England. On arrival at Netley he was found to be suffering from debility and rheumatism and was declared to be 'weakly and worn out'. Discharged as unfit for further service on 6/4/80. Intended residence, 43 East Road, Clapham. Medal for South Africa with clasp '1877–8–9'. (Incorrectly shown in medal roll as J. Shergo.) (Ref. 'B' roll only.)

25B/1005 Private   SMITH John
Born at Wigan, Lancashire; trade – labourer. Attested at Ashton 24/12/76, aged 25 years. Previously served in Royal Lancashire Militia. Description : 5′ 7½″ tall, fresh complexion, blue eyes, brown hair. Religion : C/E. Served in 'B' Company at the defence of Rorke's Drift where he was wounded in action. (Appendix A.) Examined by a medical board at Pietermaritzburg on 6/8/78 and recommended for return to England. Admit-

ted to Netley on 20/9/79 and returned to duty on 10/10/79. To Army Reserve on 21/7/80. Rejoined 46 Brigade on 1/3/81 and posted to South Africa on 5/3/81. Injured by rupture on 10/5/81 on line of march in Natal. Returned to England 19/3/82 and transferred to Royal West Kent Regiment (46B/2333) on 1/7/81. Discharged at Dublin on 25/7/82 as unfit for further service. Intended place of residence, Bury, Lancashire. Medal for South Africa with clasp '1877–8–9'. (Ref. 'B' roll only.)

25B/777 Private   STEVENS Thomas
Born at Exeter, Devonshire; trade – bricklayer. Attested at Brecon on 9/3/76, aged 22 years. Description : 5′ 5½″ tall, dark complexion, brown eyes, black hair. Religion: C/E. Next of kin : father – 'Robin Hood Inn', Dowlais, Glamorgan. Served in South Africa, Gibraltar and India. Appointed Lance-Corporal 20/1/77. Promoted Corporal 12/8/77. Confined on 13/1/78, tried and reduced to Private on 19/1/78. Served in 'B' Company at the defence of Rorke's Drift. Served in South Wales Borderers from 1/7/81 but did not transfer to regiment. Transferred to Army Reserve on 17/3/82 and recalled to Army Service on 2/8/82. Re-transferred to Army Reserve on 8/2/83. Married Ellen Calvert at Merthyr on 1/9/83. Discharged from Army Reserve on 16/3/88. Medal for South Africa with clasp '1877–8–9'. (Ref. 'C' roll which names him incorrectly as Stephens, named correctly on 'Ba' roll, also on 'D' list.)

2–24/1812 Private   TASKER William
Born at St. Martin's, Birmingham; trade – buffer. Attested at Sheffield on 20/9/66, aged 20 years 7 months. Description : 5′ 6¼″ tall, fair complexion, grey eyes, fair hair. Next of kin : brother – J. Tasker, 68 Church Street, Birmingham. Served in India, South Africa and Mediterranean. Re-engaged at Warley on 20/8/73. Deserted on 10/3/74, rejoined on 25/3/74. Confined, tried and imprisoned on 30/3/74, released on 10/5/74. Appointed Lance-Corporal 13/8/75. Reverted to Private 26/5/77. Confined on 26/5/77, tried on 2/6/77 and sentenced to 28 days imprisonment with hard labour. Served in 'B' Company at the defence of Rorke's Drift where he was wounded in action. (Appendix A.) Served in South Wales Borderers but did not transfer to regiment. Married Elizabeth Ridney at Brecon on 29/9/83. 'Prematurely discharged for the benefit of the public service' on 31/1/85. Medal for South Africa with clasp '1877–8–9'. (Ref. 'C' and 'B' rolls, also on 'D' list.)

25B/973 Private   TAYLOR Frederick
Attested at Newport on 9/12/76. Previously served in Royal Monmouth Militia. Posted to 2/24th on 22/1/77. Served in 'B' Company at the defence of Rorke's Drift. Died of disease at Pinetown, Natal, on 30/11/79. (Medal for South Africa with clasp '1877–8–9' issued on 29/8/81. (Ref. 'C' and 'B' rolls.)

25B/889   Private   TAYLOR   Thomas
Attested 16/11/76. To 2/24th, 25/11/76. Served in South Africa, Gibraltar and India. Served in 'B' Company at the defence of Rorke's Drift. Returned to England 27/1/83. Date of discharge not recorded. Medal for South Africa with clasp '1877–8–9'. (Ref. 'C' and 'B' rolls, also 'D' list.)

25B/1280   Private   THOMAS   John
(Alias Peter Sawyer.) Born at Liverpool, Lancashire; trade – labourer. Attested at Liverpool on 23/2/77, aged 24 years. Description: 5' 5¾" tall, sallow complexion, blue eyes, brown hair. Religion: R/C. Served in South Africa, Gibraltar and India. Served in 'B' Company at the defence of Rorke's Drift. To South Wales Borderers on 1/7/81 but did not transfer to regiment. On 26/5/82, whilst stationed at Secunderabad, India, he signed (with his mark since he was illiterate) a declaration before the Cantonment Magistrate. The document states that he had enlisted under the assumed name of John Thomas and his true name was Peter Sawyer, as confirmed by his baptismal certificate. Married Annie Louisa Kelsey at Portsea, Hants., on 5/7/83. Discharged from Army Reserve on 25/2/89. Medal for South Africa with clasp '1877–8–9'. (Ref. 'C' roll only and 'D' list.)

25B/1394   Private   THOMPSON   John
Attested at Brecon on 3/5/77. Posted to 2/24th on 26/1/78. Served in South Africa and India. Served in 'B' Company at the defence of Rorke's Drift. Appointed Lance-Corporal on 15/5/79. Reduced to Private 6/12/79. Returned to England from India in October 1883. Date of discharge not recorded. Medal for South Africa with clasp '1877–8–9'. (Ref. 'C' roll only and 'D' list.)

25B/879   Private   TOBIN   Michael
Born at Windgap, Co. Kilkenny; trade – labourer. Attested at Monmouth on 6/11/76, aged 20 years. Description: 5' 9½" tall, fresh complexion, grey eyes, brown hair. Religion: R/C. Served in South Africa, Gibraltar and India. May have served in 'B' Company at the defence of Rorke's Drift. Confined on 4/7/79, tried and sentenced to receive 50 lashes – sentence remitted. Served in South Wales Borderers from 1/7/81 but did not transfer to regiment. Transferred to Army Reserve on 28/3/83. Married Margaret Mohan at Windgap in February 1886. Discharged from Army Reserve on 10/11/92. Intended residence: Ninemile House, Tipperary. Medal for South Africa with clasp '1877–8–9'. (Ref. 'B' roll only – see next entry.)

25B/641   Private   TOBIN   Patrick
Attested at Newport on 17/9/75, aged 18 years. Posted to 2/24th on 21/3/77. May have served in 'B' Company at the defence of Rorke's Drift. Appointed Lance-Corporal

in 1880 (precise date not recorded), but wrongly shown as 'Michael Tobin'. Promoted Corporal in April 1881, being again incorrectly named as 'John Tobin' – evidently he had been confused with 2698 Lance-Corporal John Tobin who received the medal for South Africa without clasp. Returned to England on 28/10/81. Date of discharge not recorded. Medal for South Africa with clasp '1877–8–9'. (Ref. 'C' roll only and 'D' list. In view of the confusion regarding this man and 879 Pte. Michael Tobin, it is impossible to determine whether either or both were present at the defence of Rorke's Drift.)

25B/1281   Private   TODD   William John
Attested on 2/3/77. Posted to 2/24th on 21/3/77. Served in South Africa and India. Served in 'B' Company at the defence of Rorke's Drift. Returned to England from India on 26/4/83. Date of discharge not recorded. Medal for South Africa with clasp '1877–8–9'. (Ref. 'C' and 'B' rolls, the latter gives his initials incorrectly as W.G., also on 'D' list.)

25B/1315   Private   TONGUE   Robert
Born at Ruddington, Nottingham; trade – frame knitter. Attested at Nottingham on 26/2/77, aged 19 years. Previously served in Nottinghamshire Militia. Description: 5' 7" tall, fresh complexion, grey eyes, brown hair. Religion: Wesleyan. Served in South Africa, Gibraltar and India. Served in 'B' Company at the defence of Rorke's Drift. Served in South Wales Borderers but did not transfer to regiment. Transferred to Army Reserve on 21/6/83. Married Mary Wright at Ruddington on 27/6/84. Discharged from Army Reserve on 28/2/89. Medal for South Africa with clasp '1877–8–9'. (Ref. 'C' and 'B' rolls, also on 'D' list.)

25B/1497   Private   WALL   John
Born at St. James's, Deptford, Kent; trade – labourer. Attested at Chatham on 1/12/77, aged 18 years. Previously served in West Kent Light Infantry (8100). Description: 5' 5½" tall, fresh complexion, blue eyes, brown hair. Served in South Africa and India. Confined on 17/10/78, tried on 19/10/78 and sentenced to 21 days imprisonment with hard labour. Released on 8/11/78. Served in 'B' Company at the defence of Rorke's Drift. Embarked at Bombay for England in H.M. Troopship *Malabar* on 28/11/81. Following a medical examination at Netley on 25/10/81 he was found to be insane 'as a result of intemperance'. He was declared insane and discharged from the service on 27/12/81. Intended residence: Lunatic Asylum, Barming Heath, Maidstone, Kent. Medal for South Africa with clasp '1877–8–9'. (The medal roll gives his initial incorrectly as 'F'.) Medal returned to the Mint on 7/11/82. (Ref. 'C' and 'B' rolls, also on 'D' list.)

2–24/977   Private   WHETTON Alfred

Born at St. Luke's, London; trade – labourer. Attested at Westminster on 24/3/59, aged 17 years 10 months. Description : 5' 5½" tall, fresh complexion, hazel eyes, brown hair. Served in Mauritius, East Indies, South Africa and Gibraltar. Re-engaged at Secunderabad, India, on 15/4/69. Served in 'B' Company at the defence of Rorke's Drift. (Confirmed by an entry on his service documents, 'Present at the defence of Rorke's Drift'.) Awarded LSGC Medal with gratuity of £5. Discharged at Gibraltar on 27/5/80 on completion of his service. Intended residence : 5 Tower Hamlets Road, London, later amended to Shoreditch, London. Medal for South Africa with clasp '1877–8–9'. Medal sent to Depot under 60/2–24/129. (Ref. 'C' roll incorrectly shown as 'Whatton', 'B' roll shown as 'Whitton', which, according to his own signature, was his correct name, also on 'D' list as Whetton.)

25B/1187   Private   WILCOX William

Attested on 14/2/77. Posted to 2/24th on 23/2/77. Served in 'B' Company at the defence of Rorke's Drift. Convicted of disgraceful conduct and confined to prison at Pinetown in January 1880. He was still in prison when the battalion was posted to Gibraltar. Medal for South Africa with clasp '1877–8–9'. Medal forfeited. (Ref. 'C' and 'B' rolls, also on 'D' list.)

25B/1395   Private   WILLIAMS John V.C.

(Alias John Williams Fielding.) Born at Abergavenny, Monmouthshire, on 24/5/57. Attested at Monmouth on 22/5/77; trade – labourer. (He ran away from home to enlist and used his second Christian name as a surname to avoid being traced.) Posted to 2/24th on 3/8/77. Served in South Africa and India. Served in 'B' Company and assisted in the defence of the hospital at Rorke's Drift. Mentioned in Lieutenant Chard's report on the action, and also in his letter to Queen Victoria. Mentioned in Private Hook's accounts of the battle. Private Williams was awarded the Victoria Cross and received his decoration from Major-General Anderson at Gibraltar on 1/3/80, the citation (L.G. 2/5/79) reading : 'Was posted with Private Joseph Williams (2nd Battalion, 24th Foot) and Private William Horrigan (1st Battalion, 24th Foot) in a distant room at the hospital at Rorke's Drift, 22nd and 23rd January 1879, which they held for more than an hour, so long as they had a round of ammunition left. As communication was for a while cut off, the Zulus were enabled to advance and burst open the door; they dragged out Private Joseph Williams and two patients and assegaied them. While the Zulus were occupied with the slaughter of these men a lull took place during which Private John Williams, with two other patients, who were the only men left alive in this ward, succeeded in knocking a hole through the partition and taking the two patients into the next ward, where he found Private Hook.' After serving in India, he returned to England in October 1883. Transferred to Army Reserve (date of transfer not recorded). Discharged from Army Reserve on 22/5/93. He was married and had three sons, the eldest was killed during the retreat from Mons in the 1914-18 War, and two daughters. For many years he was attached to the civilian staff at the Regimental Depot at Brecon, and retired from this post on 26/5/20. In 1932 he was taken ill whilst living at the home of his daughter in Cwmbran, his wife having died some years previously. He died at Cwmbran on 25/11/32 and was buried at St. Michael's Churchyard, Llantarnam. Medal for South Africa with clasp '1877–8–9'. (Ref. 'C' and 'B' rolls, also on 'D' list.)

25B/934   Private   WILLIAMS John

Born at Barristown; trade – collier. Attested at Pontypool on 28/11/76. Previously served in Glamorgan Artillery. Posted to 2/24th on 15/12/76. Served in 'E' Company at the defence of Rorke's Drift. Died of disease at Rorke's Drift on 5/2/79, leaving the sum of £8-4-6. Medal for South Africa with clasp '1877–8–9' issued on 29/3/81, AGL 82. (Ref. 'C' and 'Ba' rolls.)

25B/1398   Private   WILLIAMS Joseph

Attested at Monmouth on 23/5/77. Posted to 2/24th on 3/8/77. Served in 'B' Company and assisted in the defence of the hospital at Rorke's Drift. Killed in action. (Appendix A.) Effects claimed by his father. Mentioned in Lieutenant Chard's report on the action, also in Private Hook's account of the battle. Mentioned in the citations for the award of the Victoria Cross to Privates Hook and John Williams. (It is thought, and not without reason, that had Joseph Williams survived he also would have received the Victoria Cross for his exceptional gallantry. He is buried in the cemetery at Rorke's Drift and his name appears on the monument. Medal for South Africa with clasp '1877–8–9' issued under 68/2–24/260. (Ref. 'C' and 'B' rolls.)

25B/1316   Private   WOODS Caleb

Attested on 6/3/77. Posted to 2/24th on 26/1/78. Served in South Africa and India. Served in 'B' Company at the defence of Rorke's Drift. Transferred from 'B' to 'G' Company on 29/1/79. Appointed Drummer on 1/2/81. Returned to England from India on 1/5/83. Served in South Wales Borderers but did not transfer to regiment. Date of discharge not recorded. Medal for South Africa with clasp '1877–8–9'. (Ref. 'C' and 'Ba' rolls, also on 'D' list.)

APPENDIX A

Casualties at Rorke's Drift, 22nd/23rd January 1879

1st BATTALION

135	Pte.	BECKETT William	Dangerously wounded – assegai penetrating abdomen. DIED on 23/1/79.
568	Pte.	DESMOND Patrick	Slightly wounded – gunshot through fleshy part of thumb.
1861	Pte.	HORRIGAN William	KILLED (in hospital).
841	Pte.	JENKINS James	KILLED.
625	Pte.	NICHOLAS Edward	KILLED – gunshot through head.
447	Pte.	WATERS John	Severely wounded – gunshot through arm and shoulder.

2nd BATTALION

623	Sgt.	MAXFIELD Robert	KILLED (in hospital). Assegaied to death.
1328	L/Sgt.	WILLIAMS Thomas	Dangerously wounded – gunshot left side of chest fracturing ribs. Ball not lodged. DIED on 25/1/79.
1240	Cpl.	ALLEN William (V.C.)	Severely wounded – gunshot through arm and shoulder.
1112	Cpl.	LYONS John	Dangerously wounded – gunshot through neck (?) fracturing spine. Ball lodged – later removed.
987	Pte.	ADAMS Robert	KILLED.
2350	Pte.	BUSHE James	Slightly wounded – struck on nose by ball which had previously killed Pte. Thomas Cole.
1335	Pte.	CHICK James	KILLED.
801	Pte.	COLE Thomas	KILLED – gunshot through head.
969	Pte.	FAGAN John	KILLED.
1769	Pte.	HAYDEN Garret	KILLED (in hospital). Stabbed in 16 places, abdomen cut open in 2 places and part of cheek cut off.
1362	Pte.	HITCH Frederick (V.C.)	Dangerously wounded – gunshot through shoulder joint.
1373	Pte.	HOOK Alfred H. (V.C.)	Slightly wounded – assegai contusion of forehead.
716	Pte.	JONES Robert (V.C.)	Slightly wounded – assegai contusion of abdomen.
1051	Pte.	SCANLON John	KILLED.
1005	Pte.	SMITH John	Slightly wounded – ablation of abdomen.
1812	Pte.	TASKER William	Slightly wounded – gunshot, splinter of ball breaking skin of forehead.
1398	Pte.	WILLIAMS Joseph	KILLED (in hospital). Body mutilated and possibly dismembered.

REFERENCES

Casualty Returns – 22nd January to 24th February 1879.
Soldiers' papers.
Lieutenant Chard's dispatch.
Lieutenant Chard's letter to Queen Victoria.
Personal narratives, letters, etc.

APPENDIX B

An analysis of the various sources of reference utilised in compiling the list of Rorke's Drift defenders

The probability that an individual soldier was present at the defence of Rorke's Drift is made certain if he was (1) decorated for gallantry, (2) killed or died of wounds, (3) wounded, no matter how slightly, (4) his service documents contain a specific reference to his being present at the action. This probability tends to diminish slightly where the other sources of reference are concerned, however it is accepted that a man was also present at the action if his name appears in a report or letter, or if he himself provided a detailed personal narrative which can be substantiated. The four contemporary and semi-contemporary lists of defenders are, in certain instances, at variance with each other and therefore no single list may be considered as being totally accurate. (* Indicates the men named by Lieutenant Chard in his dispatch.)

1st BATTALION

NUMBER, RANK AND NAME	Decorated	Killed/died of wounds	Wounded	Service documents	Chard's letter to Queen	The 'Chard' roll	Bourne's roll	Bourne's amended roll	Dunbar's list	Letters, accounts, etc.
Sergeant										
56 WILSON Edward						1		1		
Privates										
135 BECKETT William		1			1	1	1	1		*1
568 DESMOND Patrick			1			1		1		
1861 HORRIGAN William		1			1	1	1	1		1
841 JENKINS James		1			1	1				
625 NICHOLAS Edward		1				1	1	1		1
372 PAYTON Thomas						1		1		
1542 ROY William D.C.M.	1					1	1			*1
104 TURNER Henry						1		1		
447 WATERS John			1		1	1		1		1

2nd BATTALION

NUMBER, RANK AND NAME	Decorated	Killed/died of wounds	Wounded	Service documents	Chard's letter to Queen	The 'Chard' roll	Bourne's roll	Bourne's amended roll	Dunbar's list	Letters, accounts, etc.
Lieutenant										
BROMHEAD Gonville V.C.	1				1	1	1	1	1	*1
Colour-Sergeant										
BOURNE Frank D.C.M.	1					1	1	1	1	*1
Sergeants										
81 GALLAGHER Henry						1	1	1	1	
623 MAXFIELD Robert		1			1	1	1	1		1
1387 SMITH George						1	1	1	1	1
735 WINDRIDGE Joseph					1	1	1	1	1	*1
Lance-Sergeants										
82 TAYLOR James						1	1	1	1	
1328 WILLIAMS Thomas		1			1	1	1	1		*1
Corporals										
1240 ALLEN William W. V.C.	1		1		1	1	1	1	1	1
582 FRENCH George						1	1	1	1	
2389 KEY John							1	1		
1112 LYONS John			1			1		1	1	
849 SAXTY Alfred						1	1	1	1	
Lance-Corporals										
1287 BESSELL William						1	1	1	1	
1282 HALLEY William						1	1	1	1	
Drummers										
1713 GALGEY Patrick						1		1	1	
2067 HAYES Patrick						1	1	1	1	
2381 KEEFE James						1	1	1	1	
2383 MEEHAN John						1		1	1	
Privates										
987 ADAMS Robert		1				1	1	1		
913 ASHTON James						1	1	1	1	1
1381 BARRY Thomas							1	1		
918 BENNETT William						1	1	1		

NUMBER, RANK AND NAME	Decorated	Killed/died of wounds	Wounded	Service documents	Chard's letter to Queen	The 'Chard' roll	Bourne's roll	Bourne's amended roll	Dunbar's list	Letters, accounts, etc.
Privates										
2427 BLY John							1	1		
1524 BROMWICH Joseph						1		1	1	
1184 BUCKLEY Thomas						1	1	1	1	
1220 BURKE Thomas							1	1		
2350 BUSHE James			1		1	1	1	1	1	
1181 CAMP William H.						1	1	1	1	
1241 CHESTER Thomas						1	1	1	1	
1335 CHICK James		1				1	1	1		1
755 CLAYTON Thomas						1	1	1		
1459 COLE Robert						1		1	1	
801 COLE Thomas		1				1	1	1		1
1396 COLLINS Thomas						1	1	1	1	
906 CONNOLLY John						1		1	1	1
2310 CONNORS Anthony						1	1	1	1	
1323 CONNORS Timothy						1	1	1	1	
2453 COOPER William						1		1	1	
470 DAVIS George							1	1		
1363 DAVIS William H.							1	1		
1178 DAW Thomas							1	1		
1467 DEACON George						1	1	1		1
1357 DEANE Michael						1	1	1	1	
1697 DICK James							1	1		
1634 DICKS William						1			1	
971 DRISCOLL Thomas						1	1	1	1	
1421 DUNBAR James					1	1	1	1	1	1
922 EDWARDS George						1	1	1	1	
969 FAGAN John		1				1	1	1		1
2429 GEE Edward						1	1	1	1	
798 HAGAN James						1			1	
1062 HARRIS John				1		1		1	1	
1769 HAYDEN Garret		1				1	1	1		1
1362 HITCH Frederick V.C.	1		1		1	1	1	1	1	1
1373 HOOK Alfred H. V.C.	1		1		1	1	1	1	1	*1
1061 JOBBINS John						1	1	1	1	1
1426 JONES Evan						1	1	1	1	
970 JONES John						1	1	1	1	
1179 JONES John						1	1	1	1	
716 JONES Robert V.C.	1		1		1	1	1	1	1	*1
593 JONES William V.C.	1				1	1	1	1	1	*1
2437 JUDGE Peter						1	1	1	1	
972 KEARS Patrick				1		1	1	1	1	

NUMBER, RANK AND NAME	Decorated	Killed/died of wounds	Wounded	Service documents	Chard's letter to Queen	The 'Chard' roll	Bourne's roll	Bourne's amended roll	Dunbar's list	Letters, accounts, etc.
Privates										
1386 KILEY Michael						1	1	1	1	
963 LEWIS David							1	1		
1528 LINES Henry						1		1	1	
1409 LLOYD David						1	1	1	1	
1176 LOCKHART Thomas						1		1	1	
1304 LODGE Joshua						1	1	1	1	
942 LYNCH Thomas M.							1	1		
1441 LYONS John						1		1	1	
1731 MANLEY John						1		1	1	
964 MARSHALL James						1			1	
876 MARTIN Henry						1	1	1	1	
1284 MASON Charles						1	1	1	1	
1527 MINEHAN Michael						1	1	1	1	1
968 MOFFATT Thomas						1	1	1	1	
1342 MORRIS Augustus						1	1	1	1	
525 MORRIS Frederick						1	1	1	1	
1371 MORRISON Thomas						1	1	1	1	
662 MURPHY John						1		1	1	
1279 NEVILLE William						1		1	1	
1257 NORRIS Robert							1	1		
1480 OSBORNE William						1	1	1	1	
1399 PARRY Samuel							1	1		
1410 PARTRIDGE William						1		1	1	1
1186 PITTS Samuel						1			1	
1286 ROBINSON Thomas						1	1	1	1	
1065 RUCK James							1	1		
1185 SAVAGE Edward						1			1	
1051 SCANLON John		1				1	1	1		1
2404 SEARS Arthur						1		1	1	
1618 SHEARMAN George						1			1	
914 SHERGOLD John							1	1		
1005 SMITH John			1				1	1		
777 STEVENS Thomas						1		1	1	
1812 TASKER William			1			1	1	1	1	
973 TAYLOR Frederick						1	1	1		
889 TAYLOR Thomas						1	1	1	1	
1280 THOMAS John						1			1	
1394 THOMPSON John						1			1	
879 TOBIN Michael							1	1		
641 TOBIN Patrick						1			1	

NUMBER, RANK AND NAME	Decorated	Killed/died of wounds	Wounded	Service documents	Chard's letter to Queen	The 'Chard' roll	Bourne's roll	Bourne's amended roll	Dunbar's list	Letters, accounts, etc.
Privates										
1281 TODD William J.						1	1	1	1	
1315 TONGUE Robert						1	1	1	1	
1497 WALL John						1	1	1	1	
977 WHETTON Alfred				1		1	1	1	1	
1187 WILCOX William						1	1	1	1	
1395 WILLIAMS John V.C.	1				1	1	1	1	1	*1
934 WILLIAMS John						1		1		
1398 WILLIAMS Joseph		1				1	1	1		1
1316 WOODS Caleb						1		1	1	

APPENDIX C

Nationality (as determined by those instances where the place of birth
is known) of the officer and other ranks, 1st and 2nd Battalions
24th Regiment present at the defence of Rorke's Drift,
22nd - 23rd January 1879

1st BATTALION

ENGLAND
Staffordshire	1

SCOTLAND
Midlothian	1

IRELAND
Dublin	1

OTHER
Peshawur (India) (of British parents)	1

2nd BATTALION

ENGLAND		WALES	
Cheshire	1	Breconshire	1
Gloucestershire	1	Glamorgan	3
Herefordshire	3	Monmouthshire	5
Kent	2	Pembrokeshire	1
Lancashire	9	**IRELAND**	
Leicestershire	1	Antrim	1
London	11	Clare	2
Middlesex	2	Cork	2
Nottinghamshire	1	Dublin	3
Somerset	4	Kilkenny	2
Surrey	1	Limerick	1
Sussex	1	Tipperary	2
Warwickshire	3	**OTHER**	
Worcestershire	1	Versailles (France) (of British parents)	1
Yorkshire	1		

N.B. – The place of attestation does not indicate the place of birth.